D0847841

The Lorette Wilmot Library
Nazareth College of Rochester

AN ACOUSTIC ANALYSIS OF
VOWEL VARIATION
IN NEW WORLD ENGLISH

AN ACOUSTIC ANALYSIS OF
VOWEL VARIATION
IN NEW WORLD ENGLISH

ERIK R. THOMAS

North Carolina State University

Publication of the
American Dialect Society

·

Number 85

·

Published by Duke University Press

for the American Dialect Society

WITHDRAWN
LORETTE WILMOT LIBRARY
NAZARETH COLLEGE

Copyright © 2001
American Dialect Society
ISBN: 0-8223-6494-8

Library of Congress Cataloging-in-Publication Data

Thomas, Erik R.
    An acoustic analysis of vowel variation in New World English /
Erik R. Thomas
        p. cm. — (Publication of the American Dialect Society ; no. 85)
    Includes bibliographical references.
    ISBN 0-8223-6494-8 (alk. paper)
        1. English language—Vowels. 2. English language—Variation—
United States. 3. English language—United States—Pronunciation.
    I. Title. II. Publication of the American Dialect Society ; no. 85.

PE1702.A5 no. 85
[PE2815]
421'.54—dc21   2001023063

British Library Cataloguing-in-Publication Data available

CONTENTS

PREFACE

This collection of vowel formant plots from various American dialects is an attempt to depict visually some variations that occur in vowels. It is not intended to show a complete representation of the variation in any single community; instead, it displays part of the range of variations. It is intended as a reference for researchers on how each vowel is realized in different dialects, on what vowels might be important variables for sociolinguistic studies, and on linguistic aspects of sound change. It is also intended as a refinement of past descriptions of vowel variants, which, based largely on impressionistic transcription, were often uncertain or inaccurate (especially for the glides of diphthongs, which are difficult to judge by ear). The concentration is on speakers from three states, Ohio, North Carolina, and Texas, with speakers from other areas for comparison. Locations of the speakers' hometowns are shown on the maps in appendix A.

Not all areas are represented. Perhaps the most noticeable void is that there are only two speakers (speakers 50 and 192) from western North America. This omission may not be as important as it appears, however, because most Western dialects are quite similar to dialects that I have included. The speech of western Canada is practically identical to that of Ontario. The dialects of the Dakotas and parts of Montana are similar to those of Minnesota. The speech of a broad swath from Kansas and Colorado to California—and probably to Oregon and Washington—resembles that of central Ohio in many ways (see speaker 50). Mexican American speech in California and Arizona probably differs little from Mexican American speech in Texas. Other important omissions are St. Louis and Baltimore, which have distinctive dialects of their own but for which I did not have access to recordings. In addition, although I have placed considerable emphasis on ethnic variation, no Asian Americans are included, and this group deserves more attention (see Mendoza-Denton and Iwai 1993).

In spite of these omissions, however, this monograph contains several items that no other study of New World English has attempted to show. It has the biggest collection of vowel plots of African Americans and Mexican Americans assembled to date. Both of these groups need more vocalic study, even though other aspects of their speech have been researched extensively. It also includes an intensive acoustic examination of Southern English. Past acoustic study of sound changes has examined Northern dialects more carefully than Southern dialects and has left many aspects of Southern speech unanalyzed, and I hope to rectify that situation here. Finally, I have included analyses of a number of archival recordings, including those of several people born before the Civil War, which give this monograph as much historical depth as any study of New World English. I have accordingly placed a great deal of emphasis on the historical development of dialects.

Chapter 1 describes the form of the vowel formant plots, how to read them, and the methods used to create them. Chapter 2 discusses the variants of each vowel, with separate sections for vowels in special contexts, such as before /r/ and before /l/. Chapters 3, 4, and 5 contain the vowel plots of whites from the North, the Southeast, and the South-Central states, respectively, with discussions of the vocalic traits of each dialect that is covered. Finally, chapters 6, 7, and 8 contain the vowel plots of African Americans, Mexican Americans, and Native Americans, respectively, with descriptions of the vocalic traits that typify those dialects.

Numerous people enabled me to undertake this project. Guy Bailey provided most of the recordings of Texans and those of the ex-slaves, the Oklahomans, and speakers 50 and 53, as well as a great deal of encouragement. The fieldwork that produced many of those recordings was supported by NSF Grants BNS-8812552, BNS-9009232, and BNS-9109695. Walt Wolfram and the rest of the staff of the North Carolina Language and Life Project (especially Natalie Schilling-Estes, Kirk Hazen, Bridget Anderson, Elaine Green, Clare Dannenberg, Jeffrey Reaser, and Jason Sellers) provided most of the recordings of North Carolinians and of the Bahamian, and Walt provided much encouragement as well. This fieldwork was supported by NSF Grants SBR-93-19577 and SBR-96-16331. Some of the analysis was supported by NSF Grant 9809385. Ronald R. Butters provided the recordings of speakers from

Wilmington, North Carolina, helped to spur my early interest in this topic, and provided editorial advice; his data collection was supported by a grant from the National Endowment for the Humanities. Other recordings were provided by Larry Beason, J. K. Chambers, Maurice Crane (of the Michigan State University Voice Library), the *Dictionary of American Regional English*, Amerylis McCullough, Mitchell Million, Michael B. Montgomery, Peter Patrick, John Rickford, Martin Tomasi, F. Milton Walters, and John Wheat (of the Benson American History Center at the University of Texas at Austin). Robert Benson provided access to the Bioacoustics Laboratory at Texas A&M University. The Department of Linguistics at the University of Texas at Austin and the North Carolina Language and Life Project provided me access to acoustic equipment later on. Access was provided by my mother, Mary C. Thomas, to most of the speakers from Johnstown, Ohio; by my father, Robert B. Thomas, to the speakers from Fredericktown and Bladensburg, Ohio; by Scott and Terry Miller to the speakers from Lino Lakes, Minnesota, and Leander, Texas; and by Donna Starks to the speaker from St. John's, Newfoundland. Sandra Clarke, Harold Paddock, and Donna Starks provided information on Newfoundland English. I am grateful to all of these people and to the speakers whose voices are depicted in this collection, as well as to my wife, Barbara Hunter, for her patience while I was preparing this monograph.

1. INTRODUCTION
AND METHODS

THIS MONOGRAPH FOLLOWS a small but growing body of acoustic studies of dialectal variation in American English vowels. Within sociolinguistics, acoustic measurement is beginning to encroach upon impressionistic transcription as the analysis technique of choice for vowel production. The seminal socioacoustic work was by Labov, Yaeger, and Steiner (1972), who examined vowel shifting patterns in the Great Lakes region and in the South, as well as in several other areas, such as New York City, southeastern England, and Scotland. They named four patterns of vowel shifting observed across different languages and established several principles for vowel shifting that were later refined by Labov (1991, 1994). They also described two chain-shifting patterns of vowels that occur in American English: the Northern Cities Shift and the Southern Shift. Briefly, the Northern Cities Shift, which occurs in the Great Lakes region (especially in large urban centers), involves raising of /æ/ to [eə], fronting of /ɑ/ to [a ~ æ], unrounding of /ɔ/ to [ɑ], backing of /ʌ/ to [ɔ], backing of /ɛ/ to [ʌ] or lowering toward [a], and sometimes lowering or backing of /ɪ/. The Southern Shift includes fronting of /u/, /ʊ/, and /o/; lowering of the nuclei of /e/ and /o/ and sometimes of the nuclei of /i/ and /u/; fronting and raising of /ɪ/ and /ɛ/; and either monophthongization of /ai/ to [aː] or backing of the /ai/ nucleus to produce [ɑˀi ~ ɒi].

Several other acoustic studies by Labov and his colleagues at the University of Pennsylvania have appeared as well. A number of these papers are investigations of the Philadelphia dialect, including Graff, Labov, and Harris's (1986) comparison of white and African American speech in Philadelphia; Labov's (1980) study of the direction of vowel changes in Philadelphia; Hindle's (1980) analysis of /æ/ spoken by a woman from Philadelphia; Labov, Karen, and Miller's (1991) study of the near-merger of words such as *ferry* and *furry*; Kroch's (1996) study of upper-class speech; and Roberts's (1997) study of the acquisition of the dialect by children.

Other acoustic studies produced by this team include Herold's (1990) analysis of the merger of /ɑ/ and /ɔ/ in the Scranton/Wilkes-Barre, Pennsylvania, area; Veatch's (1991) analysis of the vowels of four very different dialects of English; Ash's (1996) analysis of /u/ fronting in the Midwest; and Labov and Ash's (1997) examination of cross-dialectal perception. Most recently, this research group has been conducting the Telephone Survey of Sound Change in Progress in North American English (TELSUR; Labov, Ash, and Boberg 1997, forthcoming). This project aims to plot numerous vowel shifts across the United States and Canada and is the first systematic and comprehensive continent-wide survey of American dialects to use acoustic data. It has already yielded a great deal of useful information on, for example, exactly where the merger of /ɑ/ and /ɔ/ occurs. A spinoff article is Boberg's (2000) comparison of vowel configurations along the United States/Canada border. Information on and updated findings from TELSUR can be found at the home page for the Phonological Atlas of North America (http://www.ling.upenn.edu/phono_atlas/home.html).

A number of other researchers have conducted acoustic research on vowels of American English. An early study was Habick's (1980) dissertation on the fronting of /o/, /ʊ/, and /u/ in Farmer City, Illinois (see also Habick 1993). Feagin (1986) compared the vowels of different generations of natives of Anniston, Alabama. Di Paolo and Faber (1990), Di Paolo (1992), Faber (1992), and Faber and Di Paolo (1995) investigated how phonation could be used to maintain vowel distinctions in Utah English that were not realized as formant differences. Esling (1991) and Esling and Warkentyne (1993) examined the social differentiation of vowel variants in Vancouver, British Columbia, the latter study focusing on the retraction of /æ/. Clarke, Elms, and Youssef (1995) included a few formant plots in their otherwise impressionistic study of vowel shifting in Canadian English. Schilling-Estes (1996) and Schilling-Estes and Wolfram (1997) compared vowel changes in two insular communities, Ocracoke, North Carolina, and Smith Island, Maryland. Wolfram, Hazen, and Schilling-Estes (1999) examined local variants of /ai/ and /ɔ/ in Ocracoke and another North Carolina coastal community, Harkers Island. Niedzielski (1996) analyzed Canadian raising of /au/ (which produces realizations such as [ʌu]) in the Detroit area. Ito and Preston (1998) and Ito (1999) examined the spread of the Northern Cities Shift in rural parts of Michigan. Fridland (1998, 2000) conducted a detailed analysis of vowel shifts among whites in Memphis.

There have also been a few acoustic studies of the vowels of African Americans and Mexican Americans. Graff, Labov, and Harris (1986) provided comparative vowel formant plots of a white and an African American Philadelphian. Deser (1990) examined /ai/, /æ/, and vowel duration within African American families from Detroit, finding some correlation between children's realizations of these variables and whether the parents were natives of Detroit or the South. Denning (1989) traced the shift from [ɪ] to [i] in unstressed syllables (e.g., in *happy*) among African Americans in East Palo Alto, California; his study was primarily impressionistic, but he included acoustic data for comparison. Godinez (1984) and Godinez and Maddieson (1985) compared the vowels of Mexican Americans and Anglos in Los Angeles. Fought (1999) examined how vowel realizations are correlated with gang affiliation among Mexican Americans in Los Angeles. Veatch (1991) and Patrick (1996) examined Jamaican vowels acoustically.

Finally, much of my own previous research has involved acoustic analysis of vowels. Thomas (1991) inquires into the origin of Canadian raising. Thomas and Bailey (1992) investigates the /ɑr/-/ɔr/ and /ɔr/-/or/ mergers in Texas. Thomas (1993) describes vowel variants in Mexican American English. More recent work includes an investigation of how phonetic factors led to dialectal differences in /ai/ (Thomas 1995); a study of the role of individuation in linguistic changes in Johnstown, Ohio (Thomas 1996); a comparison of /ai/ and /e/ realizations among rural and metropolitan Anglo Texans (Thomas 1997); two studies of the history of African American Vernacular English vowels (Thomas and Bailey 1998; Bailey and Thomas 1998); a comparative study of African American and white vernaculars in Hyde County, North Carolina (Wolfram, Thomas, and Green 2000; Wolfram and Thomas forthcoming); and a study comparing production and perception of pre-/t/ and pre-/d/ /ai/ glides of white Anglos from Ohio and Mexican Americans from Texas (Thomas 2000).

1.1. ORGANIZATION AND SYMBOLS USED

This collection is organized to emphasize the most salient dialectal divisions that occur among the speakers that are included. For this reason, speakers are divided first by ethnicity, second by geography, and third by year of birth. Linguistic differences that follow other factors, such as socioeconomic group, gender, and personal aspirations, are beyond the scope of this work, as are intraspeaker differences such as style and register variation. Special groupings are made occasionally for speakers who show unusual patterns, such as African Americans from the Pamlico Sound area or Mexican Americans who show considerable assimilation to Anglo speech. Descriptions of the general features of the dialects covered are given in the introductions to chapters 3–8. For each speaker, a short demographic description is provided, followed by some distinctive "field marks" of the person's speech. The hometown listed indicates where the speaker grew up; a few lived in different communities as adults.

For those not familiar with vowel formant plots, the squares and lines can look like gobbledygook. The numbers representing Hertz (Hz) on the horizontal and vertical axes can be misleading as well. The following tips should help readers. First, the Hz readings are best ignored. They vary with a speaker's mouth size, and listeners' auditory systems normalize them. What is important is where a vowel appears relative to the speaker's vowel system as a whole: for example, is the /o/ of *coat* more backed (on the right half of the vowel system) or more fronted (on the left side)? Second, a useful method of familiarizing oneself with vowel formant plots is to focus on a particular vowel, such as /o/, and follow it across many different plots. By looking at enough plots, one can see that younger speakers tend to have fronter /o/s than older speakers and whites tend to have fronter /o/s than African Americans or Mexican Americans. Tracing several vowels in this manner should make dialectal patterns evident and should initiate readers into the spatial "language" of vowel plots. Third, the text is designed to point out the salient features of different dialects and idiolects. As noted earlier, the descriptions at the beginning of chapters 3–8 discuss the features that characterize each dialect depicted in the plots. The descriptions below the vowel plots point out important features of individual speakers' vowels, such as particular mergers that a speaker has. These descriptions should help the reader to focus on what is dialectally distinctive in a given vowel plot.

Throughout this work, F1 refers to the first formant, F2 to the second formant, F3 to the third formant, and f_o to the fundamental frequency, as is conventional in acoustic phonetics. Symbols in brackets (e.g., [ei]) stand for phonetic realizations. The most recent (1993) version of the International Phonetic Alphabet (see appendix B) is followed, with a few exceptions: I use [ü] instead of [y] to avoid possible confusion with the palatal approximant, and I use the shift symbols [ᵛ ^ > <] instead of [ˌ ˌ ˍ ˍ] because they are more familiar to most readers.

The symbols for vowel phonemes are enclosed in slashes (e.g., /e/) in the text, but not on the plots. They are listed in table 1.1 with an example word for each. These symbols are used because most of them are conventional symbols for the vowels of American English. For /ai/, /au/, and /oi/, I have designated the glide with [i] or [u]

TABLE 1.1
Vowel Symbols

/i/, as in *eat*	/ɪ/, as in *zip*
/e/, as in *day*	/ɛ/, as in *check*
/æ/, as in *back*	/ɑ/, as in *cot*
/ɔ/, as in *caught*	/ʌ/, as in *cut*
/o/, as in *coat* or *towed*	/ʊ/, as in *hook*
/u/, as in *do*	/ai/, as in *size*
/au/, as in *how*	/oi/, as in *boy*
/ɜ/, as in *first* (when *r*-less)	/ɼ/, as in *first* (when *r*-ful)
/æ:/, as in *pass* or *half,* where it differs from the vowel in *back, pad,* or *have*	/ə/, as in *coat* or *toad,* when it is distinct from the vowel in *towed* (in old-fashioned New England speech)
/ir/, as in *hear*	/er/, as in *hair*
/ɑr/, as in *hard*	/ɔr/, as in *horse*
/or/, as in *hoarse*	/ur/, as in *tour*
/air/, as in *tire*	/aur/, as in *tower*

instead of with a semivowel symbol because most speakers of English treat them as a single vocalic unit, not as a sequence of a vowel and a semivowel. However, I did not attempt to create a unitary symbol for any of these diphthongs because such a contrived symbol would make it harder for readers to recognize what sound I was referring to. Otherwise, the symbols are not intended to imply any particular phonological content. They are intended to represent a set of diaphones that are historically connected. The arbitrariness of the actual symbol used is exemplified by /ɑr/, which I use for the sequence in *hard* even for Newfoundland English, which preserves a form with the vowel [æ] that is older than the form with [ɑ]. While it is possible to use symbols that are supposed to represent phonological relationships, I find it pointless to do so. For example, one could use /o/ instead of /ɑ/ for the vowel in *cot* because of the relationship between words such as *cone* and *conical*. As Ohala (1992) points out, however, the relationships between many such words with sound alternations are more opaque to speakers than phonologists have generally acknowledged (e.g., in *suppose* and *suppository*). They are also less productive than many have assumed: nonlinguists who are asked to create new words from existing words and affixes tend not to employ the alternations (see Ohala 1974, 1992). I suspect that most nonlinguists, when asked—for example—to add *-ical* or *-itory* to a nonsense word like *sustose* /sɔstoz/, would produce *sustosical* and *sustository* with the vowel of *coat*, not the vowel of *cot*. Thus, it is questionable whether there is any real synchronic connection between the vowels of *cot* and *coat*. It is better to use arbitrary symbols than to use symbols that are tied to phonological theories that may become outdated.

I have chosen not to give lists of vowel realizations of the sort found in Wells (1982), with a keyword for each class (e.g., *face* for /e/) and a typical realization for a vowel in each dialect. The keywords are more important for British dialects than for American dialects because of the greater variability in British dialects. Lists of typical realizations would defeat one of the principle aims of this work, which is to show diachronic changes and other variations *within* particular dialects.

Superscript annotations are added to phonemic symbols to indicate particular phonetic contexts. These notations are listed in the following column. The first three follow Labov, Yeager, and Steiner (1972), except that I use ^v strictly for vowels before voiced obstruents.

^o	before a voiceless obstruent
^v	before a voiced obstruent
^N	before a nasal
[#]	word-final
^r	before /r/
^l	before /l/
^g	before /g/
^d	before /d/
^F	before a voiceless fricative
^t	before /t/
^{ptk}	before /p/, /t/, or /k/

When two or three superscript symbols are used together, it means either or any of those contexts: for example, /au$^{\text{v#N}}$/ refers to /au/ when it is pre–voiced obstruent, word-final, or prenasal. When a vowel symbol is used on a formant plot with a full-size consonant symbol, it means that the consonant is shown as well as the vowel; for example, *ul* on a plot (as opposed to *u^l*) indicates that the /l/ glide is shown, while *er* for an *r*-less speaker indicates that the schwa-glide is shown. Two vowel symbols separated by an equal sign indicate that the two vowels are merged for that speaker. For instance, /ɑ = ɔ/ refers to the vowel resulting from the merger of /ɑ/ and /ɔ/. Determinations of whether a speaker merged two vowels were based on both the acoustic measurements and on my impressionistic judgment from listening to the tokens. Many of the speakers read minimal pairs, and their production of the minimal pairs was also taken into consideration. Obviously, the judgments are supposed to represent speakers' production, not their perception. At times it was not completely clear whether a speaker showed a merger or not. In such cases, the judgments represent the weight of the evidence.

The filled squares on the formant plots indicate the mean value of the tokens that were measured for that particular vowel. In some cases where several vowels occur in the same area, small dots appear on the plot to link the square with its label. Arrows are used for diphthongs; the square indicates the nucleus of the diphthong and the arrow point marks the mean value of the glide. Phonetic symbols are always placed near the nucleus of a diphthong. Occasionally, when it is difficult to follow a diphthong from nucleus to glide on a plot, a smaller version of the same symbol is placed near the glide.

The use of mean values allows the gliding of diphthongs to be shown. The glides of diphthongs have often been neglected in past sociophonetic studies, but they are vital to understanding dialectal variation and sound change. Showing each token of a vowel would make the plots too cluttered to depict both the nucleus and the glide of diphthongs. Error bars that depict the standard deviation might seem at first to offer a way of showing the degree of spread of the individual tokens, but I have chosen not to use them for two reasons. First, error bars would still clutter the plots to the point that they would be hard to read. This factor would not be too much of a problem if I were showing only monophthongs and nuclei of diphthongs, but with diphthong glides included, there would simply be too many lines on the plots.

Second, the nature of the data makes error bars deceptive. Although the standard deviation is not, of course, a function of whether the data show a normal or skewed distribution, error bars leave the visual impression with readers that the data have a normal distribution. Because of the effects of different adjacent consonants, the effects of variations in duration and stress, and the limiting effect of the margin of the vowel envelope, however, the distribution of tokens is almost always skewed. Furthermore, if the sample of tokens is biased toward phonetic contexts that cause, for example, lowering of F_2, the bias may not be reflected in the error bars. Thus, generally speaking, information about the phonetic context and duration of tokens should tell researchers more than the standard deviation would, especially when the number of tokens is small. Although space limitations preclude listing this information (since 150–200 vowels were measured for most speakers), I have attempted to compensate by regularly excluding vowels in contexts that show the greatest consonantal influence—for example, front vowels before /g/, vowels before /l/ (except where considered separately), and (usually) vowels after /w/ and /j/. Vowels do not all show the same degree of spread of tokens, but these differences are to some degree predictable. /u/, for example, typically shows a wide range of F2 values, either because its articulatory position makes it particularly susceptible to coarticulatory influence (see Ohala 1981) or because it lies in a region in which a small articulatory difference translates into a large acoustic difference (see Stevens 1989), or both. Diphthongs also typically show a wide range of formant values because durational variations can cause large fluctuations in the amount of truncation that they exhibit. Recognition of these predictable effects should reduce the need for error bars.

Another argument for error bars is that speakers of a dialect may show greater variation in their production of a vowel when it is shifting in that dialect (as implied in Labov, Yeager, and Steiner 1972, 79–91, and Labov 1991, 14; 1994, 158). That is, speakers may develop extensive allophonic conditioning during a shift, or they may have more variants at their disposal to use for stylistic purposes. This notion may be true to some extent, but it is easy to overstate the case for it, and some of the evidence cited for it can be explained in other ways. For example, Labov cites a Buffalo, New York, native who shows the Northern Cities Shift fronting of /ɑ/ and says that certain of her tokens of /ɑ/ are leading the shift, among which "the word *got* is the most characteristic of these: it is the leading element in the fronting" and that, in isolation, the vowel in *got* sounds more like [ɛ] (Labov 1994, 183). However, the vowel in *got* shows considerably higher F2 values than most other examples of /ɑ/ in any dialect, including those in which /ɑ/ is being merged with /ɔ/ and thus may be undergoing BACKING as well as those in which /ɑ/ is stable. What is needed are controlled acoustic studies demonstrating specifically that vowels really do show a wider range of formant values when they are undergoing shifting (though see Hindle 1980). At any rate, error bars showing the standard deviation cannot distinguish between this sort of vowel shift-related spread of formant values and spread caused by the phonetic contexts of the tokens that were measured.

Nevertheless, it should be remembered that any mean value has a margin of error. When reading the vowel plots, one should not take the exact placement of a vowel too seriously but instead should consider the mean values to be in the right neighborhood. The usual 7–10 tokens measured for a particular vowel by a particular speaker are not a large number, and a different sample of tokens by the same person would yield a somewhat different mean. The phonetic contexts of the tokens can have a noticeable effect on the mean value, especially if they are strongly skewed in some way. I took steps to reduce such skewing, however, by excluding certain contexts that show an especially strong coarticulatory effect (as noted above) and, with few exceptions, by measuring no more than two examples of the same word. In fact, it is not possible to determine a single definitive spot at which a vowel truly lies because the context pervades all aspects of vowel production. For example, should the definitive form of a vowel be the production in isolation, which usually (barring stereotyping of certain variants) represents a "target" value, or the production in connected speech, which usually shows some reduction? If certain words that contain a particular vowel are far more common than other words with that vowel (as is the case with /au/, for which *out, about, how, now, down, around,* and *house* are by far most frequent), should those words be considered most representative of that vowel, or should a context-neutral value be the goal?

All of the vowels are shown on each plot except for a few of the archival recordings, for which there were no tokens of some of the less common vowels (especially /oi/). The glides of /i/ and /u/, which are usually minimal, are not shown for all speakers. Vowels before /l/ are not shown except where they are relevant to pre-/l/ mergers or to the overall configuration of the vowel system. /er/, /ir/, and stressed syllabic /r/ are omitted for the majority of speakers, largely because I did not recognize their dialectal importance in the earlier stages of the acoustic measurement. /r/-glides, schwaglides in *r*-less varieties, /l/-glides, and the glides of /æ^N/ are seldom shown because they would have cluttered the plots too much.

In the note accompanying the plot for each speaker, speakers from the *Dictionary of American Regional English* (*DARE*) are identified by their *DARE* label (e.g., *DARE* OH 015). "Completely *r*-less" refers only to syllable rhymes, not to syllable onsets or intervocalic /r/. At the end of the note, two labels are found. The first indicates whether the analysis is based on conversational speech, reading passage speech, or both. This information is included because its importance for stylistic variation is so well established now. Tokens from word lists were never included except for a very few tokens of /ai/ and /au/ for speaker 1. The second label indicates where the analysis was conducted: the Bioacoustics Laboratory at Texas A&M University (TAMU), the Linguistics Laboratory at the University of Texas at Austin (UT), or the William C. Friday Linguistics Laboratory at North Carolina State University (NCSU) (see §1.2).

1.2. METHODS OF ACOUSTIC ANALYSIS

It is futile to try to list the models of recording devices on which the recordings analyzed in this work were created. The recordings came from a wide variety of sources, including several sociolinguistic surveys and a number of archives. For some of them, the type of recording device used is unknown.

I conducted all analyses of speakers myself except for those from Graham County, North Carolina (speakers 64–66 and 192), and two from Hyde County, North Carolina (speakers 152 and 155), which were conducted by Bridget Anderson. Measurements taken at Texas A&M University or at the University of Texas at Austin (except for speakers 10, 14, 27, and 55) were made with a Kay Sonagraph, model 5500. Measurements taken at North Carolina State University were made with a Kay Computerized Speech Laboratory (CSL), model 4300B. For both the Sonagraph 5500 and the CSL, signals were digitized at a sampling rate of 10 kHz with 16-bit resolution and Blackman windowing and were lowpass filtered at 4 kHz, with 6 dB/oct preemphasis at a factor of 0.8.

Measurements for speakers 10, 14, 27, and 55 were taken with a VaxStation II/GPX at the University of Texas; signal processing was identical to that of the Sonagraph 5500 and the CSL except that the preemphasis occurred at a factor of 0.85.

Spectrographic displays of the vowels and diphthongs measured were examined in order to determine where to take formant readings. Normally a Fast Fourier Transform (FFT) frame length of 100 points was used to produce the displays, but frame lengths of 75 points were used for many of the female speakers analyzed at the University of Texas. While there are various ways to determine where to take readings, such as taking one each a quarter, a half, and three quarters through the vocoid or even creating formant tracks, the most practical method for my purposes was to take one reading for a monophthong, two for a diphthong, and three for a triphthong. Measurements were taken in the center of the vowel for monophthongs. For diphthongs, the methods used at Texas A&M University and the University of Texas and those used at North Carolina State University differed slightly. At Texas A&M and the University of Texas, readings were taken in the center of steady states, or where F2 changed trajectory if no steady state was present (but not closer than 25 ms to the edge of the vocoid), or 25 ms from the edge of the vocoid if there was no steady state or change in F2 trajectory. The purpose of the 25-ms limit is to eliminate most of the transitional effects of adjacent segments. At North Carolina State, median linear predictive coding (LPC) values were taken for the region between 25 and 45 ms from the beginning of the vocoid for the nucleus and between 25 and 45 ms from the end for the glide. Tokens with durations of 70 ms or less were not measured as diphthongs. The effects of the two different methods on the mean values shown in the plots are small. Methods used for triphthongs were the same as for diphthongs except that a third reading was taken where the change in formant trajectory occurred, which often coincided with a steady state.

An LPC program (Atal and Hanauer 1971) was available for the Sonagraph 5500 at Texas A&M, the VaxStation at the University of Texas, and the CSL at North Carolina State, but not for the Sonagraph 5500 at the University of Texas. Formants were estimated with LPC when it was available, using the autocorrelation method. The default LPC settings are 12 coefficients for the Kay products and 14 coefficients for the VaxStation, and most LPC measurements were taken with these settings. However, anywhere from 8 to 20 coefficients were used when the default setting either failed to produce a reading for a formant or produced two readings for a single formant.

With the Sonagraph 5500 at the University of Texas, for which LPC was not available, formants were estimated from harmonic values. Harmonics were examined using FFT power spectra with a frame length of 512 points. If a single harmonic in the neighborhood of a formant had a greater amplitude than neighboring ones, its value was taken as the formant estimate. If two adjacent harmonics in the neighborhood of a formant had approximately equal amplitudes, a value halfway between them was taken as the formant estimate. This method was also used with the CSL at North Carolina State for taking follow-up measurements for speakers analyzed earlier without LPC at the University of Texas. A comparison of vowels measured with and without LPC showed that the difference in techniques did not affect the formant readings greatly (Thomas 1995). It should be remembered that readings taken with LPC, like those made with the harmonic estimation method, can be influenced by harmonic frequencies (especially when f_0 is high), though usually to a lesser extent. LPC is also susceptible to background noise.

The plots show only F1 and F2. From 1990 until 1993, when I was conducting analyses of most of the Texans, I recorded only F1 and F2 values. In 1993, when I turned to analyses of Ohioans, I began recording F3 as well. Since 1996, the period when most of the North Carolinians were analyzed, I have regularly recorded f_0, too. F3 is important largely for lip rounding, /r/-coloring, /l/-coloring, certain other consonant transitions, and certain vowel normalization techniques, while f_0 is important for phonation and some normalization techniques, as well as, of course, various prosodic functions.

Ordinarily, seven to ten tokens of each vowel were measured. However, for some of the less-frequent vowels, such as /oi/ and /ʊ/, and for some of the vowels in special contexts, such as /er/ and /ul/, fewer than seven tokens were available in most cases, and the mean values are based on whatever tokens were present. In addition, some of the archival recordings used were rather short and did not contain the desired number of tokens. When possible, all the tokens were of different lexical items, and with only a few exceptions, no more than two tokens of the same lexical item were measured. When only one token of a vowel class was measured, the word is shown on the formant plot inside angled brackets (e.g., <tour>).

2. VOWEL VARIANTS
IN NEW WORLD ENGLISH

THIS CHAPTER DESCRIBES and discusses the variants, or diaphones, of each stressed vowel. Section 2.1 progresses from the high front vowels, starting with /i/, to the low vowels and then through the back vowels to /u/, with the diphthongs /ai/, /oi/, and /au/ at the end. Section 2.2 covers vowels in certain phonetic contexts that frequently cause conditioned sound changes, namely (1) before /r/, (2) before /l/, (3) before nasals, (4) before certain palatals and velars (especially /g/ and /ʃ/), and (5) in word-final and hiatus positions. Throughout this chapter, references to particular dialects are fairly vague because the emphasis here is on the processes affecting each vowel. However, descriptions of each dialect covered are given in the introductions to chapters 3–8. The descriptions given here are based not only on the vowel plots, but also on the large body of past research by others and on my casual observations of speakers.

2.1. MAIN DIAPHONES OF THE VOWELS

2.1.1. /i/. /i/, as in *see* and *keep*, shows less variation in New World English than most of the other vowels. Much of its meager variation involves the amount of gliding that it exhibits. In general, /i/ tends to be monophthongal at short durations and to show a slight upglide at long durations. It is probably for this reason that it tends to show a wider diphthongization in the South than in the North (assuming that the "Southern drawl" involves longer durations of stressed syllables; see Wetzell 2000). This trend is visible in those plots for which I showed /i/ as a diphthong. Some of the Northerners (e.g., speakers 6, 11, and 15) show little or no gliding, that is, spectral change in the formants from nucleus to glide. Some of the Southerners, conversely, show considerable gliding (e.g., speakers 61, 64, and 84). Wide diphthongization to [əi ~ ɛi], while common in dialects of England, is rare in New World English, though an [əi] type occurs for speaker 87, from Harkers Island, North Carolina. Ingliding [iə] has been reported from the Low Country of coastal South Carolina and Georgia (Kurath and McDavid 1961).

2.1.2. /ɪ/. Most of the diaphones of /ɪ/, as in *bid*, involve varying degrees of fronting and backing, though lowering is also reported. Fronted forms, which may have an inglide (i.e., [i ~ iə]), are most common in the southeastern states (e.g., speakers 59 and 68). They are also predominant in African American speech and in Caribbean varieties. In the North, /ɪ/ tends to be quite central and might best be rendered as [ɨ]. Although this centralization is reported mainly in the Inland Upper North as part of the Northern Cities Shift (e.g., Labov 1994), it appears in many other Northern dialects, such as those in central Ohio. Central forms of /ɪ/ are also reported in old-fashioned Southern speech in such words as *sister* and *dinner*; the distinctiveness of this variant led Trager and Smith (1957) to include it in their /ɨ/ phoneme, but Sledd (1966) countered convincingly that the central and front forms of /ɪ/ simply formed a phonetic continuum. Some Southerners, especially African Americans, appear to have reanalyzed the stressed vowel in *sister* as /ʊ/, so that they produce this word as /sʊstə/. I have shown *sister* on the plots for several such speakers. Lowering of /ɪ/ toward [ɛ] is reported to occur within the Northern Cities Shift as well as in the San Francisco Bay area of California (Luthin 1987) and in Canada (Clarke, Elms, and Youssef 1995; Hoffman 1999; Meechan 1999).

2.1.3. /e/. In most dialects of the North, as well as African American speech, the speech of most white Southerners born in the nineteenth century, and (apparently) most Mexican American English, the usual realization of /e/, as in *day* or *eight*, is [ei]. However, /e/ shows widening, with lowering of the nucleus, in some dialects and may also show monophthongization in other dialects. Lowering, though noted around Philadelphia and Pittsburgh (Kurath and McDavid 1961; Labov 1994), is found mostly in Southern white dialects (see Kurath and McDavid 1961; Labov, Yaeger, and Steiner 1972; Armour 1983; Buckingham 1983; Feagin 1986; Labov 1991;

Mock 1991; Fridland 1998, 2000). Moderate lowering, to [ɛi] ~ [ɛe], is common over much of the South, such as in central Alabama (speakers 59–62) and central North Carolina (speakers 71–74) and also around Pamlico Sound (speakers 79–86). Centralization of the nucleus may occur, too, as in speakers 80 and 87 (from the Pamlico Sound area), speaker 65 (from the southern Appalachians), and speaker 110 (from Texas). Extreme lowering of the nucleus, which results in an [æi] diphthong, is found in the southern Appalachians, in Texas and Oklahoma, and undoubtedly in many other areas, such as Robeson County, North Carolina (see speaker 68). Lowering to [æi] is almost always associated with unconditioned monophthongization of /ai/. While this extreme lowering can be accompanied by retraction of the nucleus to produce an [ai] diphthong, as with speakers 64 and 66 (from the southern Appalachians), the retraction is often absent. Many of the Texans who show the lowering to [æi] have the nucleus very close to the front edge of the vowel envelope (e.g., speakers 117, 118, 120, and 125).

Monophthongization of /e/ to [e:] is usually associated with dialects that show influence from other languages. Perhaps the most obvious examples are found in Minnesota and adjacent states (Allen 1976; see speaker 10, who shows variably monophthongal /e/), which were settled largely by Germans and Scandinavians, and in the Pennsylvania German area (Kurath and McDavid 1961). It is also reported in Louisiana Cajun English (Rubrecht 1971) and among older Japanese Americans in California (Mendoza-Denton and Iwai 1993). Monophthongization should be expected among Hispanic groups, though most of the Mexican Americans featured in chapter 7 show upgliding diphthongal forms. Monophthongal /e/ occurs in Caribbean English and English-based creoles (see speakers 136 and 138) and in very old-fashioned African American speech (see Dorrill 1986a, 1986b, and the discussion in chap. 6), in which it is probably due to influence from African languages. Linguistic atlas records show monophthongal /e/ in white speech in the Low Country of South Carolina and Georgia (as described in the next paragraph) and sporadically elsewhere in the South Atlantic states, especially in the Virginia Piedmont (Kurath and

McDavid 1961; Thomas and Bailey 1998). It is also known from parts of Newfoundland with strong Irish influence (Clarke 1991). Paddock (1981) and Colbourne (1982, cited in Paddock 1986) reported that some speakers from the northeastern coast of New-foundland retain the Middle English distinction between words like *pain/pane* and *maid/made*, the latter of each pair being pro-duced as a monophthong.

Ingliding forms of /e/, i.e., [eə] ~ [iə], also occur and are usually associated with monophthongal forms, probably as a subse-quent development following monophthongization. They occur in Jamaican English, as with speaker 137, where they are clearly derived from earlier monophthongal forms. In old-fashioned white speech of the Low Country of coastal South Carolina and Georgia, some speakers show monophthongal /e/ (e.g., speaker 57) and others show ingliding /e/, but only in checked (non-word-final) position (McDavid 1955). Kurath and McDavid (1961) assert that these variants are survivals of forms formerly predominant in English, but Thomas and Bailey (1998) argue that they (or monophthongization, at any rate) spread from African American speech to white speech. O'Cain (1977) notes that ingliding and monophthongal forms of /e/ are being replaced by upgliding forms in Charleston, and that is undoubtedly true of the rest of the Low Country, too (see also Hopkins 1975).

Schematically, the apparent diachronic development of vari-ants of /e/ is as follows, with [ei] as the oldest extant form in New World English:

[eə ~ iə] < [eː] < [ei] > [ɛi ~ ɛe ~ ɜi] > [æi ~ ai]

2.1.4. /ɛ/. /ɛ/, as in *seven* and *head*, shows various degrees of lowering and raising. In general, lowering is more common in Northern dialects and raising more common in Southern dialects, but each region shows some variation. Lowering has been cited as character-istic of certain Northern and Western dialects: lowering and/or retraction occurs as part of the Northern Cities Shift (Labov 1991, 1994), and lowering is reported from the San Francisco Bay area of California (Luthin 1987) and Canada (Clarke, Elms, and Youssef 1995; Hoffman 1999; Meechan 1999). Speakers 15 and 16 show the Northern Cities Shift mutation of /ɛ/. Although in other dialects /ɛ/ almost always shows a lower mean F1 than /ʌ/, for these two speakers it is the same or slightly higher. In Northern dialects that show slightly raised /æ/ and lowered /ɛ/, it appears that /ɛ/ is distinguished from /æ/ by shorter length. Lowering of /ɛ/ reaches an extreme for speaker 51, from the Bahamas, who may have merged /ɛ/ with /æ/.

Not all Southerners have raised /ɛ/, but forms that are raised and often slightly fronted are common across the South as far west as Texas. Such forms may show inglides. Among the Southeasterners who are featured in this work, the raising of /ɛ/ is most extreme for speakers 57 (from coastal South Carolina), 65 (from the southern Appalachians) and especially 87 (from Harkers Island, North Carolina). It is also obvious among most of the white Texans who preserve the distinction between /ɑ/ and /ɔ/ (see chap. 5). For them it appears that /ɑ/ causes /æ/ to be raised, and /æ/ in turn causes /ɛ/ to be raised. Raised forms of /ɛ/ are common in African American English, too, for the same reason (see chap. 6). They are common as well in Mexican American English (see chap. 7), but there they may be due to Spanish influence. Many Southerners show strongly raised and broken forms of /ɛ/ before /d/ (and perhaps before /n/, though the merger of /ɪ/ and /ɛ/ before nasals among many Southerners obscures the pattern). Thus utterances such as *dead* [deiəd] and *head* [heiəd] are common among Southerners born before about 1960 and are shown on the plots for speakers 53, 58, 72, 88, and 189 (though many of the other speakers produced such forms as well). It is not clear whether the raising before /d/ is phonologized or is part of a phonetic gradient. One non-Southern dialect in which raising of /ɛ/ occurs is that of northeastern Newfoundland, where some speakers merge /ɛ/ into /ɪ/ (Colbourne 1982, cited in Paddock 1986).

2.1.5. /æ/. /æ/, as in *back* and *that*, shows a variety of diaphones, many of them related to the split between /æ/ and /æː/ that occurs in some dialects. /æː/ is covered in §2.1.6; this section discusses variants in dialects that lack the split and the short /æ/ in dialects that have the split. Variants of the short or unsplit /æ/ generally fall into three groups: slightly raised [æ^], strongly raised [eə ~ eɛ ~ iə], and slightly lowered [æ˅ ~ a]. The difference between the slightly raised and slightly lowered forms can often be detected by comparing /æ/ with /ɑ/ to see which has the higher F1 mean. When /æ/ has a lower F1 than /ɑ/, it is raised, and when it has a higher F1, it is lowered. This method works because /æ/ and /ɑ/ seem to affect each other: when /ɑ/ shifts toward [a] (with increased F1 and F2 values), /æ/ is raised, but when /ɑ/ shifts to the back (with decreased F1 and F2), /æ/ is lowered. The slightly raised [æ^] predominates in most older speech and is associated with retention of the /ɑ/-/ɔ/ distinction, though it also occurs in eastern New England speech that has an [a:] vowel deriving from /ar/. It is especially characteristic of African American speech, in which the raising may go as far as [ɛ]. The most strongly raised forms, [eə ~ eɛ ~ iə], typify contemporary speech of the Inland Upper North as part of the Northern Cities Shift, as speakers 14–16 demonstrate. They also occur in Minnesota (see speaker 10), in the St. Louis area (Labov, Ash, and Boberg forthcoming), and in eastern New England (Laferriere 1977).

Lowered /æ/ was until recently restricted to a few dialects. It occurs in Caribbean varieties (see speakers 51 and 136–38), of course, in some of which /æ/ and /ɑ/ are merged to [a], and in Gullah (speaker 139). It also occurs in some speech of the Pamlico Sound area (e.g., speakers 79, 85, and 86) and among older Lumbees (speaker 189) and is reported in words such as *hammer* from old-fashioned speech of northern New England and the South Carolina and Georgia Low Country (Kurath and McDavid 1961; see also speaker 57). In addition, it is found in some dialects with the /æ/-/æ:/ split, such as in Philadelphia (speaker 11; see also the New Orleans native, speaker 88). In the latter half of the twentieth century, however, it has begun to appear much more widely in North America. This sudden spread is closely associated with the merger of /ɑ/ and /ɔ/ and seldom occurs among speakers who do not show that merger. It can be seen in the speech of the western Pennsylvanian (speaker 12), among several of the central Ohioans featured in chapter 3 (most obviously for speakers 26, 27, 43, 45, and 47–50; see also Thomas 1996), and among some of the young Texans in chapter 5 (e.g., speakers 122, 126, 129, 132, and 135). In addition, it has been reported in California (Luthin 1987) and in Canada (Esling and Warkentyne 1993; de Wolf 1993; Clarke, Elms, and Youssef 1995; Warkentyne and Esling 1995; Hoffman 1999), where the merger of /ɑ/ and /ɔ/ also occurs.

Lengthened and ingliding forms, often depicted as [æə] but probably more accurately [æɐ], are common across the South (see, e.g., Feagin 1996). They occur whenever /æ/ has a sufficient duration. They can occur as triphthongal forms, i.e., [æɛɐ ~ æɛæ], and for some Southerners this breaking obscures or obliterates the distinction between /æ/ and /æ:/.

2.1.6. /æ:/. As mentioned in chapter 1, the occurrence of /æ:/, as in *past* and *half*, with respect to /æ/ is often—in fact, usually—phonetically predictable, so it is not truly phonemic in the traditional sense. Its most frequent occurrence is before voiceless fricatives, especially the anterior fricatives /f/, /θ/, and /s/, which seems to derive from the fact that vowels tend to be longer before fricatives than before stops (House and Fairbanks 1953). However, it may also occur in other contexts. As is well known, in British English it occurs before certain nasal clusters, as in *dance* and *command*, in *-alm* words such as *calm* and *palm*, in *father* and *rather*, and in various borrowed words such as *rajah*, and this pattern is mimicked to various degrees in eastern New England. Labov (1971, 427), using a wave model framework, showed how /æ:/ has spread to other phonetic contexts in the Mid-Atlantic states, where it is realized as [eə]. In Philadelphia, /æ:/ occurs before the anterior nasals /n/ and /m/, anterior voiceless fricatives, and in three words before /d/ (*bad*, *mad*, and *glad*). In New York City, /æ:/ occurs before all consonants except voiceless stops, /l/, /ŋ/, and (usually) voiced fricatives. Various communities in New Jersey show intermediate patterns. The patterns are further complicated by the fact that function words (such as auxiliary *can*), irregular verb tenses (e.g., *ran*) and polysyllabic words (e.g., *manager*) tend not to have /æ:/ and by various other factors (see Labov 1989; 1994, 335). Strassel and Boberg (1996) found that /æ:/ had spread to even more contexts in Cincinnati than in New York City, occurring in all environments except before voiceless stops and /l/.

/æ:/ occurs in various incarnations in different dialects. The oldest stage in the split of /æ:/ from /æ/ involves a difference in length but not quality, so that /æ:/ is realized as [æ:] and /æ/ as [æ]. Speakers 2, from Newfoundland, and 53, a Virginia native born in 1846, show this stage. A similar opposition is found in some Caribbean speech (see speakers 136 and 137). What is probably the next oldest development is the backing of /æ:/ to [aː], the "broad *a*," that occurred in eastern New England. As speakers 3 and 4 show, /æ:/ was merged with /ɑr/ in eastern New England, though in contemporary New England speech the short /æ/ has bled most of the former /æ:/ words (see the discussion in the introduction to chap. 3). Some New Englanders have backed the "broad *a*" to [ɑː], the form found in standard British English. At present it is uncertain whether the broad *a* in New England was brought by the settlers from East Anglia who dominated Massachusetts Bay (see Fischer 1989), emerged as an imitation of fashionable British usage, or was an independent development in New England.

In the South a quite different development of /æ:/ occurred: it underwent breaking. A few very old Southerners such as speaker 63 and speakers from the margins of the South such as speaker 22 show forms that could be transcribed as [æɛæ]. However, the usual form is an upgliding diphthong [æɛ] (e.g., for speakers 58, 64, 72, and 100), which may be backed to [aɛ] (e.g., for speaker 65). This form normally consists of an offset steady state but no onset steady state, suggesting that it may have arisen from an earlier [æɛæ] form. Feagin (1996) notes that some speakers intermix the two variants. [æɛ] occurs before [f], [θ], and [s], as is usual in other dialects for /æ:/, but it also usually occurs before palatals, especially /ʃ/ (Kurath and McDavid 1961). The informant sketches in Kretzschmar et al. (1994) indicate that a few speakers in eastern North Carolina had [æɛ] in *-alm* words, though those particular speakers did not have it before palatals. The presence of /æ:/ realized as [æɛ] does not prevent /e/ from being lowered, but the two vowels normally do not become merged because /e/ is realized as [æi], with a higher glide (e.g., speaker 100). The informant sketches in Kretzschmar et al. (1994), however, report that a few eastern North Carolinians did merge /æ:/ and /e/, with the result that pairs such as *past* and *paste* were homophonous. It is unfortunate that none of those informants was recorded so that the transcription could be checked acoustically. According to Kurath and McDavid (1961), /æ:/ realized as [æɛ] occurs throughout the South Atlantic states except for the areas around Chesapeake Bay and Pamlico Sound and in coastal South Carolina. The *Linguistic Atlas of the Gulf States* (*LAGS* 1986–92) reports that, although [æɛ] is widespread in the region, it is most frequent in the highland regions of Tennessee and Arkansas and in the coastal Piney Woods belt of the southern parts of Georgia, Alabama, and Mississippi and northern Florida, with a disjunct area in eastern Texas.

Raising of /æ:/ occurs in the Mid-Atlantic region from New York City to Philadelphia (see the extensive discussion in Labov 1994, as well as in his earlier work, especially Labov 1966, 1971, 1989) and also in Cincinnati (Strassel and Boberg 1996) and formerly throughout the southern three-quarters of Ohio (see Humphries 1999; Thomas and Boberg in preparation). The phonetic distribution in different dialects is described above. The realization varies from slightly raised [æ^:] to moderately raised and ingliding or downgliding variants [eə ~ eɛ ~ eæ] to extreme forms such as [iə].

Labov (1994, 203–4) reports that the vowel in words such as *father, calm,* and *rajah* remains distinct from /ɑ/ in New York City, often being more backed, [ɒ:]. Speakers with this distinction may identify this vowel with /ɑr/, as Kurath and McDavid (1961) note for some *r*-less Southerners for the same words.

2.1.7. /ɑ/. /ɑ/, as in *cot* and *hospital,* is reported to show a range of values from [æ] to [ɒ] in New World English. Fronted variants, [a], can be recognized on the vowel plots because they are found at the bottom corner of the vowel envelope, approximately on the midline of the envelope—that is, a line that divides the envelope into equal front and back halves. [a] occurs in three general regions. The first is a broad area that includes the Inland Upper North, Connecticut, and parts of the northern Great Plains (especially Minnesota). In this region the Northern Cities Shift, of which the fronting of /ɑ/ is one component, operates. Speakers 7, 8, 13–16, and to a lesser extent, 10 exhibit the fronting. Labov, Yaeger, and Steiner (1972) and Labov (1991, 1994) have stated that fronting as far as [æ] occurs, but an examination of the vowel formant plots in those sources suggests that [æ] forms occur mainly in phonetic contexts that induce raising of F2, particularly the words *got* and *not*, and that /ɑ/ seldom otherwise occurs as [æ]. The description of /ɑ/ as [æ] may have been influenced by misperceptions by listeners from other dialects—for example, Labov's (1994, 186) account of his own misperception of a Chicagoan's pronunciations of *John* and *locks*.

The other regions in which /ɑ/ may be fronted to [a] are Newfoundland and the Caribbean. In Newfoundland, the fronting seems to be due to Irish influence (see speaker 2; also described by D'Arcy 1999). In the Caribbean, [a] occurs as a residue of creole formation, often as a result of merger of /ɑ/ with /æ/ (see speakers 136 and 137).

Forms of /ɑ/ that are nearly as front can be recognized on the plots by their position just back of the midline of the vowel envelope. These variants might best be described as [ɑ˂] and are widespread in dialects that maintain the distinction between /ɑ/ and /ɔ/ (e.g., Philadelphia, north-central Ohio, and most of the South). They are characteristic of African American English.

A more backed variant, [ɑ˲], usually occurs when /ɑ/ and /ɔ/ are merged. On the vowel plots, this variant lies at a point that is clearly on the back edge of the vowel envelope, not at the bottom corner. The linguistic atlas records from eastern New England and western Pennsylvania, where this merger occurs, usually depicted the merged vowel as [ɒ]. Speakers 3 and 4, who were linguistic atlas informants, did not impressionistically sound to me as if their /ɑ = ɔ/ vowel was as rounded as the form usual in standard British *hot*, but lip rounding is a gradient feature and some rounding may well have been present. The *Linguistic Atlas of New England* (*LANE* 1939–43) did not have a symbol for a low back unrounded vowel and field-workers may have used [ɒ] for that value. Several studies have reported rounding of the merged /ɑ = ɔ/ in Canada (Woods 1979, 1991, 1993; de Wolf 1993; Clarke, Elms, and Youssef 1995;

Warkentyne and Esling 1995). Some Mexican Americans with the merger show more fronted forms (e.g., speakers 181 and 182). /ɒ/ forms have been reported in two American dialects that retain the /ɑ/-/ɔ/ distinction, the Pamlico Sound dialect (Howren 1962) and the dialect of the Low Country of South Carolina and Georgia (McDavid 1955, 1958; Kurath and McDavid 1961). However, the Pamlico Sound natives featured here (speakers 79–87 and 150–156) do not show any such rounding. Many Southerners who maintain the /ɑ/-/ɔ/ distinction do have forms of /ɑ/ in the range of [ɑˀ].

2.1.8. /ɔ/. /ɔ/, as in *caught* and *off*, shows a wide range of variation, much of it analogous with variation in /æː/. The form that apparently predominated in early Modern English, [aː ~ ɑː], still occurs in Newfoundland, where it was brought by settlers from Ireland and southwestern England (see speaker 2). It also occurs in some Caribbean speech, especially when /ɔ/ is merged with /æː/, as with speaker 136. More widespread in New World English are rounded but still monophthongal forms, [ɒ ~ ɔ]. They occur in many dialects in which the distinction between /ɑ/ and /ɔ/ is maintained and even in some Southern speech, for which they may be considered more prestigious than the upgliding forms that predominate in the South.

Upgliding forms are widespread in the South in both white and African American speech. Older Southerners usually produce rather raised forms, [ɔo]. Some older Southerners, such as speaker 58, produce forms with a wider glide, [ɑo]. Younger Southerners are more likely to produce lower forms that might be best depicted as [ɑʊ]; speakers 62, 74, and 115 are examples. Outside the South, upgliding forms are rare or restricted to favorable phonetic contexts, such as before [g].

Raised and monophthongal forms approaching [o], though common in British dialects, have a restricted distribution in New World English. They are most prevalent around Pamlico Sound in North Carolina, mostly among speakers born before 1960 (see speakers 79–81, 83–87, 150, 152, 154, and 155; the weak glides shown on the plots are largely inconsequential). More discussion is found in Wolfram, Hazen, and Schilling-Estes (1999, 120–41). Similar forms are found in the Low Country of South Carolina and Georgia (speaker 57), in white Bahamian English (speaker 51), in old-fashioned African American speech (e.g., speakers 140 and 142), and in the speech of some older Southerners who do not show appreciable upglides (e.g., speakers 53 and 97).

Raised and ingliding or downgliding variants of /ɔ/ are associated with the dialects of New York City, New Jersey, and Philadelphia. Their realizations include [oə ~ oɔ ~ uə]. Speakers 9 and 11 exhibit such forms.

Unrounded forms of /ɔ/ that are not retentions from early Modern English (as in Newfoundland) occur in two situations. The first is in dialects that merge /ɑ/ and /ɔ/, for which the resulting vowel is normally partially or fully unrounded. The resulting realization is most commonly [ɑ>], though more fronted forms occur and more rounded forms, denoted as [ɒ], are reported (see discussion in §2.1.7). The merger of /ɑ/ and /ɔ/ is found over large parts of North America: eastern New England; Canada; a region including western Pennsylvania, West Virginia, eastern Kentucky, and much of central and southern Ohio, with extensions into Indiana and Illinois; and the West, extending east to portions of Minnesota, western Missouri, and Oklahoma (see, e.g., Wetmore 1959; Kurath and McDavid 1961; Avis 1972; Metc 'f 1972a; Mills 1980; and esp. Labov, Ash, and Boberg forthcomi). The merger is spreading in many areas. The plots in chapter 5 show that it has spread across most of Texas recently (also reported in Tillery 1989; Bailey, Wikle, and Sand 1991; and Bernstein 1993), and Fridland (1998, 2000) has found it in Memphis, Tennessee. Partial neutralizations of /ɑ/ and /ɔ/ occur as well. DeCamp (1959) reported that some speakers in Washington state could perceive the distinction only in final syllables, thus recognizing the distinction between *cot* and *caught* but not that between *knotty* and *naughty*. Speaker 29, from Columbus, Ohio, shows the same distribution in his production. Linguistic atlas informants from southeastern Ohio and northern West Virginia have /ɑ/ and /ɔ/ neutralized before /t/, but apparently not in other contexts; this alignment is shown by speakers 25 and 157 (see also the discussion in chap. 3). Labov, Ash, and Boberg (1997) reported that some speakers neutralize /ɑ/ and /ɔ/ before nasals (e.g., *Don* and *dawn*) but not in other contexts. Di Paolo (1992) reported that /ɑ/ and /ɔ/ may be distinguished in Utah, where they are usually assumed to be merged, through either the F_1/F_2 pattern or phonation, with /ɔ/ breathier than /ɑ/.

The second situation in which unrounded /ɔ/ occurs as an innovation is in the Northern Cities Shift. In this shift, /ɔ/ may simply be lowered to [ɒ] or may be unrounded to [ɑ], which still remains distinct from /ɑ/. Speakers 15 and 16, who show the Northern Cities Shift, both have this [ɑ ~ ɒ] variant.

2.1.9. /ʌ/. The most widespread variant of /ʌ/, as in *cut*, is one that appears on the midline of vowel plots. It is probably best described as [ɜ] because it is more central than back. It occurs consistently for the speakers from Johnstown, Ohio (speakers 31–50), and for most of the Texans in chapter 5, but it is found in many other dialects.

Backed variants of /ʌ/ are more restricted in distribution, but occur in several dialects. Most commonly they may be backed and unrounded, [ʌ], but they may be rounded to [ɔ]. They can be recognized on the plots by their appearing back of center. They are found in six of the dialects covered in this monograph. The first is the dialect of Newfoundland (speaker 2), in which backed [ʌ] is common and rounded [ɔ] occurs where Irish influence is strong. The second is the Northern Cities Shift dialect, where backing and rounding occur as a recent development, as with speaker 16. Eckert (1987) first noted this aspect of the Northern Cities Shift, and she found that a few of her subjects from a suburb of Detroit showed variants approaching [ʊ]. The third is the Philadelphia accent (speaker 11). The fourth is Caribbean English and English-based creoles, in which the usual realization is [ɔ] (speakers 51 and 136–38). The fifth is African American English, in which backing of /ʌ/ is common but not universal (see chap. 6). Sixth is old-fashioned white Southern speech, mainly in coastal plain and Piedmont areas in which the plantation culture once flourished. Examples are speakers 57, 59–61, 69, and 88. Surprisingly, backed forms do not appear to be frequent in Mexican American speech, though a few Chicanos, such as speaker 177, have them. They may be more common in the speech of Mexican Americans who acquired English as a second language.

Other variants of /ʌ/ occasionally appear as well. Fronted forms are occasionally reported (Luthin 1987; Clarke, Elms, and Youssef 1995); on some of the plots /ʌ/ may seem to squeeze in between /æ/ and /e/, as for speakers 30, 87, 93, and 188. Raised forms, [ə], occur for a few Southerners, such as speakers 123 and 147. The linguistic atlas records mapped in Kurath and McDavid (1961) showed raised forms, transcribed as [ɤ] or [ʌ>^] depending on the field-worker, for most of the South, but such forms did not appear in the vowel formant plots from that region; the [ɤ ~ ʌ>^] form shown in the lingusitic atlas transcriptions may have referred to the backed variant described above.

2.1.10. /o/. /o/, as in *coat* and *know*, undergoes four processes in different dialects: fronting of the nucleus, fronting of the glide, lowering of the nucleus, and monophthongization, the last of which may be associated with ingliding. To complicate the picture, some dialects show both fronting and lowering. Fronting of the nucleus may be moderate, so that /o/ is produced as [ɵu ~ əu], or strong, with /o/ produced as [øʉ ~ eʉ]. According to linguistic atlas records, as shown in Kurath and McDavid (1961) and in field records from the *Linguistic Atlas of the Middle and South Atlantic States* (*LAMSAS* 1982–86) and the *Linguistic Atlas of the North Central States* (*LANCS* 1976–78), the fronting was originally confined to three geographical centers. The first center is Philadelphia and adjacent parts of southeastern Pennsylvania, southern New Jersey, and Delaware (for this area, see also Tucker 1944). The second center is an area including western Pennsylvania, northern West Virginia, and parts of central and southern Ohio. In Ohio, the older *LANCS* informants show less fronting than the younger ones, so fronting of /o/ probably was not as old there as in Pennsylvania (see also chap. 3). The third center is eastern North Carolina. In the *LAMSAS* records, all of the informants from around Pamlico Sound show some fronting, but it occurs irregularly elsewhere in the North Carolina coastal plain, mostly among younger informants. The linguistic atlas data suggest that fronting of /o/—

moderate fronting, at least—was established in Philadelphia and western Pennsylvania and around Pamlico Sound by the time of the Civil War and spread across central and southern Ohio and inland parts of the North Carolina coastal plain around 1900. The Delmarva Peninsula soon followed (Greet 1933). Wells (1982) notes that there was a fourth center of /o/ fronting, white Bahamian speech (as can be seen for speaker 51), and La Ban (1971) reports that the Bahamians who settled in the Florida Keys brought fronted /o/ with them.

Fronting of the nucleus has spread rapidly in American English in recent years. It has been reported in east-central Illinois (Habick 1980, 1993); Kansas City (Lusk 1976), Wichita, Kansas (Wyatt 1976); the Bay area of California (Luthin 1987); Canada (Clarke, Elms, and Youssef 1995); Texas (Bailey and Maynor 1989, 21); eastern Tennessee (Pederson 1983); Anniston, Alabama (Feagin 1986); southeastern Georgia (Hall 1976); Wilmington, North Carolina (Thomas 1989); Baltimore (Kerr 1963; Schnitzer 1972); and central Ohio (Thomas 1989/93, 1996). See also Hartman (1984) and Murray (1992). It now seems to predominate in the speech of young whites throughout the South and as far north as Pennsylvania, north-central Ohio, central Illinois, Kansas, and California, and possibly farther north in the West (see Labov, Ash, and Boberg forthcoming, though they exclude the West from its main distribution). The main regions that have resisted it are New England, the Inland Upper North, the northern Great Plains, and perhaps New York City. The progression of fronting can be seen for the central Ohio speakers in chapter 3, for whom only the oldest (speakers 25, 29, and 31, all born before 1910) show backed forms, and several of those born after 1960 show strongly fronted forms. The Texans in chapter 5 show a similar, but delayed, distribution: backed forms predominate among those before World War II, fronted forms among those born after. The fronting is largely confined to white speech (and Asian American speech; see Luthin 1987). However, a few African Americans and Mexican Americans do show it, as noted in chapters 6 and 7 (see speakers 152–57, 170, and 186–88), as do young Lumbee Indians in North Carolina (speaker 190).

Fronting of the glide of /o/ results in forms such as [ʌü] and [ɜü] and even, as with speaker 73, [ɛü]. Glide fronting of /o/ is largely confined to the Southeastern states. It has been present in eastern North Carolina for some time (see the analysis in Labov, Yaeger, and Steiner 1972, 135–44). However, together with fronting of the nucleus, it has spread throughout the Southeast since World War II. I have heard speakers with front gliding /o/ from as far north as Roanoke, Virginia, central West Virginia, and Kentucky and as far west as Arkansas. It is mostly absent in Texas, however. Because rounding increases through the course of the /o/ diphthong and rounding decreases F2, front-gliding /o/ appears on the vowel formant plots not only when the vector moves leftward (i.e., when F2 increases), but also when the vector moves straight upward (i.e., when F2 shows little change). The only older speakers who have front-gliding /o/ are from eastern North Carolina (speakers 67, 80, 81, and 152), but it appears for many younger people (speakers 62, 68, 70, 71, 73, 74, 78, 82, 118, 156, and 190).

Lowering of the nucleus of /o/ results in forms such as [ʌu] if the lowering is moderate and [ɐu] if it is strong. It typically occurs in tandem with lowering of the nucleus of /e/ and thus is largely restricted to the South. Speakers 112–14 and 117 exemplify the [ɐu]-type variant. Lowering often occurs together with fronting, which results in forms such as [æʉ ~ ɜʉ]. Examples of speakers with both lowering and fronting of the nucleus are speakers 66, 115, 122, and 127.

Like the relationship between lowering of /o/ and lowering of /e/, monophthongization of /o/ to [oː] is analogous with monophthongization of /e/ and occurs in the same dialects. In fact, practically everything mentioned in section 2.1.3 for monophthongal /e/ is true of monophthongal /o/ as well. It occurs in Minnesota and adjacent states (Allen 1976 and speaker 10), in the Pennsylvania German area (Kurath and McDavid 1961), in Irish-influenced Newfoundland speech (Clarke 1991), in Louisiana Cajun English (Rubrecht 1971), among older Japanese Americans in California (Mendoza-Denton and Iwai 1993), among Hispanic groups (e.g., speaker 182), in Caribbean English and English-based creoles (e.g., speakers 136 and 138), in old-fashioned African American speech (Dorrill 1986a, 1986b, and speakers 140 and 142), and in old-fashioned white speech of the Low Country of South Carolina and Georgia (speaker 57) and sporadically elsewhere in the South Atlantic states. Just as with ingliding forms of /e/, ingliding or downgliding forms of /o/, [oə ~ ɔɔ ~ uə ~ uo], occur in some areas, notably Jamaica (speaker 137) and the Low Country, where they are associated with monophthongal forms as an apparent subsequent development following monophthongization. Like ingliding /e/, they are confined to checked phonetic contexts in the Low Country (see Kurath and McDavid 1961). Also like /e/, O'Cain (1977) found that ingliding and monophthongal variants of /o/ are being supplanted by upgliding forms in Charleston, South Carolina.

The diachronic processes that affected /o/ are shown in table 2.1. I assume [ou] as the starting form, though, as with monophthongal /e/, there is disagreement as to whether monophthongal /o/ resulted from monophthongization of [ou], the position that I favor, or was brought from England, which Kurath and McDavid (1961) favor; see also the discussion of /ɵ/ that follows.

A sidelight on the story of /o/ is /ɵ/, which occurred in very old-fashioned New England speech (see speakers 3 and 4). /ɵ/ was a residue of the Middle English distinction between such words as *toad/towed, road/rowed, moan/mown*, and *toe/tow*. In each of these pairs, the first member had Middle English /ɔː/ and the second had Middle English /ɔu/. This distinction has been lost in all other forms of New World English. In New England, some words from

TABLE 2.1
Diachronic Processes Affecting /o/

Caribbean, Low Country, and other language contact situations

[ou]	>	[oː] (monophthongization)	>	[oə ~ ɔɔ ~ uə ~ uo] (ingliding/downgliding)

Elsewhere in North America	*Without Lowering*	*With Lowering*
Without fronting	[ou] (i.e., no change)	[ʌu ~ ɐu]
Fronting of nucleus	[ɵu ~ əu ~ øʉ ~ eʉ]	[æʉ ~ ɜʉ]
Fronting of nucleus & glide	[ɵü ~ əü ~ øü ~ eü]	[ɜü ~ ɛü]

the Middle English /ɔː/ class, such as *toad, road, most, home, stone, folks,* and *whole,* formed a class distinct from the one that included *towed,* and this class has previously been called /ɵ/ or the "New England short *o.*" Fuller descriptions are given in Avis (1961) and Kurath and McDavid (1961). /ɵ/ never occurred word-finally, but otherwise the distribution of words with Middle English /ɔː/ that were transferred to Modern English /o/ and those that remained as /ɵ/ was lexically and idiolectally specific. Kurath and McDavid (1961, 111) described /ɵ/ as "a fronted and lowered mid-back [o<ᵛ ~ ɔ<ᶺ] sound," but the data for speakers 3 and 4 (based on only a few tokens) suggest that /ɵ/ may not have been fronted at all. Avis (1961) noted that /ɵ/ showed inglides in certain words but not in others, but the words with inglides that he listed are ones in which the phonetic context would favor a rising F2, that is, words with /ɵ/ in the final syllable followed by an alveolar stop.

2.1.11. /ʊ/. Most of the variation that /ʊ/, as in *took* and *put,* exhibits involves the front/back dimension. Many dialects show backed forms, [ʊ], but fronting to [ʉ] and even as far as [ʏ] is common, especially in white Southern speech. The plots can make /ʊ/ appear more central than it really is. Speakers who also show backed /u/, such as speakers 2 (Newfoundland) and 3 (Massachusetts) and many of the African Americans in chapter 6, have higher F2 values for /ʊ/ than for /u/. This difference is not due to centralization of /ʊ/, but to the facts that /u/ shows stronger rounding than /ʊ/ and rounding decreases F2. A number of other speakers, such as speakers 11 (Philadelphia), 51 (Bahamas), and 57 (Low Country of South Carolina), show /ʊ/ in the same position as the previously named speakers, but show mean /u/ values with a higher F2. This alignment reflects the fact that /ʊ/ is less likely to be fronted than /u/.

Most of the speakers with strongly fronted variants of /ʊ/ are Texans (e.g., speakers 121, 122, 124, 129, 131, 134, and 135), though some North Carolinians, such as speakers 67 and 68, also show strongly fronted forms. A comparison of the Texans in chapter 5 with the Ohioans in chapter 3 would make it seem that the fronting of /ʊ/ lags behind the fronting of /u/ in Ohio but not in

Texas. Nevertheless, this apparent difference could be an artifact of the words used. Different reading passages were used in Texas and Ohio. One of the six words with /ʊ/ measured for the Texans was *good*. /ʊ/ typically shows a high F2 value in *good* because of coarticulation with the /g/ and with the alveolar /d/. *Good* was not one of the seven words with /ʊ/ measured for the Ohioans. With only six or seven tokens, one word could skew the formant readings enough to produce the apparent difference.

2.1.12. /u/. Like /ʊ/, /u/, as in *too* and *move*, shows most of its variation in the front-back dimension. Like /i/, however, it also varies in the amount of gliding that it shows. The front-back variation applies not only to the nucleus, but also, as with /o/ and /au/, to the direction of gliding. I have not shown the gliding of /u/ on the plots of many speakers because the relative rarity of /u/ meant that fewer examples of /u/ were available in the recordings than of other vowels. As a result, I was forced to use more tokens of /u/ in contexts with nasals and approximants, for which the high degree of coarticulation makes the gliding less certain. Thus, in many cases it seemed best simply to take one reading in the center of /u/.

That said, there are still clear trends in the development of /u/. Kurath and McDavid (1961) found that, for the birth cohorts represented in the linguistic atlas projects, the fronting of /u/ was essentially a Southern feature, though a few Northerners showed it as well. The linguistic atlas transcriptions showed [ʉ], not [ü], as the most advanced form at the time, which my analyses of speakers of that vintage support. Since the time that the linguistic atlas research was conducted, however, /u/ has changed considerably. First, the fronting process has spread widely. It has spilled out of the South: it is now firmly entrenched in areas such as central Illinois (Habick 1980, 1993), central Ohio (Thomas 1989/93, 1996), and Philadelphia (Labov 1994) and is making inroads into California (Luthin 1987), the Inland Upper North (Ash 1996) and even New England (see speaker 6) and Canada (Clarke, Elms, and Youssef 1995). In most areas where fronting of both /u/ and /o/ occurs, /u/ fronting leads /o/ fronting, and it occurs in a number of areas where /o/ fronting is rare such as the Inland Upper North. However, it has not become predominant in African American speech, even though a few African Americans show it (e.g., speakers 152, 154, 155, 163, and 164), and avoidance of it may have become an identity marker for African Americans. It is also absent from most Mexican American speech (see chap. 7).

Second, the most advanced form is now the fully fronted [ü]. This form is common throughout the South but is found in other areas, too. Almost all of the young central Ohioans (speakers 27, 28, 30, and 44–49) show it. Some authors have asserted that /u/ is undergoing unrounding as it is fronted, but I am skeptical about that.

When /u/ has a duration long enough to show a glide, it normally shows a falling F2, as with speakers 4, 11, 23, and 52. The fall in F2 is probably accomplished in large part by an increase in rounding through the course of /u/. If so, the weaker initial rounding may have been what led some, as noted in the preceding paragraph, to assert that /u/ was being unrounded. In the Southeast, /u/ can show a fronting glide, as with speaker 74, so that forms such as *too* [tʰʉˇü] are possible (see also Labov, Yaeger, and Steiner 1972, 135–44). A few Southerners, such as speaker 66, show some widening of the /u/ diphthong.

2.1.13. /ai/. This sound, as in *sight* and *side*, is one of the most heavily studied vowels because much of its variation is stereotypical. In general, three basic processes affect it: backing and sometimes rounding of the nucleus, fronting and/or raising of the nucleus, and weakening of the glide or outright monophthongization. I am using [ai ~ ae] here as the basic form because it is the most widespread variant.

Backing of the nucleus produces forms such as [ɑˀːe ~ ɑˀːɛ], and subsequent rounding produces forms like [ɒːe ~ ɒːɛ], though rounded forms are less common than backed unrounded forms in New World English. Forms of /ai/ with a strongly backed nucleus are most prevalent around Pamlico Sound in eastern North Carolina, as with speakers 79–81, 83–87, 152, 154, and 155. In this area, triphthongization to [ɐɑˀɛ] may occur, as it does for speakers

79 and 80. Backing may also occur in North Carolina in old-fashioned Lumbee speech; for example speaker 189 shows rounding of the nucleus, as indicated by the fact that his /ai/ nuclei appear higher in the plot relative to the other vowels than the /ai/ nuclei for the Pamlico Sound speakers. Backing of the /ai/ nucleus is known from several other dialects, too. Strongly backed forms occur in New York City (Labov 1966) and are reported in Philadelphia, though it is not clear that variants with anything more than moderate backing occur in Philadelphia. They occur in white Bahamian speech (see speaker 51). They also occur in Newfoundland, where /ai/ may be merged with /oi/, as with speaker 2. They can occur as well across the South before voiceless consonants in dialects that retain /ai/ as a diphthong in that context, as in *sight* [sɑˀˑet] (e.g., speakers 59–62, 70, 71, 75–78, and 88). Moderate backing to [ɑˤe ~ ɑe] is widespread. Many of the central Ohio speakers, most prominently speakers 23, 26, 30, 33, 37, and 42, as well as people from other regions, such as speaker 132, exhibit moderate backing.

There is no clear-cut distinction between fronting and raising of the /ai/ nucleus. Both are products of truncation of the onset of the diphthong, and they ordinarily occur together, resulting in [æˀi ~ ɜi]. They have been spreading rapidly in recent years in the northern United States. I described the fronting part of the process in Thomas (1996) for Johnstown, Ohio, where some young natives, such as speaker 49, show it robustly. Other young Ohioans who show fronting/raising are speakers 20 and 27. These three speakers show the fronting/raising in all phonetic contexts. Some Caribbeans, such as speakers 136 and 138, do so as well. More commonly, however, it appears only before voiceless consonants, (e.g., *sight* [sɜit] vs. *side* [saed]). Though first described from Virginia (Shewmake 1920, 1925) this contextual distribution has been associated with Canadian English since Joos (1942) first described it from Canada and was dubbed "Canadian raising" by Chambers (1973). Traditionally, it was found in parts of the South Atlantic states (Kurath and McDavid 1961), in some Caribbean varieties (Trudgill 1986), and in Canada. During the twentieth century, however, it has declined in the South but has spread into

New England, the Inland Upper North, the New York–Philadelphia area, and apparently western Pennsylvania. Discussions of the literature on these changes are given in chapters 3 and 4. In the Inland Upper North, the raising may be extended to /ai/ before /r/, as in *tire*, as shown for speakers 15 and 16. Some speakers with the raising show subsequent backing of the nucleus to produce an [ʌi] form, as do speakers 2 and 16; speaker 3 shows a similar form in all contexts.

One controversy surrounding "Canadian raising" is the question of whether it truly represents raising from an earlier [ai] form or represents failure to lower during the Great Vowel Shift from Middle English [iː] to Modern English [ai]. Chambers (1973) and I (Thomas 1991) have argued that it is raising, but various other authors (e.g., Gregg 1973; Picard 1977) have argued that it represents failure to lower. In my opinion, the latter view stems from slavish adherence to the doctrine of parsimony. An [ai] > [ɜi] shift has been demonstrated in Philadelphia (see Labov 1994), though it could be argued that it could have resulted from a spread of [ɜi] from other regions. Nevertheless, I now think that both views are partly correct because the phonetics of /ai/ are more complicated than anyone has acknowledged. Some very old speakers, such as speakers 3, 4, 7, and 13, show a pattern in which /ai/ has a low nucleus when it has a long duration but a higher nucleus when it has a short duration. Thus their target values are [ai ~ ɑi], but they show a wide range of phonetic realizations. These old speakers do not have the variants limited to positions before voiceless or voiced consonants. Because vowels and diphthongs tend to be shorter before voiceless consonants than elsewhere and because shorter durations can result in truncation of the onsets of diphthongs, however, eventually the raised forms gravitated to contexts before voiceless consonants and the lowered forms to other contexts. The result was Canadian raising. Younger speakers who show Canadian raising exhibit narrower ranges of variation for each phonetic context than the old speakers did.

The final process affecting /ai/, glide weakening or monophthongization, involves weakening of the glide to produce [aɛ], [aːæ ~ aːɐ], and ultimately [aː]. It is usually associated with the

South, and its distribution coincides closely with the South and with a few Southern-settled areas, such as southern Illinois (Frazer 1978, 1987b) and eastern New Mexico. However, some other Northerners show it, too (e.g., speaker 12, from western Pennsylvania), and it is widespread in favored environments such as before /l/. Some early accounts disputed whether it involved simply weakening of the glide (e.g., Greet 1931, Edgerton 1935) or complete monophthongization (e.g., Evans 1935). The fact is that both forms occur, as Hall (1942) noted.

Glide weakening and monophthongization show two contextual distributions. The first, and presumably older, is for them to occur in all phonetic contexts except before voiceless consonants, so that *side* is [saːæd ~ saːd] and *sight* is [saet ~ sɑet]. This pattern is usual in African American speech. It also predominates in white speech in parts of the South in which the plantation culture once flourished. It is almost certainly derived from the pattern that still appears in Northern dialects in which /ai/ glides approach a high front position more closely before voiceless consonants than in other contexts, resulting in *side* [saed] versus *sight* [sait] (see Thomas 1991, 1995, 2000). The other distribution pattern is for /ai/ to be weak-gliding or monophthongal in all contexts, as in *side* [saːæd ~ saːd] and *sight* [saæt ~ saˑt]. This pattern predominates in the southern Appalachians (see Hall 1942 and speakers 64–66), in some parts of the North Carolina coastal plain, mainly in the Cape Fear valley (speakers 67, 68, and 190), and in rural parts of Texas (see chap. 5). *LAGS* data show that it predominates not only in the southern Appalachians (especially eastern Tennessee and northern Alabama), but also in the Ozark region and in the southerly Piney Woods belt. In the South Atlantic states it is associated with regions settled heavily by Ulster Scots or Highland Scots, and west of the Appalachians it is associated with regions where the plantation culture was never strong. In many parts of the South it is considered less prestigious than the pattern that has strong glides before voiceless consonants. Completely monophthongal /ai/ can vary in its quality. Some speakers, such as speaker 126, have a form approaching [ɑː] and others, such as speaker 110, produce [æː], but most have an intermediate [aː].

The following summarizes the processes that have affected /ai/:

Backing: [ai ~ ae] > [ɑˀ:e ~ ɑˀ:ɛ] > [ɒ:e ~ ɒ:ɛ]
Canadian raising: [ɐi ~ ai ~ ae] > [ɐi ~ ɜi] before voiceless consonants/
  [ae] in other contexts > [ʌi] before voiceless consonants/[ɑe] in
  other contexts
Glide weakening: [ai] before voiceless consonants/[ae] in other
  contexts > [ai ~ ɑi] before voiceless consonants/[a:æ ~ a:] in
  other contexts > [a:] in all contexts

2.1.14. /oi/. /oi/, as in *boy* and *voice*, shows more variation than might
be expected. Some of this variation involves one of the least-noted
but most widespread shifts in American English: the raising of /oi/
from [ɔi] to [oi] and occasionally to [ui]. Forms closer to [ɔi] are
found mainly among the oldest speakers featured here (e.g., speakers 4, 13, 22, 25, 53, 54, 63, 72, 95, and 139). Almost all of the
speakers born in the twentieth century—and some born earlier,
such as speakers 97 and 141—show higher nuclei.

Two other variations are found mainly in the South: triphthongization, to [ɔoi], and lowering or weakening of the glide.
Triphthongization is common among Southerners born before
World War II, but is apparently absent among those born after
1970. It is shown for many of the speakers in chapters 4–6 (e.g.,
speakers 58–61, 100, 104, 110, 112, 117, and 166). It becomes
most extreme for the speakers from Montgomery, Alabama—the
mean /oi/ value for speaker 60 is equivalent to [ɑoɨ].

Lowering of the glide to produce forms such as [oɛ] and [oæ]
is most frequent in African American speech. African Americans
who show glide lowering most strongly include speakers 141, 146,
152, 154, 155, 162, 168, and 171. Weakening of the glide results in
forms such as [oɤ] and [ɔʌ], as shown by speaker 145. These
processes are much less common in white Southern speech, but
glide weakening appears for speakers 75–77, from the North Carolina Piedmont. Glide weakening also occurs in Cherokee English,
as for speaker 191 (see Anderson 1999). Unlike for /ai/, glide
lowering and weakening of /oi/ are apparently little affected by the
voicing of the following consonant, though the sparseness of tokens of /oi/ precludes firm conclusions about that.

Merger of /oi/ with /ai/ occurs in a few dialects. It is common in Caribbean varieties, as shown for speaker 137 from Jamaica, though some Caribbeans maintain the distinction by producing /oi/ as [wai] and /ai/ simply as [ai] (Veatch 1991). It also occurs in Newfoundland, as for speaker 2.

2.1.15. /au/. /au/, as in *house* and *now*, shows a bewildering array of variations. Variation in the nucleus of /au/ is well known. However, at least as much variation occurs for the glide, and this variation is not well documented. The phonetic target of the glide may be [u], [ü], or, most commonly in American English, [ɔ] (and there may be other possibilities, too). To add to the confusion, the glide seldom reaches its target. For example, in dialects that seem to have a glide target value of [u], the most common realization of the glide is [o].

There are relatively few dialects that show what is commonly regarded as the "normal" form of /au/, with a target value of [au] in all phonetic contexts. In such dialects, the usual realization is not actually [au], but [ao ~ ɑo]. Speakers 10 (Minnesota), 17 and 18 (north-central Ohio), and 88 (New Orleans) show this variant. Foreign language influence is likely in all three of those dialects: Scandinavian languages and German in Minnesota, German in north-central Ohio, and French in New Orleans. Even though /au/ does not occur in most dialects of Swedish or Norwegian or in French, interference could have occurred if speakers treated /au/ as a sequence of /a/ plus /u/.

[ao ~ ɑo] occurs more widely as part of the process called Canadian raising, described in §2.1.13 above. For /au/, Canadian raising is manifested as [ʌu ~ ʌo ~ ɜü] before voiceless consonants (as in *house*) and [ao ~ ɑo ~ æɔ] in other phonetic contexts. Dialects that show the backed form [ʌu ~ ʌo] before voiceless consonants show [ao ~ ɑo] in other contexts, while those that show the fronted form [ɜü] before voiceless consonants show [æɔ] in other contexts. The [ʌu ~ ʌo]–versus–[ao ~ ɑo] pattern predominates in Canada, as with speakers 1 and 2, and probably in the contemporary speech of eastern New England, as with speakers 5 and 6. It appears in old-fashioned speech of the Low Country of South

Carolina and Georgia, as for speaker 57, and in old-fashioned African American speech in Virginia and adjacent areas, as for speaker 140. The [ɝü]-versus-[æɔ] pattern is usually associated with white speech in Virginia and adjacent parts of Maryland and North Carolina and is most obvious for speakers 55 and 69. Chambers and Hardwick (1986) note that a similar pattern can occur for some young Canadians. The frontward progression of the form found before voiceless consonants is clear for speakers 53–55: speaker 53 shows [ɐʉ], 54 shows [əʉˁ], and 55 shows the fully fronted [ɝü]. Another variation occurs for speaker 75, who has [aʉ] before voiceless consonants. It should be noted that speaker 53 does not have [ɐʉ] confined to contexts before voiceless consonants. It also appears before voiced obstruents, as in *thousand*. This pattern appears for many of the older linguistic atlas informants in eastern Virginia, especially in rural areas and around Petersburg, and appears to be older than the pattern in which the raised forms were found only before voiceless consonants. The raised forms could also appear word-finally, as in *cow*. Lowman (1936) described this pattern; he noted that the lowered forms occurred mainly before /l/, as in *owl*, and before and after /n/, as in *down* and *now*. The plot for speaker 53 suggests that the difference between the raised and lowered allophones was more robust for the glides than for the nuclei, despite the long tradition of describing the difference in terms of the nuclei. If so, the pattern that Lowman discussed is easily explained: coarticulation with the velar /l/ and the nasal /n/ would result in an [o]- or [ɔ]-like formant pattern for the glide, whereas an [ʉ] glide would remain elsewhere. Later, along the margins of the raising territory and in the larger cities (Washington, Richmond, Newport News, and Norfolk), the lowering was extended to contexts before any voiced consonant or word-finally.

[ʌu] forms can occur in all contexts in a few dialects. This pattern is found, most notably, in the Caribbean, as for speakers 137 and 138, and in Gullah, as with speaker 139. It can also appear in very old-fashioned New England speech, though speaker 3's realizations vary with the duration of the diphthong and his nuclei could be as low as [ɑ] when the diphthong was long enough.

Forms in the range of [ɑɔ ~ ɑɒ ~ ɑɔ ~ ɑɒ], which show central or back nuclei and lowered glides, predominate in several important dialects. Among the dialects included are those of the region extending from Connecticut through the Inland Upper North. In this region, /au/ has usually been described as [ɑʊ], but as speakers 7–8 and 13–16 show, the glide tends to be considerably lowered, to the point that speaker 13 shows a monophthongal [ɑː]. Higher glides may be more common along the Canadian border, but the lowering of the glide in this region is clearly an important trend that has been overlooked. Similar forms are also common in western Pennsylvania (see speaker 12), where monophthongization is also reported. They are probably widespread in the West as well, though of course I present no evidence of that here. They occur throughout the area in which [æɔ], described below, predominates, either as an old-fashioned feature (e.g., speakers 25 and 29), as a recent innovation (e.g., speakers 27–28, 128–35, and to a lesser extent 47–50; see also Frazer 1983), or often under weak stress, which can cause truncation of the onset of the diphthong. They also predominate in the speech of two other important groups: African Americans (see chap. 6) and Mexican Americans (see chap. 7). /au/ for some African Americans, such as speaker 145, approaches a monophthongal value, especially before voiceless consonants (Thomas 1989/93; Wolfram and Thomas forthcoming).

Fronting of the nucleus of /au/ to [æ] is a common and widespread feature. It predominates, but only in white speech, throughout the South and has spread as far north as New York City (Labov 1966), central Ohio (Thomas 1989/93), central Illinois (Frazer 1983, 1987a), Kansas City (Lusk 1976), Utah (Cook 1969), and the Bay area of California (Luthin 1987). Results from TELSUR (Labov, Ash, and Boberg forthcoming) confirm this general distribution. Fronted /au/ has been regarded as unprestigious (see Thomas 1958), especially in certain areas such as New England (formerly; Kurath and McDavid 1961) and central Illinois (Frazer 1987a), though Murray (1992) found it to be a trendy feature among fraternity and sorority members in Kansas. Frazer (1994) found it to be associated with female speech among *DARE* informants from Virginia.

When the nucleus of /au/ is fronted, the glide nearly always undergoes one of two shifts: either it is lowered to [ɔ], [ɒ], or even [ɑ], or it is fronted to [ɵ], [ø], or [ɛ]. Lowering of the glide is by far more common in American English. Labov (e.g., 1994) has described this lowering for Philadelphia, but it is by no means confined to that city. [æɔ ~ æɒ] is the predominant form across a large part of the United States that includes almost all of the territory in which fronting of the nucleus occurs. This fact is obvious for the speakers from central and southern Ohio featured in chapter 3 and for most of the speakers featured in chapters 4 and 5.

Subsequent developments of this [æɔ] type include raising of the nucleus and triphthongization. Raising of the nucleus, resulting in [ɛɔ], predominates in white Philadelphia speech (Labov 1994; see speaker 11) and occurs sporadically elsewhere. Some Southerners, such as speakers 70, 91, 108, 115, and 116, have taken this process a step further and produce /au/ as [ɛɑ]. The forms of /au/ described in *LAGS* as monophthongal or ingliding, which were reported as most common in the Tennessee highlands and in the southerly Piney Woods belt, may represent this form. Triphthongal forms of /au/, [æɛɒ ~ æɛɑ], as exhibited by speakers 59–61, are also Southern in distribution.

Fronting of the glide of /au/ when the nucleus is low, though apparently common in England, occurs only marginally in New World English. It is found mainly in the Chesapeake Bay area, the Pamlico Sound area in North Carolina, old-fashioned Lumbee Indian speech in North Carolina, and white Bahamian speech, but it occasionally appears elsewhere, as with speaker 33, from central Ohio. The speakers featured in this monograph show three recognizable stages of this fronting. In the earliest stage, /au/ is realized as [æɵ]. Speakers 33, 79, 83, 150–51, 154, and 189 represent this stage; speaker 4, from New England, where fronting of /au/ became stigmatized and was eventually driven to extinction, appears to represent this form as well. In the next stage, the glide becomes more fronted and the nucleus may or may not show some retraction, resulting in [æø ~ aø]. Speakers 51, 52, 81, 84, 87, and 155

TABLE 2.2
Diachronic Processes Affecting /au/

	Archaic or Creole	Canadian Raising	Nuclear Fronting	Glide Lowering	Glide Fronting
[ʌu]	✔				
[ao ~ ɑo]					
[ʌu ~ ʌo] vs. [ao ~ ɑo]		✔			
[ɜü] vs. [æɔ]		✔	✔	(✔)	(✔)
[aɔ ~ aɒ ~ ɑɔ ~ ɑɒ]				✔	
[æɔ ~ æɒ ~ ɛɑ]			✔	✔	
[æø ~ aø ~ aɛ]			(✔)		✔

represent this stage. Finally, the glide may become unrounded and retraction of the nucleus may be completed, leading to production of /au/ as [ae]. Speakers 80, 85, 86, and 152 exhibit this form. It is distinct from /ai/ because /ai/ has a backed nucleus in these dialects, but it can create confusion for speakers of other dialects, as Schilling-Estes's (1997) account of the experiences of natives of Smith Island, Maryland, shows. In some areas, such as Smith Island (speaker 52), and Ocracoke, North Carolina (as for speakers 85 and 86; see also Howren 1962), the fronting may not occur in certain contexts: word-finally and before /r/, in which an epenthetic [w] may cause the glide to be backed, and before /l/, in which coarticulation with the velar [ɫ] backs the glide.

Table 2.2 charts the diachronic developments that have affected /au/.

2.2. VOWELS IN CONTEXTS THAT COMMONLY INDUCE CONDITIONED SHIFTS

This section discusses vowel variants in contexts that have an especially strong effect on vowels. All of these contexts involve what follows the vowel and illustrate the strength of the effects of anticipatory coarticulation. The first is before /r/, for which the vowels in many dialects are no longer readily identifiable with the vowels that occur in other contexts. The second is before /l/, which appears to be following in the footsteps of the pre-/r/ context. The others include contexts before nasals, the formants of which can affect vowel quality considerably; before certain dorsal consonants, whose rising F2 transitions can be reinterpreted by listeners as upglides; and in hiatus positions, especially word-finally. These contexts cause conditioned sound changes most often.

2.2.1. VOWELS BEFORE /r/. Of all the contexts that lead to conditioned sound changes, the pre-/r/ environment has had the most drastic effects on vowels. Its effects are complicated by the variation between *r*-fulness and *r*-lessness, that is, whether the *r* in words such as *here*, *four*, and *first* is produced as *r*-ful (rhotic) [ɹ ~ ɻ]—often denoted as [ɚ]—or as *r*-less [ə ~ Ø]. In *r*-ful varieties, whether /r/ is the more common "bunched-tongue" [ɹ] or the retroflex [ɻ] (see Lindau 1985 for an articulatory description), it has F1 and F2 values in the same range as [ə ~ ɨ], though its F3 values are quite different, of course. Coarticulation with /r/ shrinks the vowel space of pre-/r/ vowels and obliterates certain cues such as gliding that are used to distinguish vowels. These effects, in turn, lead to difficulty by speakers in identifying pre-/r/ vowels with particular vowel phonemes, as Guenter, Lewis, and Urban (1999) have demonstrated. They also lead to mergers, which are also common in /r/-less varieties, perhaps because [ə] glides show similar effects. Although vowels followed by /rV/, as in *ferry*, *carrot*, and *orange*, show their own patterns of variation, I will not attempt to discuss them here.

2.2.1.1. /ir/. /ir/, as in *here* and *fear*, is relatively tame in the amount of variation that it shows. Whether *r*-ful or *r*-less, its nucleus is usually [i ~ iˀ]. Other than rhoticity, the principal variation that it exhibits is merger with /er/, so that *here* and *hair* are homophonous. Though this merger has attracted attention in other parts of the English-speaking world, especially New Zealand (e.g., Maclagan and Gordon 1996), its frequency in New World English is limited. It is most prevalent among *r*-less varieties: it is reported in New York City (Labov 1966), in the Low Country of South Carolina and Georgia (Primer 1887; McDavid 1955; Kurath and McDavid 1961; O'Cain 1977; see speaker 57), and in various Caribbean varieties (see speakers 51 and 137). It also occurs in one *r*-ful area, New-foundland (see speaker 2).

2.2.1.2. /er/. /er/, as in *there* and *stairs*, used to show a broad range of variants in New World English but is presently undergoing a dramatic reduction in its dialectal variation. Young speakers nearly everywhere show /er/ in the range of [eɹ ~ eᵛɹ ~ eˀɹ] if *r*-ful and [eə ~ eᵛə ~ eˀə] if *r*-less . In the past, however, and among speakers born before World War II, there has been considerable variation.

The most common variation of /er/ is lowering. Thus, the nucleus can be realized as [ɛ], [æ], or even [a]. Kurath and McDavid (1961) show this variant to have been common over much of New England and throughout the South Atlantic states from Maryland southward except for the Low Country. *LAGS* reports it to be especially common in the *r*-ful Tennessee and Arkansas highlands and in *r*-less Louisiana and southeastern Texas. Lowered forms of /er/ can be seen in the plots of speakers 3 and 4 from New England, of many of the speakers born before 1960 in chapter 4, and of speakers 102, 103, and 110 from Texas. The extreme form, [aɹ], can be seen in the plots for speakers 64 (from the southern Appalachians) and 79, 80, 85, and 86 (from the Pamlico Sound area). In the New York City–Philadelphia area, the nucleus of /er/ is usually identified with the /æː/ of *pass* and *half,* but its quality is in the range of [e ~ eᵛ ~ eˀ].

Two other developments are centralization to [ɜɹ] and upgliding, both of which may be related to lowering. Centralization is visible in the plots for speakers 22, 66, 71, 87, and perhaps 24. Upgliding is usually found in *r*-less varieties and results in forms such as [eiə] and [ɛiə]. Speakers 51, 55, and 72 show such forms. The extreme is reached by speaker 59, who shows [ajæ], e.g., *stairs* [stajæz].

2.2.1.3. /ɑr/. /ɑr/, as in *hard* and *start*, shows a continuum of variants in its nucleus from [æ] to [ɒ]. [æɹ] has a very restricted distribution in New World English. It appears in Newfoundland, as with speaker 2, and in some other areas of Canada with prominent Irish settlement (Pringle and Padolsky 1983). [aɹ] occurs in scattered places. Speaker 1, from Toronto, shows [aɹ], and this variant has been reported from the Inland Upper North; speakers 13 and 14, from the Cleveland area, have a form approaching [aɹ]. R-less [aː] is stereotypical of eastern New England speech, and speakers 3–5 indeed show that form. [aː] also occurs in some Caribbean speech, as with speaker 137.

[ɑɹ] is the most common variant outside the South, and it or forms close to it appear on most of the plots in chapter 3. It also appears in very old-fashioned speech in r-ful parts of the South, as with speaker 63 from the southern Appalachians, and as a recent innovation in some areas of the South, as with speakers 62, 122, 126, and 129. Some Mexican Americans in Texas, such as speakers 175, 182, and 184, show it, too. Coarticulation with /r/ can cause the nucleus of the [ɑɹ]-type variant to approach [ʌ] in quality, most prominently for speakers 15, 20, 45, and 50. R-less [ɑː] occurs as an old-fashioned variant in some r-less dialects: in New York City (Labov 1966), in some African American speech (speakers 143, 144, and 161), and in some white Southern speech (speakers 53, 58, and 94). [ɑː] also occurs in eastern New England alongside [aː] (Kurath and McDavid 1961) and is probably still common there.

Rounded nuclei are common in certain areas. [ɒɹ] predominates in Philadelphia, as with speaker 11 (see also Labov 1994). R-ful [ɒɹ] and r-less [ɒː] predominate throughout the South, both in white speech (see chaps. 4 and 5) and in African American speech (see chaps 6). They also occur in the speech of younger natives of New York City (Labov 1966). [ɒɹ] occurs as well in some areas bordering the South, such as southern Ohio (e.g., speakers 22 and 24). When /ɑr/ is rounded, it is sometimes merged with /ɔr/, as discussed in the following section.

2.2.1.4. /ɔr/. /ɔr/, as in *horse, morning,* and *for,* is rapidly losing its status as a distinct class because its merger with /or/ (which makes *horse* and *hoarse* homophonous) is so pervasive now. In former times, it was realized as [ɔɹ ~ ɒɹ] (if r-ful) or [ɔː ~ ɒː] (if r-less). These variants can still be seen on the plots for speakers who maintain /ɔr/ as a distinct class, including speakers 3, 4, 7, and 13 and many of the speakers in chapters 4–6. The merger of /ɔr/ with /or/ used to be more confined; Kurath and McDavid (1961) found

that, for linguistic atlas informants, almost all of whom were born
in the nineteenth century, the only part of the Atlantic states in
which the merger predominated was a region including New York
City, New Jersey, most of Pennsylvania, and northern Maryland.
Nobbelin (1980), who analyzed records from *LANCS*, found the
merger predominant in Ontario, most of Ohio, and northern
Illinois and scattered elsewhere in the region. The distinction
subsequently disappeared in Connecticut and the Inland Upper
North: while speakers 7 and 13 from these regions maintain the
distinction, speakers 8 and 14–16 do not (see also Thomas 1961).
More recently, the distinction has become moribund across the
South as well. Almost none of the speakers featured in chapters 4–
6 who were born after World War II maintain it (see also Thomas
and Bailey 1992). It is possible that the distinction is still maintained by some young eastern New Englanders, but even there the
/ɔr/-/or/ merger is making inroads (see Laferriere 1979 and speaker
6). In the traditional eastern New England dialect, /ɔr/ (but not
/or/) was merged with /ɑ = ɔ/, so that *order, odder,* and *awed 'er* were all
homophonous. Perhaps the last stronghold of the /ɔr/-/or/ distinction will be the Caribbean, in which it still appears to be strong in
some areas, such as Jamaica (see speaker 137).

The quality of the nucleus of the merged /ɔr = or/ is often
described as [ɔ]. However, the speakers featured in this monograph suggest that [o] is more common. Some of the older speakers with the /ɔr/-/or/ merger, such as speakers 1, 21, 25, and 29, do
show a form in the range of [ɔɹ]. Almost all of the younger
speakers and some of the older ones with the merger, however,
have a value more like [oɹ] (*r*-ful) or [oə] (*r*-less), and some show a
quality approaching [uɹ]. Like the shift of /oi/ from [ɔi] to [oi], the
shift of /ɔr = or/ from [ɔɹ] to [oɹ] has largely escaped notice.

Before the /ɔr/-/or/ merger swept over North America, there
were a few areas in which /ɔr/ merged with /ɑr/, so that *lord* and *lard*
were homophonous. This merger has been reported from the
Delmarva Peninsula (Kurath and McDavid 1961), the lower Mississippi valley (Pilch 1955; Rubrecht 1971; Hartman 1985), the area
from St. Louis to Evansville, Indiana (Hartman 1985; Labov, Ash,
and Boberg forthcoming), Texas (Norman 1956; Labov, Yaeger,

and Steiner 1972; Walsh and Mote 1974; Thomas and Bailey 1992), and Newfoundland (Colbourne 1982, cited in Paddock 1986). A near-merger is reported in Utah (Cook 1969). The resulting form was usually [ɒɹ ~ ɔɹ] except in Newfoundland, where it was apparently [aɹ]. Speakers 22, from southern Ohio, and 105, 109, and 110, from Texas, display the /ɔr/-/ɑr/ merger.

2.2.1.5. /or/. /or/, as in *hoarse, mourning,* and *four,* is generally realized as *r*-ful [oɹ] or *r*-less [oə] when it is distinct from /ɔr/. Some Southerners show an upglide, so that it is produced as [ouɹ], as by speakers 83–86 and 154, or [ouə ~ ou], as by speakers 58–60, 69, 100, 150, 153, 160, and 161. The realization of /or/ when it is merged with /ɔr/ is described in section 2.2.1.4 above.

2.2.1.6. /ur/. /ur/, as in *tour* and *cure,* is also highly prone to mergers. Over much of the United States west of the Appalachians, it is commonly merged with stressed syllabic /r/ in certain environments. One of these environments is after a palatal consonant, as in *sure, pure, cure,* and *mature,* with the result that *surely* and *Shirley* are homophonous. The other environment occurs when the syllable containing /ur/ is followed by an unstressed syllable, as in *endurance* and *tournament.* In the remaining words (e.g., *tour, endure*), /ur/ may be interpreted as disyllabic. In some areas, some of those /ur/ words, such as *endure,* may also show stressed, syllabic /r/.

In other parts of the country, particularly New York City, New Jersey, and Pennsylvania, /ur/ may show an unconditioned merger with /or = ɔr/ (see Labov 1966 and speaker 12). Thus *sure* and *shore* are homophonous, as are *tour* and *tore.* This merger is often stereotypically associated with old-fashioned Southern speech, both white and African American. Some younger speakers in areas that show the conditioned merger of /ur/ with stressed syllabic /r/ merge words like *tour* into /or = ɔr/.

2.2.1.7. *Stressed Syllabic* /r/. Of all the contexts in which /r/ appears in a syllable rhyme, stressed syllabic /r/, as in *first, heard,* and *stir,* is the least likely to be *r*-less. In some white Southern speech (e.g., speakers 69 and 100) and in much contemporary African American, New York City, eastern New England, and white Bahamian speech, it is *r*-ful while all other syllable rhymes are *r*-less. When it is *r*-ful, it is typically produced as [ɹ], often with a falling F1, as shown for speakers 11, 12, 52, and 69. This falling F1 pattern may be so strong in some Southern speech that it is perceived as diphthongal, as for speakers 110, 119, and 124, who produce something like [ʌɹ ~ ɐ.ɹ]. Kurath and McDavid (1961) report an [ʌr] form from western Pennsylvania, but they may have been describing a variant with retroflex [ɻ]; see the discussion in the section in chapter 3 on western Pennsylvania.

When stressed syllabic /r/ is *r*-less, it may show either of two forms: a monophthongal variant or an upgliding variant. The monophthongal variant is often described as [ɜ], but it tends to be closer to [ə] or [ɤ]. It appears in old-fashioned speech in eastern New England (speakers 3–5) and parts of the South (speakers 53, 54, and 58), especially in African American speech (speakers 139, 140, 143, and 162). The upgliding variant normally occurs in complementary distribution with the monophthongal form: the monophthong appears stem-finally, as in *stir*, and the upgliding diphthong appears elsewhere, as in *first* and *thirty*, including irregular preterites such as *heard*. The upgliding diphthong is usually realized as [ɜɪ ~ əɪ], sometimes with some rounding, [ɵɪ ~ ɵɪ]. It was found in old-fashioned speech of New York City, of the region from South Carolina to Texas, and of the Bahamas (Wells 1982). It may be seen in the plots for speakers 9, 59 (in part), 88, 94, 97, 98, 141, 142, and 161.

2.2.1.8. /air/. In most dialects, /ai/ before /r/, as in *tire*, is produced much like /ai/ before other voiced consonants, though it tends to undergo more weakening of the glide because of coarticulation with /r/. Speaker 24, from southern Ohio, shows [aː] before /r/ but otherwise shows strong /ai/ glides. In some varieties, mostly old-fashioned, in the South and in western Pennsylvania, the glide weakening may lead to replacement of /air/ by /ɑr/ (Kurath and McDavid 1961). A different process affects /air/ in the Inland Upper North. There, the Canadian raising process is extended to /air/, so that *tire* is produced as [tʰɜiɹ] (see Kilbury 1983; Vance 1987; and speakers 15 and 16). /air/ is probably disyllabic in many dialects.

2.2.1.9. /aur/. /au/ before /r/, as in *tower*, tends to behave much like /air/. That is, it shows some glide weakening and occasional replacement by [æɹ] (as in mainland Maryland) or /ɑr/. In some areas around Pamlico Sound and Chesapeake Bay where /au/ is usually realized as [aø ~ aɛ], an epenthetic [w] may keep the glide backed before /r/, as in *tower* [tʰaowr̩] (see speakers 52, 85, and 86). Like /air/, /aur/ is most likely disyllabic in many dialects.

2.2.2. VOWELS BEFORE /l/. Syllable coda /l/, whether produced as the velar [ɫ] or as vocalized [o ~ u ~ w] (see Hankey 1972; Ash 1982; McElhinny 1999; vocalized /l/ is often mistranscribed as [ɯ] but is normally rounded), exerts a strong coarticulatory effect on preceding vowels. The result is that vowels show lower F2 values before /l/ than in other contexts—often much lower—and thus, like /r/, /l/ has the effect of shrinking the formant space of preceding vowels. Labov (1972), for instance, noted that /o/ is fronted in Philadelphia except before /l/, where it is backed. This coarticulation can weaken the glides of /ai/ and /oi/ before /l/, even in dialects that do not normally show glide weakening. Also like /r/, coarticulation with /l/ can neutralize phonetic cues used to distinguish vowels. Not surprisingly, a variety of pre-/l/ mergers of vowels have been reported recently. Perhaps more surprisingly, in Utah, the phonetic cues used to distinguish some pre-/l/ vowels appear to have switched from formant values to phonation (Di Paolo and Faber 1990; Faber 1992; Faber and Di Paolo 1995).

The merger of /ul/ and /ʊl/ to [ʊˀɫ ~ ʊˀ:], which makes *pool* and *pull* homophonous, seems to be the most common pre-/l/ merger. A three-way merger of /ul/, /ʊl/, and /ol/ to [oɫ ~ o:], so that *pool*, *pull*, and *pole* are all homophonous, can also occur, as can a merger only of /ʊl/ and /ol/ to [oɫ ~ o:]. The merger of /il/ and /ɪl/ to [ɪɫ ~ ɪo], making *feel* and *fill* homophonous, is widely reported, as is the merger of /el/ and /ɛl/ to [ɛɫ ~ ɛo], which makes *fail* and *fell* homophonous. Less-often reported mergers are those of /ʌl/ and /ɔl/ to [ɔɫ ~ ɔo], so that *gull* and *gall* are homophonous; of /ʌl/ and /ol/ to [oɫ ~ o:], making *gull* and *goal* homophonous; and of /ɔl/ and /ʊl/ to [oɫ ~ o:], which makes *Paul* and *pull* homophonous. A merger of /ʌl/ and /ʊl/ to [ʊˀɫ ~ ʊˀ:], which would make *gull* and *pull* rhyme, should be watched for among younger speakers.

Johnson (1971) and Hankey (1972) reported the /ul/-/ʊl/ merger from western Pennsylvania. Dickey (1997), also describing western Pennsylvania speech, reported the /il/-/ɪl/ and /ul/-/ʊl/-/ol/ mergers from that area. McElhinny (1999) analyzed the laxing of /il/ and /ul/ in Pittsburgh. Thomas (1989/93, 1996) described the occurrence of the /ul/-/ʊl/, /ul/-/ʊl/-/ol/, and /ʌl/-/ɔl/ mergers in central Ohio. Flanigan and Norris (2000) report the /ul/-/ʊl/-/ol/ and /il/-/ɪl/ mergers from southern Ohio. Bowie's (1998) study of both production and perception found both the /ʊl/-/ol/ and /ul/-/ʊl/ mergers in Waldorf, Maryland, south of Washington, D.C. Shores (1985) reported the /ɔl/-/ʊl/ merger from Tangier Island, Virginia. Guenter (2000) found the /ʌl/-/ol/ merger to be widespread in California. TELSUR (Labov, Ash, and Boberg forthcoming) investigated the /ul/-/ʊl/ and /il/-/ɪl/ mergers and found that they show similar distributions: they are found in western Pennsylvania and in scattered locations across the South, the southern Midwest, and the southern part of the West. Bernstein (1993), Bailey et al. (1993, 1996), and Tillery (1997) have reported laxing of /ul/, /il/, and /el/, which are associated with the /ul/-/ʊl/, /il/-/ɪl/, and /el/-/ɛl/ mergers, respectively, to be widespread in Texas and Oklahoma. However, the same three pairs were found to be distinguished by phonation in Utah by Di Paolo and Faber (1990), Faber (1992), and Faber and Di Paolo (1995), who examined both production and perception.

Most of the reported pre-/l/ mergers can be found among the speakers featured in this monograph. The merger of /ul/ and /ʊl/ occurs for speaker 12 (from western Pennsylvania), several of the young speakers from Ohio, a few of the young North Carolinians (speakers 68, 74, and 82), and many of the young Texans of all ethnicities. The three-way merger of /ul/, /ʊl/, and /ol/ occurs for some of the young Ohioans (speakers 27, 28, 46, and 49). The /il/-/ɪl/ merger occurs for the western Pennsylvanian (speaker 12), for speakers 68 and 82 (from North Carolina), and for a fair number of the young Texans. The /el/-/ɛl/ merger is not shown on the plots except for speakers 12 and 135. The merger of /ʌl/ with /ol/ may occur for speaker 50. Finally, the merger of /ʌl/ and /ɔl/ occurs for speaker 12, for most of the central Ohioans born after 1930, and for a few Mexican Americans from Texas.

2.2.3. VOWELS BEFORE NASALS. Nasals sometimes cause conditioned changes of preceding vowels. These changes have to do with the nasalizing effect of nasal consonants on preceding vowels. Nasalization produces nasal formants as well as antiformants that can cancel oral formants. In general, the first nasal formant occurs about where F1 is for an upper-mid or high vowel. The second nasal formant occurs where F2 would be for a back, rounded vowel and at a somewhat higher value (in Hz) than F1 is for a low vowel. The first antiformant varies; it is close to the first nasal formant for weakly nasal vowels, but its value in Hz increases as the degree of nasalization increases (Johnson 1997).

The merger of /ɪ/ and /ɛ/ before nasals, as in *pin* and *pen* or *him* and *hem*, is found throughout the South (see, e.g., Wise 1933a; Thomas 1958; Brown 1991), but also in southern California (Metcalf 1972a) and in some southerly parts of the Midwest, such as central Ohio (Hartman 1966; Thomas 1996) and Kansas (Labov, Ash, and Boberg forthcoming). Its concentration in the South may have to do with the fact that /ɛ/ is generally higher (i.e., with a lower F1) in the South than in the North. This tendency would make F1 of /ɛ/ more susceptible to being canceled by the antiformant and thus would make the first nasal formant into the perceived F1. I have not attempted to show this merger on the vowel plots because of the difficulties that nasality creates in obtaining a single F1 reading.

The raising of /æ/ before nasals, as in *hand* and *ham*, occurs widely in North American English (shown for many of the speakers in chapters 3–5; see also, e.g., Labov 1994; Clarke, Elms, and Youssef 1995; Boberg 2000). As with the preceding example, it results from canceling of the first oral formant and reinterpretation of the first nasal formant as F1. The raising of prenasal /æ/ appears to be largely a twentieth-century phenomenon; few of the nineteenth-century speakers featured in this monograph show it. It is also largely absent in Mexican American English (see chapter 7).

In very old-fashioned Virginia speech (Lowman 1936 and speaker 53), /au/ is produced as [ɐʉ] except when followed or preceded by /n/, as in *down* and *now*, in which case it is produced as [æɔ]. As discussed in section 2.1.15 above, the effect seems to be stronger for the glide than for the nucleus; the result is that the F_1 and F_2 values of the glide in *down, now,* and so on coincide with the first two nasal formants.

In central Ohio, /o/ is fronted except in *don't, won't, only,* and *home,* which have [oː] (Thomas 1996 and speakers 27 and 28). Again, F_1 and F_2 coincide with the first two nasal formants.

[æ ~ ɛ] appear for /ɪ/ before /ŋ/, as in *thing,* in parts of the South, especially Highland regions and Texas (e.g., Klipple 1945). The rising F_2 transition for the palatal /ŋ/ = [ɲ] may be more important than nasalization per se and may make the vowel seem diphthongal (see §2.2.4 below), with subsequent widening of the diphthong in these dialects.

Merger of /ɑ/ and /ɔ/ only before nasals, as in *Don* and *dawn,* is reported by Labov, Ash, and Boberg (forthcoming) from some parts of the North. Lexical-specific variation between /ɑ/ and /ɔ/ before nasals, as in *on* and *long,* is well known (e.g., Kurath and McDavid 1961). These alternations are due to the damping effects of nasality on the first oral formant, which make the height of the vowel less certain for listeners.

Lexical-specific alternations of /ɑ/ and /ʌ/ occur, e.g., *un-* /ɑn/, *want* /wʌnt/ (see Hartman 1985, li). As with the preceding example, these alternations seem to derive from the effects of nasality on F_1.

Low vowels tend to show some nasalization because of muscular connections between the tongue and velum (Johnson 1997). In dialects such as the Inland Upper North in which /ɑ/ is fronted, it is conceivable that nasalization could serve as a perceptual cue to the identity of the vowel. The result would be a merging of the first oral formant and second nasal formant, which would account for the unusually high F_1 values of /ɑ/ in these dialects.

2.2.4. VOWELS BEFORE PALATAL AND VELAR CONSONANTS. It is widely known that upglides are often perceived before palatal consonants, including not only /ʃ/, /ʒ/, /tʃ/, and /dʒ/, but also the front allophones of /g/, /k/, and /ŋ/. The main cause is the rising F_2 transition associated with palatals, which can be reinterpreted as

LORETTE WILMOT LIBRARY
NAZARETH COLLEGE

an [i] glide. The effects are strongest for /g/, /ŋ/, /ʃ/, and /ʒ/. As a result, /ɪ/, as in *big* and *sing*, can sound like /i/; /ɛ/, as in *beg* and *strength*, can sound like /e/; and /æ/, as in *bag* and *hang*, can sound like [æi]. Guenter, Lewis, and Urban (1999) found that many of their California subjects (from the San Francisco Bay area) did not identify pre-/ŋ/ vowels with the lax vowel classes. In dialects in which /æ/ is raised, speakers may identify the vowel in words like *bag* as /e/ (Zeller 1993). Because it is impossible to tell from formant readings alone whether pre-/g/ and pre-/ŋ/ vowels show a phonologized [i] upglide or not, I have not shown them on the plots.

Upglides before /ʃ/ and /ʒ/ occur in fewer dialects. Kurath and McDavid (1961) show upgliding /æ/ in *ashes* to be widespread in the South and New England. They also show front-gliding [ʊɨ] in *push* to occur in the same region, with mutation to /u/ common in certain areas, especially West Virginia. They note the occurrence of intrusive /r/ in *wash* but do not mention that upgliding [ɔi ~ oi] forms also occur in *wash*. Most of the older speakers from central and southern Ohio (speakers 18, 22, 25, 31–35, and 37; also speaker 23) show upglides or mutations of short vowels before /ʃ/ and /ʒ/. Thus, *dish* and *division* may have [ɪi] or /i/, *special* and *measure* may have /e/, *dash* may have [æe], and *gosh* may have /ai/. These forms are quite recessive now, however. Wolfram, Hazen, and Schilling-Estes (1999) noted a mutation of /ɪ/ to [i] before /ʃ/ in Ocracoke, North Carolina, and Colbourne (1982) found it as far away as Newfoundland.

Velars occasionally condition [u]-like glides on preceding vowels. In central and southern Ohio, the only contexts in which /ɔ/ is commonly realized as [ɔo] are before /g/ and /ŋ/, as in *dog, August, long,* and *honk* (see Nobbelin 1980). Such forms may be merged with the /ɔl/ sequence (Thomas 1996). Upgliding /ɔ/ before /g/ is shown for speakers 23, 27, 28, 32, 33, 36, 45, and 46.

2.2.5. VOWELS IN WORD-FINAL AND HIATUS CONTEXTS. Word-final and hiatus environments occasionally condition vowel shifts. Most commonly, the shift involves an epenthetic [j] or [w] that appears in hiatus position and may be analogically extended to any word-final position. One example, noted in section 2.1.15, is the alternation between [aø ~ aɛ] and [aɔ] on Smith Island, Maryland, and Ocracoke, North Carolina (speakers 52, 85, and 86). [aɔ] occurs before /r/ and /l/, in which the /r/ and /l/ can be treated as syllabic consonants (e.g., *tower* [tʰaɔwɹ̩]). It also occurs word-finally. In these cases, the epenthetic [w] causes the glide of /au/ to be backed. A similar effect occurs for Southerners who show front-gliding /o/ and /u/. Another example is the alternation between ingliding and monophthongal variants of /e/ and /o/ reported from the Low Country of South Carolina and Georgia, in which ingliding forms occur in checked positions and monophthongal forms word-finally (Kurath and McDavid 1961). In this case, even a slight gesture toward an epenthetic /j/ or /w/ would cancel the inglide. A third example is reported by Anderson (1999) for Cherokee speech in western North Carolina. In that dialect, /ai/ and /oi/ are monophthongal except in hiatus and prepausal contexts. In addition, the occurrence of /air/ as [ɜiɹ] in the Inland Upper North, as described in section 2.1.13, seems to be a hiatus effect. Raised /ai/ nuclei are associated with higher /ai/ glides (Thomas 1991, 1995, 2000), so an epenthetic [j] between /ai/ and /r/ could induce raising of the nucleus.

An apparent exception is the alternation between [ɜi] and [ɜ] in old-fashioned New York City and Deep South speech, discussed in section 2.2.1.7. In this case, [ɜ] occurs word-finally, as in *stir*, and [ɜi] occurs in checked position. This exception may be due to the fact that [ɹ], not [j], occurred in hiatus position in these dialects (regularly in New York City, inconsistently in the Deep South). Thus [j] would not be extended analogically to any word-final context.

2.3. SOME GENERAL REMARKS ON VOWEL SHIFTS

Although all sound changes presumably have a social motivation, most have a phonetic motivation as well. Bailey (1985) distinguished between "abnatural" linguistic changes, which involve language contact or hypercorrection, and "connatural" changes, which do not. He indicated that connatural changes are linguistically motivated, and it follows that connatural sound changes are phonetically motivated. Phonetic motivations are among the "internal factors" that Labov (1994, 1–3) discussed, even as he felt obliged to defend the notion that they could be separated from social "external factors."

I attempted to name the phonetic motivations for the conditioned vowel alternations discussed in section 2.2. I did not do so for most of the unconditioned vowel variations described in section 2.1. Some are relatively transparent. For example, as noted in section 2.1.5, /æ/ is slightly raised in dialects that have a relatively front /ɑ/, but it is slightly lowered and retracted in dialects that have a backed /ɑ/. Similarly, /e/ is widened to [æi ~ ai] only in dialects that monophthongize /ai/ in all phonetic contexts. Both of these examples have to do with the fact that vowels tend to be spaced so that perceptual differences among them are maximized. This notion has a long history. It is reflected in writings by historical linguists on the "margin of security" and the "range of dispersion," most prominently Martinet (1952) and Moulton (1962), and in phonetic writings on vowel dispersion (e.g., Liljencrants and Lindblom 1972; Disner 1984; Lindblom 1986; ten Bosch 1991; Schwartz et al. 1997). It also lies behind the notion of chain shifts of vowels. Among the better-known chain shifts in English dialects are the Northern Cities Shift and the Southern Shift, which were outlined in the preface (see Labov 1991, 1994); the "Canadian Shift," which involves lowering of /æ/, /ɛ/, and /ɪ/ (Clarke, Elms, and Youssef 1995); and the "diphthong shift" in dialects of England, which involves a shift of /oi/, /ai/, /e/, and /i/ to [oi ~ ui], [ɑi ~ ɒi ~ ɔi], [ai], and [ei ~ əi], respectively (Wells 1982). Thus, when one vowel shifts, neighboring vowels may also shift in a way that optimizes perceptual distinctions among them. Another impetus occurs when consonantal influence, often vocalization of consonants, creates new vowels. For example, coarticulation of syllable-coda /l/ with preceding vowels, often accompanied by vocalization of the /l/, has created a new series of back, rounded vowels from /ol/, /ʊl/, and /ul/. Labov (1994, 332) cites this development as a motivation for the fronting of /o/, /ʊ/, and /u/ in other phonetic contexts, which would increase the perceptual distance between, for example, *go* [gəʊ ~ geʉ] and *goal* [goɫ ~ goː]. Mergers violate this principle, but they are most likely in cases of dialect mixture or vocalization of consonants.

The motivations for other vowel shifts are not as transparent. Some are due to maximization of perceptual distance, while others are not. One that may be is the raising of /æ/ to [eə] in the Inland Upper North as part of the Northern Cities Shift. Though it is often connected to the fronting of /ɑ/ in this dialect, it may also have to do with the fact that older speakers from that region have /æ/ slightly raised and /ɛ/ somewhat low, which brings /æ/ and /ɛ/ very close to each other in formant space. Listeners probably had to rely on other cues besides formant values, especially length, since /æ/ is longer than /ɛ/. As a result, the length of /æ/ may have been exaggerated and /æ/ was reinterpreted as a long, mid vowel, with development of other correlates of tenseness (see below) and further raising as a consequence.

A number of factors besides maximization of perceptual distance are implicated in unconditioned sound changes. One that Labov, Yaeger, and Steiner (1972) and Labov (1991, 1994) have noted is a cross-linguistic diachronic tendency for tense or long vowels to rise and for lax or short vowels to fall. They treat tenseness as a phonological abstraction and instead speak mostly in terms of peripherality. The reasons are that tense vowels are usually (though not always) peripheral, which was bolstered by Lindau (1978), and that they found peripherality to be linked to shifts in vowel height. Nevertheless, it is not clear that there is any phonetic motivation for peripherality, as a phonetic factor, to cause vowels to rise or fall. The motivation may rest with other correlates of tenseness. The tense/lax distinction in English and other languages shows several phonetic attributes. Tense vowels are not only more peripheral, but also longer (as Labov notes), breathier, often more diphthongal, and—because of raising of the tongue and resultant advancement of the tongue root—produced with a lengthened pharyngeal cavity (see Lindau 1978; Kingston et al. 1997). The pharyngeal cavity lengthening certainly provides a motivation for shifts in vowel height because it lowers F_1, thereby making a vowel seem higher. Thus, tense vowels sound higher than their lax counterparts. This difference can lead to redefinitions of the phonetic targets of vowels. As a phonetic factor, peripherality is probably incidental to the vowel shifts.

Diphthongs show additional complications. Space limitations prevent me from giving them a full treatment here, but I will describe briefly the most important factors and one special case. I think that the steady-state pattern of a diphthong is more important than has usually been acknowledged. Diphthongs typically show steady states where they reach the margin of the vowel envelope and show formant movement elsewhere. Thus /e/, realized as [ei], shows an offset steady state but no onset steady state (Lehiste and Peterson 1961). /ai/, when realized as [ae ~ ɑe], usually shows an onset steady state and no offset steady state, but when it precedes a voiceless consonant, it is realized as [ae ~ ai] and may show only an offset steady state. Lengthening affects diphthongs dramatically. It may affect the steady state, which may become long or may break, in which case the diphthong becomes a triphthong. It may also affect the transition, which will cause the diphthong to widen. Shortening has the opposite effect (see Mock 1991; Thomas 1995). In the process of lowering from Middle English [iː] to its present values, /ai/ probably started with only an offset steady state and later switched to showing an onset steady state when it reached the bottom of the vowel envelope. The special case noted above is the conditioned variation that /ai/ shows in some dialects: either Canadian raising, in which it is realized as [ɜi] before voiceless consonants and [ae] elsewhere, or the Southern and AAVE pattern of [ae ~ ɑe] before voiceless consonants and [aːæ ~ aː] elsewhere. The glide is higher in these and most other dialects of American English, apparently as a cue to the voicing of the following consonant (Thomas 1991, 1995, 2000). In Canadian raising, shortening affects only the nucleus of prevoiceless /ai/ because it has no onset steady state and because the glide is too important as a perceptual cue to truncate. In the South, lengthening in nonprevoiceless contexts causes the onset (nuclear) steady state to be lengthened to the point that it overshadows the glide, making the glide sound more like a consonant transition.

3. WHITES FROM THE NORTH

THE REGION THAT THIS CHAPTER COVERS—not only the northern United States but Canada as well—is large and dialectally diverse. The vowel plots in this chapter represent a superficial coverage of the region, consisting mostly of one or more representative speakers from some of the major dialect areas within it. As in chapters 4 and 5, one area is featured with more intense coverage. In this chapter, the featured area is the state of Ohio, and central Ohio in particular, with a fairly comprehensive depiction of variation within the community of Johnstown, Ohio (my hometown). Johnstown is not particularly unusual in any obvious way. It was once a rural, agricultural community but has become a bedroom community, an "exurb" for Columbus (see Thomas 1996). The central Ohio dialect is one that is not particularly stereotyped or stigmatized, though a few features of it (e.g., the upgliding tendencies of vowels before alveopalatal fricatives among older natives) have taken on some stigma. The cross-section of speakers from Johnstown should serve as an example of the degree of variation that can occur in a relatively unstereotyped dialect. Brief descriptions of each of the dialects covered in this chapter follow.

GENERAL CANADIAN (speaker 1). Canadian sociolinguists have been quite active and have described the "General Canadian" dialect, which is spoken over most of Canada outside of Québec and Newfoundland, in more detail than most other dialects have been described (see Chambers 1991 for an overview). The best-known vocalic feature of the dialect is a process that affects /ai/ and /au/, "Canadian raising." As described in chapter 2, Canadian raising involves these two diphthongs' showing low nuclei before voiced consonants and word-finally but mid nuclei before voiceless consonants. The result is such oppositions as *side* [saɪd] versus *sight* [sɜit] and *loud* [laʊd] versus *lout* [lʌut]. Though first described for Virginia (see chapter 4), this conditioning has been discussed extensively for Canadian English (see Joos 1942; Bloomfield 1948; Avis 1956; Gregg 1957, 1973; King 1972; Chambers 1973; Bailey 1975;

SPEAKER 1

Female, Born 1927, from Toronto, Ontario
(courtesy of J. K. Chambers; college-educated; recorded in 1979)

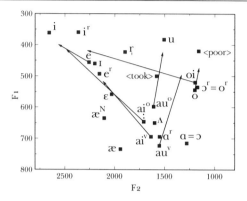

NOTE: She shows traditional Canadian traits, including the merger of /ɑ/ and /ɔ/ and Canadian raising of /au/ and /ai/. Her /o/ is nearly monophthongal and her /ɑr/ is rather front, [aɹ]. (reading passage and conversation; UT and NCSU)

Picard 1977; Warden 1979; Paradis 1980; Thomas 1991, 1995). Some recent studies have suggested that Canadian raising of /au/ is undergoing changes and that some geographical differentiation within Canada is occurring. Chambers and Hardwick (1986) found that the raised [ʌu] is undergoing nuclear rounding among some Vancouver natives, resulting in [ou]. However, Chambers and Hardwick (1986), Chambers (1989), and Hung, Davison, and Chambers (1993) noted a general fronting tendency of /au/ in Toronto, Vancouver, and Victoria, British Columbia, among young speakers, especially women. In their notation, the extreme forms are [ɛw] (before voiceless consonants) and [æw] (in any context). They noted that Canadian raising had diminished somewhat among younger speakers. Similarly, Woods (1979, 1993) found that young, urban females in the Ottawa area showed less Canadian raising of both /au/ and /ai/ than other groups in Ottawa. Meechan (1999) found that Mormons show less Canadian raising than non-Mormons in southern Alberta.

Several other distinctive vocalic traits also typify General Canadian English. /ɑ/ and /ɔ/ are merged (e.g., Avis 1972; Kinloch 1983; Boberg 2000) except in some former Loyalist enclaves in the St. Lawrence valley (Pringle and Padolsky 1983). Woods (1979, 1991, 1993), de Wolf (1993), and Warkentyne and Esling (1995) found rounding of this merged vowel to [ɒ], Woods in Ottawa and the last two studies in Vancouver. Esling and Warkentyne (1993), de Wolf (1993), and Warkentyne and Esling (1995) found retraction of /æ/ toward [a] in Vancouver. Hoffman (1999) found not only retraction of /æ/ but lowering of /ɛ/ and /ɪ/ as well in her sample of speakers from various parts of southern Ontario. Meechan (1999) also reported lowering of /ɛ/ and /ɪ/ in southern Alberta. Clarke, Elms, and Youssef (1995), who examined the vowels of young, urban Canadians, mostly from Ontario, found not only all of the above-mentioned shifts of /ɪ/, /ɛ/, /æ/, and /ɑ = ɔ/, but also fronting and lowering of /ʌ/, fronting of /u/ and /ʊ/, and incipient fronting of /o/. /u/, /ʊ/, and /o/ were traditionally backed in General Canadian English. General Canadian is strongly *r*-ful.

Speaker 1 represents a classic Canadian accent. Most of the newer developments in General Canadian English do not occur in her speech.

NEWFOUNDLAND (speaker 2). While the General Canadian dialect seems to have been established by Loyalists who fled the northern parts of the United States during the Revolutionary War (see Chambers 1991), the traditional dialect of Newfoundland was established by a quite different makeup of settlers. Irish, mainly from an area of southeastern Ireland centered around Waterford, dominated the southern coast of Newfoundland, while settlers from southwestern England, especially Devon and Dorset, predominated along the northeastern coast and in parts of the western coast (see Handcock 1977). Newfoundland English shows considerable Irish influence, though many of the "Irish" features also occur in southwestern England. Irish seem to have formed the majority in St. John's, the capital city, and its dialect traditionally exerted influence over the rest of Newfoundland. However, since

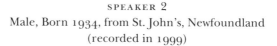

SPEAKER 2
Male, Born 1934, from St. John's, Newfoundland
(recorded in 1999)

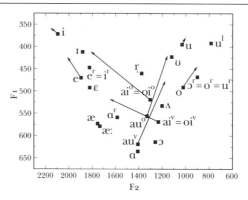

NOTE: He shows traditional Newfoundland traits, including front /ar/ (i.e., [æɹ]), as well as Canadian raising of /ai = oi/ and /au/. He distinguishes /ɑ/ and /ɔ/ mainly by length: /ɑ/ → [a], /ɔ/ → [a: ~ ɑ:]. (reading passage supplemented by conversation; NCSU)

Newfoundland joined Canada in 1949, General Canadian English has influenced Newfoundland speech profoundly (Clarke 1991).

A number of studies have documented traditional Newfoundland vowel variants. Paddock's (1981) study of the community of Carbonear (based on fieldwork conducted 1965–66) described a number of the features typical of Newfoundland English. Carbonear lies in a mainly English area but has many Irish. /ʌ/ is backed and often rounded to [ɔ]. /ai/ and /oi/ are merged to [əi ~ ʌi ~ ɔi]. /ir/ and /er/ are merged. /ɔr/, /or/, and /ur/ are also all merged. /ar/ is produced with a front nucleus, as [aɚ]. /æ/, as in *bat*, and /æ:/, as in *bath*, may be distinguished by length, with the result that *bat* and *bath* can become a minimal pair because /θ/ is often merged into [t]. /ɑ/ and /ɔ/, analogously, can be distinguished solely by length as [ɑ] (as in *cot* [kʰɑt]) and [ɑ:] (as in *caught* [kʰɑ:t]). Finally, the old distinction between words like *made/maid* and *pane/pain* was often maintained in Carbonear as [ɛ: ~ e:] versus [ɛi], respectively. This distinction has not been reported in any North American dialect outside of Newfoundland. Colbourne (1982, cited in Paddock 1986) studied the speech of Long Island, in Notre Dame Bay in northeastern Newfoundland. He found that some natives showed an unconditioned merger of /ɪ/ and /ɛ/, usually to [ɪ]. The *made/ maid* distinction appeared, as did a merger of /ɔr/ with /ɑr/, apparently to [ɑɹ]. He noted a mutation of /ɪ/ to [i] before /ʃ/, as in *fish*, and in a few other words (e.g., *pin*). Kirwin's (1993) description of Newfoundland Anglo-Irish speech pointed out that /ɑ/ tends to be quite fronted, [a]. Paddock (pers. comm., 1999) said that some Newfoundlanders distinguish /ɑ/ and /ɔ/ while others do not, and that rounded pronunciations of /ɔ/ are a prestige feature among some who make the distinction. Kirwin (1993) stated that /ai/ (but not /au/) shows Canadian raising in Irish-settled parts of Newfoundland, though /au/ apparently shows Canadian raising for many other Newfoundlanders. Except in a few communities on the west side of Conception Bay, speakers from most parts of Newfoundland, including St. John's, are *r*-ful.

Clarke (1991) and D'Arcy (1999) traced some of the recent changes occurring in the speech of St. John's. Clarke found that monophthongal /e/ and /o/, usually associated with Irish influence, are declining in St. John's, and that the lowered and retracted form of /æ/ that is common in General Canadian speech (see above) is making inroads, especially among young females. D'Arcy reported that the backed, rounded variant of /ʌ/ and the fronted forms of /ar/ and /a/ that typify classic St. John's speech are less prevalent among younger residents, especially those whose parents are from other parts of Canada. Paddock (pers. comm., 1999) notes that rounded forms of /ʌ/ are stigmatized as an Irish feature, but that backed and unrounded forms are widespread in Newfoundland.

Speaker 2 represents a classic St. John's accent. He lacks the *made/maid* distinction, but his production of /ar/ suggests that [æɹ], not [aɹ], might be the best rendition of the traditional form in Irish-influenced areas.

EASTERN NEW ENGLAND (speakers 3–6). Investigations of the dialects of New England had an ambitious start with *LANE* (1939–43;

see also Kurath et al. 1939), and there were several other studies during the following 30 years, but little has been done since. The main compilation of phonological information from *LANE* is Kurath and McDavid (1961). They found that *r*-lessness predominates in eastern New England except for a few enclaves of *r*-fulness (the opposite of Canada), and *r*-lessness makes an impact on the structure of the vowel system. The main distinguishing vocalic traits that they named for eastern New England are as follows. /ɑ/ and /ɔ/ are merged to [ɒ]. However, many of the oldest generation distinguished /ɵ/, as in *toad* and *road*, from /o/, as in *towed* and *rowed*. Kurath and McDavid, as well as Avis (1961) describe /ɵ/ as a slightly centralized [o< ~ ɔ<], often with an inglide, but the acoustic measurements of speakers 3 and 4 suggest that it may not have been centralized at all. Many speakers produced an [ɪu] diphthong in words such as *dew*, *new*, and *music*, though this feature was considered rustic and was declining. /ɑr/ and /æː/ are realized identically as [aː]. Many of the words that had originally had /æː/, such as *glass* and *after*, were being transferred to the short /æ/ class, but the [aː]

SPEAKER 3

Male, Born 1860, from North Truro, Massachusetts

(one of the Hanley recordings included on the ADS Centennial tape; recorded in 1933)

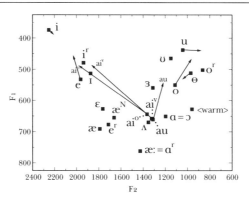

NOTE: He shows a traditional eastern New England configuration, including /ɵ/. His /au/ is generally realized as [ʌo], but varies. He is completely *r*-less. (conversation; NCSU)

SPEAKER 4
Male, Born 1844, from Belmont, New Hampshire
(one of the Hanley recordings included on the ADS Centennial tape;
recorded in 1934)

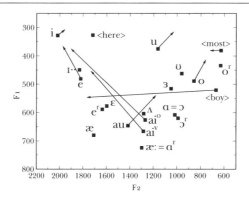

NOTE: His configuration is similar to speaker 3's except that he realizes /au/ as [æ˃ɵ]. /ɵ/ appears in *most*. He is completely *r*-less. (conversation; NCSU)

SPEAKER 5
Male, Born 1941, from Haverhill, Massachusetts
(recorded in 1994)

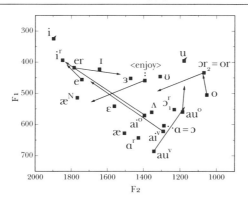

NOTE: He shows Canadian raising of /au/ and /ai/. Some of his tokens of /ɔr/ are merged with /or/, while others form a separate class. The F2 of *enjoy* is affected by coarticulation with [dʒ]. His /ɜ/ is usually *r*-less but varies; otherwise he is completely *r*-less. (conversation; NCSU)

SPEAKER 6

Female, Born 1976, from Uxbridge, Massachusetts
(college student; recorded in 1997)

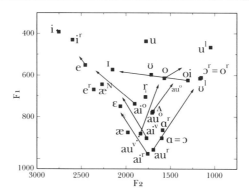

NOTE: She shows Canadian raising of /au/ and /ai/. She produces /ar/ with a backed nucleus, perhaps because she is almost completely r-ful. (reading passage; NCSU)

form carried prestige at the same time, especially in such words as *aunt* and *rather.* /ɔr/ and /or/ were kept distinct, and /ɔr/ was usually merged with /ɑ = ɔ/, so that *short* and *shot* were homophonous. /er/, though variable, was often realized as [æə], with a low nucleus. /ai/ varied between [aɪ] and [əɪ], and the [əɪ] forms were not limited to contexts before voiceless consonants; speaker 3 illustrates this situation, though he also shows some backing of /ai/, which Kurath and McDavid did not report. Finally, /au/ showed three distinct variants. The first two, [aʊ] and [əʊ], corresponded to the variants that /ai/ showed. A third variant that they described as [æʊ] occurred as a relic form, mostly in northern New England but also, sporadically, in southeastern Massachusetts (as well as in Connecticut). Speaker 4 has this fronted variant. It is likely that all three variants of /au/ had existed throughout New England since the eighteenth century, with [aʊ] and [əʊ] as the more prestigious forms and [æʊ] the less prestigious and, ultimately, stigmatized form. Thomas (1961, 228), using evidence from the speech of college students, found [əʊ] to be predominant in Maine and common in New Hampshire, Vermont, and Massachusetts before voiceless consonants. It was less frequent in the same states in other phonetic contexts.

Parslow (1967) described changes in the speech of Boston. Perhaps the most important development that he described was the formation of a new middle-class dialect distinct from both working-class speech and Brahmin aristocratic speech. It was characterized by an increased rate of *r*-fulness, the extinction of /ɵ/, the disappearance of [ɪu] in such words as *dew* and *tune*, and the replacement of [aː] in such words as *past* and *glass* with [æ]. Speaker 6, though not from the immediate vicinity of Boston, represents this emerging middle-class dialect; she was almost completely *r*-ful in the interview setting. Porter's (1965) study of Dartmouth, in southern Massachusetts, revealed some of the same vowel changes: [aː] was giving way to [æ] in many words, [ɪu] had disappeared, and /ɵ/ existed only in the memories of some elderly natives. Both Miller (1953) and Laferriere (1977) provided further evidence that [aː] is being replaced in many words by [æ], but Laferriere also found a new process, raising of /æ/, in operation in Boston. The raising was most prevalent before nasals and voiceless fricatives, but some younger speakers exhibited it in all phonetic contexts.

Laferriere (1979) found that /ɔr/ was being transferred in Boston from /ɑ = ɔ/ and being merged with /or/, though more among Jews than among Irish and more among Irish than among Italians. The best-known sociolinguistic study in eastern New England is that of Labov (1963) on Martha's Vineyard. He described how /ai/ and /au/ were being raised toward [əɪ] and [əʊ], respectively, as a sign of island identity. This raising was most frequent before voiceless consonants but was not confined to that context. As speakers 5 and 6 indicate, this raising is not restricted to Martha's Vineyard; my own observations suggest that it is widespread in eastern New England. There is some reason to think that [aː], which survives mainly as a reflex of /ɑr/, is becoming backed to [ɑː] among some *r*-less speakers. One final note about changes in eastern New England speech is that /er/ in Boston is now often produced as a triphthongal [eiə] (Labov 1988).

CONNECTICUT (speakers 7 and 8). Connecticut was the most important source of settlers in upstate New York, and upstate New York in
turn was the primary source of settlers in other parts of the "Inland
Upper North" region, which includes not only upstate New York
but also Michigan, Wisconsin, and the northern parts of Ohio,
Indiana, and Illinois (see, e.g., Wilhelm 1982). Thus, Connecticut
occupies a key position in the history of American English dialects.
Nevertheless, since *LANE* was published, Connecticut speech has
been sorely neglected in studies of language variation.

Kurath and McDavid (1961), based on information from *LANE*,
found several features that set Connecticut speech off from that of
eastern New England. Connecticut speech is basically *r*-ful west of
the Connecticut River, though *r*-lessness predominated in the
LANE records from eastern Connecticut. Also of great importance
is the fact that the distinction between /ɑ/ and /ɔ/ is maintained. A
fact that is probably linked to the preservation of the /ɑ/-/ɔ/ distinction is that /æ:/ was essentially nonexistent in most of Connecticut
in the *LANE* records. Most of the /æ:/ words (e.g., *half, aunt, pasture,*

SPEAKER 7
Male, Born 1853, from Greenwich, Connecticut
(one of the Hanley recordings included on the ADS Centennial tape;
recorded in 1933)

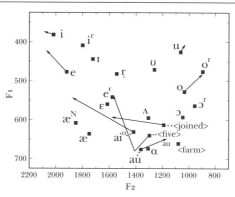

NOTE: He shows a traditional Connecticut configuration, with /ɔr/ and /or/
distinct. The F1 of *joined* is affected by nasalization. He is completely *r*-ful.
(conversation; NCSU)

SPEAKER 8
Male, Born 1907, from Meriden, Connecticut
(featured in Ayres and Greet 1930; college-educated;
recorded in 1927 or 1928)

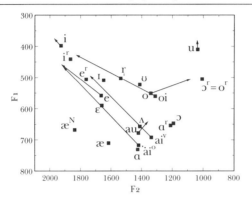

NOTE: His configuration is similar to speaker 7's, but he merges /ɔr/ with /or/. The high F_2 values of his /o/ and /oi/ nuclei are an artifact of the consonants in the words that were measured. He is completely *r*-ful. (reading passage; NCSU)

and *glass*) were merged into /æ/. A few (e.g., *father* and *calm, palm*) were merged into /ɑ/. As a result, there were three low vowels, just as in eastern New England, but the origins of the three were different: /æ = æ:/, /ɑ/, and /ɔ/ in Connecticut versus /æ/, /æ:/, and /ɑ = ɔ/ in eastern New England. Kurath and McDavid found that the distinction between /ɔr/ and /or/ was maintained in Connecticut as in eastern New England, but Thomas (1961) found that this distinction has largely been lost in Connecticut since *LANE* was conducted.

Boberg and Labov (1998), noting the key role of western New England in the settlement of the Inland Upper North, attempted to find evidence of the Northern Cities Shift in Connecticut and other parts of western New England. They found some traces of it. Raising of /æ/ was widespread in western New England, and their Connecticut speakers showed other components of the shift, such as the fronting of /ɑ/ and the backing of /ɛ/. It seems likely that New York City has had some influence on the speech of Connecticut, but studies that document it specifically are lacking.

Raised nuclei of /au/ do not seem to be common in Connecticut, a fact that both Kurath and McDavid (1961) and Thomas (1961, 228) noted. Instead, lowering of the glide occurs. The result is a realization of /au/ as [ɑɔ ~ ɑʊ], which differs noticeably from the higher-gliding forms common in eastern New England. TELSUR data (Labov, Ash, and Boberg forthcoming) show that fronting of the nucleus of /au/ is making inroads into Connecticut. Fronting of /au/ would set Connecticut off from the Inland Upper North and may result from New York City influence.

The Connecticut and eastern New England dialects are not the only dialects in New England. Rhode Island and Vermont have their own dialects that are transitional between those of Connecticut and eastern New England in many ways (Labov, Ash, and Boberg 1997; Boberg and Labov 1998).

NEW YORK CITY (speaker 9). Although there were a number of earlier studies of New York City English, the definitive study is Labov's (1966) survey of the Lower East Side of Manhattan, with acoustic analyses of the vowels of some of the speakers from that study shown in Labov, Yeager, and Steiner (1972). The two vowels that Labov studied most intensely were /æː/ and /ɔ/. /æː/ is distinct from /æ/ in New York City and is realized as a mid or even high, ingliding (or downgliding) [eə ~ eə ~ iə]. The patterning of /æː/ and /æ/ is more or less predictable (as noted in chapter 1, I am using the slashes mainly for convenience with regard to /æː/ vs. /æ/) and the contexts for each are outlined in Labov (1994, 335). /ɔ/ is quite distinct from /ɑ/ and, analogously with /æː/, is raised to [oə ~ uə]. Both the raising of /æː/ and the raising of /ɔ/ were ongoing when Labov conducted his interviews. The complicated social patterning of the variants is described in Labov (1966). Labov also noted that the nucleus of /au/ was being fronted to [æ] and the nucleus of /ai/ was being backed to [ɑ]. This pattern of /au/ → [æʊ] and /ai/ → [ɑɪ] matches that found in many British dialects. He found that r-lessness, which traditionally predominated in New York City, had become unprestigious and variable and showed its own social patterning. Pre-/r/ vowels were undergoing change as well. /ɔr/ and /or/ have long been merged in New

SPEAKER 9
Male, Born 1908, from Manhattan, New York, New York
(Irish ancestry; featured in Ayres and Greet 1930;
recorded in 1927 or 1928)

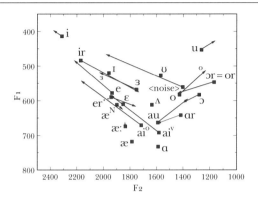

NOTE: He shows an old-fashioned New York City configuration, with /ɜ/ realized as [ɜɪ], a back /au/ nucleus, and /æː/ barely raised. He is completely *r*-less. (reading passage; NCSU)

York City (Kurath and McDavid 1961), and Labov (1966) reported that this merged /ɔr = or/ was merged with /ɔ/, though after conducting acoustic analyses he later said that they tended to remain slightly different (Labov, Yeager, and Steiner 1972; Labov 1994). Labov (1966) also reported that /ar/ was being backed and rounded to [ɒː] and that /ir/ and /er/ were often merged. Finally, he found that the [ʌɪ] variant of stressed syllabic /r/ in closed syllables, as in *first*, and the [ʌː] variant in open syllables, as in *stir*, that traditionally predominated in New York City were highly recessive and were being replaced by an *r*-ful form. Since Labov's fieldwork in the 1960s, there are undoubtedly newer developments in New York City English. For example, I have observed that many young, middle-class New Yorkers show some fronting of /o/ and /u/.

The New York City speaker featured here (speaker 9) represents an old-fashioned form of the New York accent. I have not attempted to represent this dialect more fully because of the extensive work on the New York dialect by Labov and his team.

MINNESOTA (speaker 10). Minnesota, western Wisconsin, northern Iowa, the Dakotas, and eastern Montana were all settled in large part by Germans and Scandinavians, and these groups left an important mark on the speech of this region: a tendency for /e/ and /o/ to be realized as monophthongal [e:] and [o:], respectively (Allen 1976). In other respects, the speech of this region is similar to that of the Inland Upper North, with Canadian raising of /ai/ and sometimes of /au/, backed /au/ nuclei, and raised /æ/ prevalent. One difference is that /ɑ/ and /ɔ/ are merged over some parts of this region. Data from TELSUR (Labov, Ash, and Boberg forthcoming) show that the merger predominates in northern Minnesota (around Duluth) and in the western parts of the Dakotas. Another difference is that /au/ tends to be realized as [ɑo ~ ɑu], with higher glides than in most Inland Upper North speech.

The one speaker from this region who is featured here, a native of the Twin Cities area of Minnesota, maintains the distinction between /ɑ/ and /ɔ/. He also shows monophthongal /o/ and nearly monophthongal /e/.

SPEAKERS 10
Male, Born 1940, from Lino Lakes, Minnesota
(recorded in 1994)

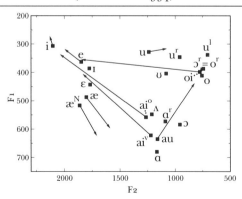

NOTE: He keeps /ɑ/ distinct from /ɔ/ and shows raised, downgliding /æ/. His /o/ (consistently) and /e/ (variably) are monophthongal. (reading passage; UT)

PHILADELPHIA (speaker 11). Although there were earlier studies (e.g., Tucker 1944), Kurath and McDavid (1961) essentially provided the historical baseline for the Philadelphia dialect. They noted several tendencies among the Philadelphia linguistic atlas informants: fronting of /o/, lowering of /e/, fronted nuclei of /au/, a clear distinction between /ɑ/ and /ɔ/, rounding of /ɑr/ to [ɒɚ], and the merger of /ɔr/ and /or/. They also noted that the Philadelphia dialect is *r*-ful. They did not detect the split of /æ/ and /æ:/ or the raising of /æ:/, though these features were certainly present. Since then, as with New York, the definitive dialectal work on Philadelphia has been conducted by William Labov and his research team. They examined cross-generational differences in all of the stressed vowels. The principal summaries of the findings on production of vowels in Philadelphia are found in Labov (1980; 1989; 1994, especially pp. 56–72; see also Hindle 1980; Payne 1980; Kroch 1996; and Roberts 1997). Almost all of the vowels were undergoing change (assuming the apparent time hypothesis that generational differences reflect real changes across time). The most noteworthy

SPEAKER 11

Male, Born 1943, from Roxboro, Philadelphia, Pennsylvania
(recorded in 1999)

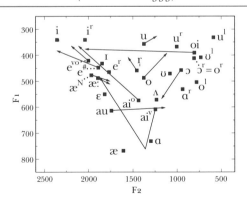

NOTE: He shows all of the typical Philadelphia traits. His /aiʸ/ is triphthongal, [ʌae]. (reading passage supplemented by conversation; NCSU)

changes were that /e/ in closed syllables (but not in open syllables) was now being raised instead of lowered; that /au/ was being shifted from [æʊ] to [ɛə]; and that Canadian raising of /ai/ was occurring, with clear raising in pre-voiceless obstruent contexts (not lowering in other contexts). The last change was unusual in that it was led by males, while females led in all the other changes that they found. Their results also indicated that /ʌ/ is backed in Philadelphia and is becoming more backed (Labov 1994, 58–59). Labov (1989) described the complex conditioning of the split between /æ/ and /æ:/ in Philadelphia. As in New York City, /æ:/ is raised to [ɛə ~ eə ~ eæ] and /ɔ/ is raised to [oə ~ oɔ].

Labov's team has also conducted some perceptual work on the Philadelphia dialect. Labov, Karen, and Miller (1991) investigated the ability of Philadelphians to distinguish pairs of words like *ferry/furry* and *merry/Murray*. Labov and Ash (1997) examined cross-dialectal recognition of the Philadelphia dialect, as compared with the dialects of Birmingham, Alabama, and Chicago.

WESTERN PENNSYLVANIA (speaker 12). Perhaps the most distinctive trait of the Western Pennsylvania dialect is that it is a hotbed of vowel mergers. The merger of /ɑ/ and /ɔ/ is a long-established feature in it (Wetmore 1959; Kurath and McDavid 1961; Hankey 1972; Herold 1990, 1997). Several mergers of vowels before /l/ are also well-established and are found in the speech of natives born as early as the 1930s. Johnson (1971) reported the merger of /ul/ and /ʊl/ (i.e., *pool = pull*) in western Pennsylvania. Hankey (1972) reported both the /ul/-/ʊl/ merger and the merger of /il/ and /ɪl/ (*feel = fell*); see also Brown (1982). Dickey (1997) reported the mergers of /il/ and /ɪl/ and of /el/ and /ɛl/ (*fail = fell*), as well as a three-way merger of /ul/, /ʊl/, and /ol/ (*pool = pull = pole*). McElhinny (1999) analyzed the laxing of /il/ and /ul/, which are correlates of the /il/-/ɪl/ and /ul/-/ʊl/ mergers in Pittsburgh. The data from TELSUR (Labov, Ash, and Boberg forthcoming) show a strong presence of the /ul/-/ʊl/ and /il/-/ɪl/ mergers in western Pennsylvania. The merger of /ɑl = ɔl/ with /ʌl/ (*gall = gull*) also occurs. These mergers have brought about some stereotyping; popular publications such as Abel (1996) list pronunciations like "still mill" (for *steel mill*), "dill"

SPEAKER 12

Female, Born 1971, from Burgettstown, Pennsylvania

(recorded in 1990)

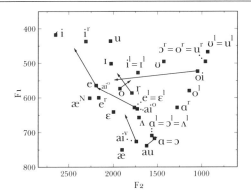

NOTE: She shows all of the mergers described in the text for western Pennsylvania except that her /ol/ is distinct from her /ʊl = ul/. Her /ai/ shows Canadian raising. Her /aiʸ/ and /au/ both show weakening of the glide. (reading passage; TAMU and NCSU)

(*deal*) and "Pittsburgh Stillers" (*Steelers*). Other mergers occur before /r/. Kurath and McDavid (1961) noted that the merger of /ɔr/ and /or/ was practically universal among linguistic atlas speakers. Among younger speakers, the merger of /ur/ with /or = ɔr/ in all contexts (*tour* = *tore, sure* = *shore*) seems to be common.

A number of other features have been noted as typical of western Pennsylvania, too. Kurath and McDavid (1961) and Hankey (1972) cited fronting of /o/ as predominant. Kurath and McDavid also said that lowering of /e/ was common, though it is uncertain whether that is still true. They note that the western Pennsylvania dialect is *r*-ful, and also describe a distinctive pronunciation of syllable-coda /r/, which they say is produced as "an alveolar tongue tip consonant" in western Pennsylvania (109), as opposed to the more widespread form produced "with the sides of the tongue drawn away from the gums and the body of the tongue bulging upward" (107). It is not entirely clear what they meant, but the former may refer to a retroflex /r/ and the latter to the "bunched-tongue" /r/, which is produced with constrictions in the pharyngeal and palatal-velar areas (Lindau 1985). It is also not clear whether the variant that Kurath and McDavid described is still common in western Pennsylvania. At any rate, stressed syllabic /r/ with that variant was apparently quite distinctive.

A final vowel variant considered characteristic of western Pennsylvania is monophthongization of /au/. While stereotypical of Pittsburgh English—Abel (1996) lists "dahntahn" and "aht" as Pittsburgh pronunciations of *downtown* and *out*—it has not attracted much scholarly attention. However, Hankey (1972) states that weak-gliding forms of both /au/ and /ai/ are occasional in western Pennsylvania, and Johnstone, Bhasin, and Wittkofski (2000) found that monophthongal /au/ occurs mainly among Pittsburghers born after 1920. The latter study also noted that monophthongization seemed to be absent in word-final contexts.

Philadelphia and western Pennsylvania do not represent all of the dialectal diversity in Pennsylvania. The Pennsylvania German region and the northeastern section of the state are dialectally quite distinctive in their own right.

INLAND UPPER NORTH (speakers 13–16). This dialect, spoken from upstate New York to eastern Wisconsin, has been studied intensely in recent years by William Labov, his students, and several other researchers. Before Labov came on the scene, however, McDavid (1958), using data from linguistic atlas informants born in the nineteenth century, listed a few vocalic features that typified the old-fashioned speech of this region: /ɑ/ was fronted, sometimes as far as [a]; the [ɪu] variant that occurred in old-fashioned New England speech in *dew* and *music* was found there; /ɔr/ and /or/ were kept distinct; and the dialect was highly *r*-ful. Since then, fronted /ɑ/ and *r*-fulness have remained in the Inland Upper North, but the /ɔr/-/or/ distinction and the [ɪu] diphthong have died out. Pederson (1965, 33) found that only 13 of his 55 mostly middle-aged and older Chicago informants maintained the /ɔr/-/or/ distinction. Thomas (1958) noted the presence of fronted /ɑ/ in this region, though his base of data was college students born in the twentieth century. Gordon (1997) reviewed a number of other pre-Labovian sources on vowel shifting in the region and found possible (but inconclusive) evidence that the raising of /æ/ may have begun before 1900.

As described briefly in chapter 1, the Inland Upper North is now characterized by a set of vowel changes called the Northern Cities Shift. Labov and his team have described this shift extensively (see Labov, Yeager, and Steiner 1972; Labov 1991, 1994; Labov, Ash, and Boberg 1997). Except for the last-named study, their evidence is based largely on acoustic analyses of speakers from in or near Rochester, Buffalo, Detroit, and Chicago. The vowel shifts form a chain. /æ/ is raised to [eə] or something similar. Its glide tends to be a downglide, so that it may be produced as [eæ]. The fronting of /ɑ/ to [a], though apparently an old development, is considered to be part of the Northern Cities Shift; Labov says that it may be fronted as far as [æ]. /ɔ/, while generally produced as [ɒ] or, less often, as [ɔ] in older Inner Upper North speech (see, e.g., Kurath and McDavid 1961; Pederson 1965), is lowered and often unrounded to [ɑ] in the Northern Cities Shift. /ʌ/ is backed and may be rounded to [ɔ], though it tends to be

SPEAKER 13
Female, Born 1878, from Madison, Ohio
(*DARE* OH 015; recorded in 1967)

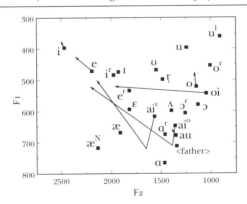

NOTE: She shows a pre–Northern Cities Shift configuration. <father> is based on five tokens. Her /au/ is a monophthongal [ɑː]. Her /ai/ is triphthongal; the apparent backing of /aiᵒ/ is an artifact of the words used. She keeps /ɔr/ and /or/ distinct. (conversation; NCSU)

shorter than /ɔ/ had been. /ɛ/ may be lowered toward [a] or backed toward [ʌ]. Finally, /ɪ/ may be lowered or, more often, centralized. Centralization of /ɪ/ is not unique to the Inland Upper North; it appears to be rather widespread in Northern dialects, as well as in some other areas, such as Texas. Labov (1991) notes that /e/ and /o/ do not undergo shifting in the Inland Upper North. He, as well as Ash (1996), also states that /u/ is often centralized, but this shift is probably an extension of the general fronting of /u/ that occurs over most of the United States. See also the data, mostly from Michigan natives, presented in Hillenbrand et al. (1995).

Several other studies based mostly on impressionistic phonetic analyses have contributed important information about the spread of the Northern Cities Shift. Callary's (1975) analysis of the speech of college students found that, in northern Illinois, the raising of /æ/ to [eə] is directly correlated with the size of a speaker's hometown. Herndobler (1993) found that women led men in Chicago in the raising of /æ/ but not in the fronting of /ɑ/. This situation makes sense if the raising of /æ/ is an innovation and the fronting

SPEAKER 14
Male, Born 1946, from Mentor, Ohio
(father of speaker 16; college-educated; recorded in 1994)

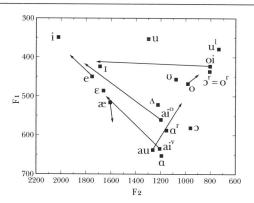

NOTE: He shows the Northern Cities Shift for /æ/ and /ɑ/ and a moderate degree of Canadian raising of /ai/. His /o/ is nearly monophthongal. (reading passage; UT)

of /ɑ/ an old development. Eckert's (1987, 1988, 1989a, 1989b) studies of the speech of high schoolers in Livonia, Michigan, a suburb of Detroit, also suggested that the Northern Cities Shift was associated with urbanness. Although the older shifts—those of /æ/, /ɑ/, and /ɔ/—were well integrated into Livonia speech and were correlated mainly with gender, the newer shifts—the backing of /ʌ/ and /ɛ/—were associated with students with a nonschool and largely blue-collar orientation, who had more contacts in inner-city areas. Knack (1991) found that Jewish women in Grand Rapids, Michigan, resisted the lowering of /ɔ/, perhaps because of their connections with Jews from New York City, where /ɔ/ is raised. Gordon (1997, 2001) examined shifting of the six vowels involved in the Northern Cities Shift (/æ/, /ɑ/, /ɔ/, /ʌ/, /ɛ/, and /ɪ/) in two small towns in southern Michigan, Paw Paw and Chelsea. In contrast with Callary's findings, he found that speakers in Paw Paw, which is farther from any large city, consistently led speakers from Chelsea, which is near Ann Arbor and fairly close to Detroit, in the vowel

SPEAKER 15
Female, Born 1969, from Euclid, Ohio
(college-educated; recorded in 1996)

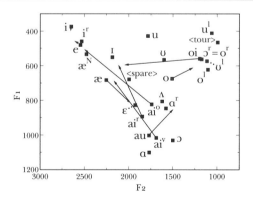

NOTE: Her /æ/, /ɑ/, and /ɔ/ all show the Northern Cities Shift. Her /ai/ shows strong Canadian raising; her /aiʳ/ (e.g., *tire*) shows raised nuclei. Her /ɑr/ nucleus is raised and centralized. (reading passage; NCSU)

shifts. One possible explanation was that Paw Paw is less affluent and thus more blue-collar than Chelsea, but another possible factor was that some Chelsea residents may have been reacting to a rapid influx of outsiders there. Gordon also noted that the backing of /ʌ/ was barely evident, though all five of the other vowels showed definite shifting. Ito and Preston's (1998) acoustic analysis of the shifting of /æ/, /ɑ/, and /ɔ/ in rural north-central Michigan suggested that local identity retards the shifting of those vowels. Ito's (1999) acoustic study of variation in /æ/ raising in another rural community, Clare, Michigan, found that the raising seemed to be more advanced among females and working-class residents, but was not correlated with the age of a speaker. She also examined phonetic conditioning of the raising intensively, finding that /æ/ was most raised before nasals and least raised before voiceless stops and fricatives. Gordon (2000) found Northern Cities Shift features to only a limited degree in Gary, Indiana.

Apart from the Northern Cities Shift, the other major development in the Inland Upper North is Canadian raising, which affects

SPEAKER 16
Male, Born 1977, from Brunswick, Ohio
(son of speaker 14; later matriculated to college; recorded in 1991)

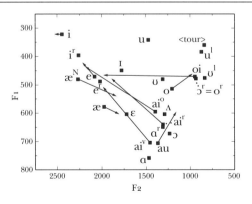

NOTE: His /æ/, /ɑ/, /ɔ/, /ʌ/, and /ɛ/ show the Northern Cities Shift. /ai/ shows strong Canadian raising; /aiʳ/ shows raised onsets. (reading passage; UT)

/ai/ and, less commonly, /au/ in this region. Kilbury (1983) described Canadian raising from his own Chicago speech. He observed that the raising occurred not only before voiceless consonants but also before /r/, even if there were intervening consonants between /ai/ and /r/ (as in *spider*), though the raising was blocked by morpheme boundaries. He noted that Canadian raising of /au/ was much more restricted in his speech. Vance (1987) depicted a similar pattern for /ai/ in the speech of his three speakers and discussed how syllable structure affects the distribution of raised and nonraised variants. Niedzielski (1996) reported that Canadian raising of both /ai/ and /au/ occurs in Detroit (see also Niedzielski 1999). Likewise, Eckert (1996) discussed the spread of /ai/ raising in the Detroit area. Dailey-O'Cain (1997) found Canadian raising of /ai/ to be well-established and that of /au/ to be incipient in Ann Arbor, Michigan. In Thomas (1991), I noted the occurrence of Canadian raising of /ai/ in various dialects of the North, and I described its phonetic development in the Cleveland area in Thomas (1995). The fact that Canadian raising of /ai/ is far more common than Canadian raising of /au/ in this region has not been explained, but it may have to do with the structure of /au/ in this dialect. As with Connecticut and many regions to the south, but unlike eastern New England and Canada, the glide of /au/ typically does not reach a high position in most parts of the Inland Upper North. In common with Connecticut, the typical realization is [ɑɔ ~ ɑʊ], with a low back nucleus and a lower-mid back or low back glide. In fact, speaker 13 produced /au/ as a monophthongal [ɑː]. (A few speakers do show higher glides, however.) I have shown before (Thomas 1991, 1995, 2000) that /ai/ glides are higher before voiceless consonants than in other contexts and have argued that this difference in the glides is essential for the development of Canadian raising, which is an analogous difference in the nuclei. I suspect that /au/ operates similarly, so if /au/ glides do not reach an upper-mid to high position, it would follow that Canadian raising cannot develop.

The Inland Upper North is represented here by four speakers (speakers 13–16) from the vicinity of Cleveland, Ohio. According to Labov, Ash, and Boberg (1997), the entire Inland Upper North

shows a high degree of dialectal uniformity, and since other researchers have covered much of the rest of this region, providing
more than this superficial coverage is not necessary. The progress
of the Northern Cities Shift in the Cleveland area has received less
attention than that in most of the other metropolitan centers in
the Inland Upper North (though see Lance 1994, 357–59). The
oldest speaker (speaker 13) predates both the Northern Cities
Shift and Canadian raising of /ai/, while the three younger speakers
show various stages of them.

CENTRAL AND SOUTHERN OHIO (speakers 17–49). This region consists of several weakly differentiated dialectal areas. The whole area
was settled by varying mixtures of Pennsylvanians and Virginians,
with small numbers of Marylanders, New Yorkers, New Englanders,
and New Jerseyans who were often concentrated in colonies—for
example, New Englanders in Marietta and New Jerseyans in Cincinnati (Wilhelm 1982). The largest group of Pennsylvanians came
from south-central and southwestern Pennsylvania, but significant

SPEAKER 17
Male, Born 1898
(lived near Kalida, Ohio, a German American community, until age 11,
then moved near Findlay, Ohio; father of speaker 18; recorded in 1978)

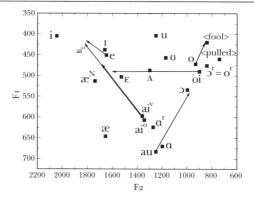

NOTE: His /ai/ nucleus is lower-mid in all contexts. His /o/ is backed and
nearly monophthongal (possibly from German influence). (conversation;
UT)

numbers from the Pennsylvania German region settled in some sections. Most of the Virginians came from the northern part of the Blue Ridge Mountains (Thomas and Boberg in preparation). The speech of the region reflects these origins. Very similar dialects are found across much of Indiana, central Illinois, western Missouri, Kansas, and a large swath of the western states as far as the Pacific coast (see speaker 50).

A number of trends characterize the region. The area is strongly *r*-ful except for a few communities along the Ohio River that were settled by Kentuckyans. /ɔr/ and /or/ are merged in most areas (Nobbelin 1980). Among older speakers, /ʃ/ and /ʒ/ have a strong effect on preceding vowels. Thus, the stressed vowel in *fish*, *dish*, *official*, *division*, and so on may be produced with an upglide ([ɪi]) or may actually have /i/; *special* and *measure* may have [ei] = /e/; *ash*, *cash*, and *trash* may have [æe]; and *gosh* may have /ai/. *Wash* and *squash* with /oi/, [oə] ~ /ʊ/, or /ɔr/ and *push* with [ʊi] or /u/ are also heard. This effect is common or predominant among speakers born before 1930, but it seems to have attracted a stigma (especially with regard to /ɪ/, /ʊ/, and /ɔ/) and is much less common

SPEAKER 18

Female, Born 1924, from Near Findlay, Ohio

(daughter of speaker 17 and mother of speaker 19; recorded in 1993)

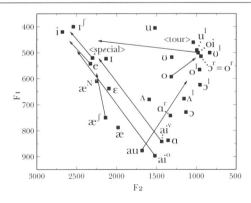

NOTE: Her /ai/ nucleus is low, and her /au/ nucleus is not front. Her /o/ is back. (reading passage; UT)

among speakers born after 1930. It is certainly not limited to Ohio, as it is found in many parts of the South and the Midwest and probably elsewhere.

Other trends in central and southern Ohio are the merger of /ɑ/ and /ɔ/, the fronting of /u/ and /o/, and the fronting of the nucleus of /au/. Judging by the field records of *LANCS*, the merger of /ɑ/ and /ɔ/ and the fronting of /u/ and /o/ seem to have started in the southeastern part of the state and then spread more widely. Most of the *LANCS* informants from southeastern Ohio have /ɑ/ and /ɔ/ merged before /t/ (so that *caught* and *cot* are homonyms) but perhaps not in other phonetic contexts, with the result that *caught* is pronounced [kʰɑt] and *off* [ɔf] (see also Nobbelin 1980). Most of the *LANCS* informants with central variants of /o/ are from southern Ohio, especially the southeastern part, and the central forms are more frequent among younger informants than among older ones. For /au/, the *LANCS* informants as well as *DARE* informants (as shown in Frazer 1978) from the southern part of the state show fronted nuclei, which in all likelihood are related to Virginia and Kentucky settlement. Fronted forms have since spread

SPEAKER 19

Female, Born 1950, from Benton Ridge, Ohio

(daughter of speaker 18 and mother of speaker 20; recorded in 1993)

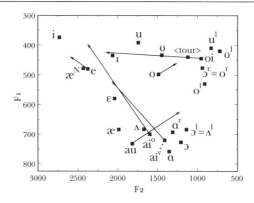

NOTE: Her /au/ nucleus is front, and her /o/ nucleus is central. She merges /ʌl/ with /ɔl/. (reading passage; UT)

SPEAKER 20
Female, Born 1970, from Jenera, Ohio
(daughter of speaker 19; recorded in 1993)

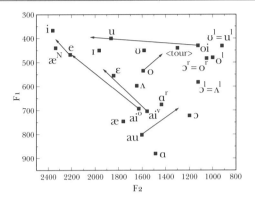

NOTE: Her /ai/ and /ɑr/ nuclei are somewhat raised. Her /o/ nucleus is central. She shows mergers of /ʌl/ and /ɔl/ and of /ʊl/ and /ul/. (reading passage supplemented by conversation; UT)

SPEAKER 21
Male, Born 1918, from Cheviot, Ohio
(*DARE* OH 076; recorded in 1968)

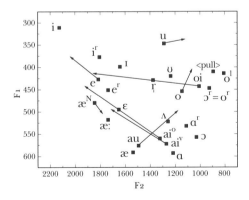

NOTE: His /o/ is back (fronted forms are more common in the Cincinnati area), but he shows the Cincinnati split of /æ/ and /æ:/. (reading passage and conversation; NCSU)

into central Ohio (see Thomas 1989/93), though young speakers show some retraction of /au/ nuclei. Frazer (1983) found a similar pattern of fronting of /au/ and subsequent retraction in McDonough County, Illinois.

Recent developments in central and southern Ohio include several additional mergers. Some back vowels may be merged before /l/ (see Thomas 1989/93, 1996; Flanigan and Norris 2000). The merger of /ɑl/ = ɔl/ with /ʌl/ (*gall* = *gull*) is common among speakers born as early as the 1930s. The merger of /ul/ with /ʊl/ is restricted to speakers born after about 1960, and a three-way merger of /ul/, /ʊl/, and /ol/ occurs among some young speakers. Mergers of front vowels before /l/ do not appear to be common. /ur/ is commonly merged with syllabic /r/ after palatals (e.g., *surely* = *Shirley*) and in nonfinal syllables (as in *endurance* and *tournament*), and sometimes in other contexts (e.g., the local stereotypical pronunciation of *Newark* as "Nerk"). This merger, while widespread in American English, sets Ohio speech off from that of western

SPEAKER 22

Male, Born 1897, from Ripley, Ohio
(*DARE* OH 058; recorded in 1968)

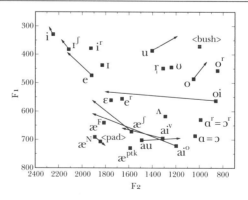

NOTE: He shows mergers of /ɑ/ with /ɔ/ and of /ɑr/ with /ɔr/. His /aï/ shows weak glides. He appears to have a split of /æ/ and /æ:/, with /æ:/ (represented by /æ^F/ and apparently *pad*) produced as [æɛæ] (only the highest point is shown on the plot). Often *r*-less in unstressed syllables, but otherwise *r*-ful. (reading passage and conversation; NCSU)

SPEAKER 23
Female, Born 1950, from Long Bottom, Ohio
(*DARE* OH 040; recorded in 1968)

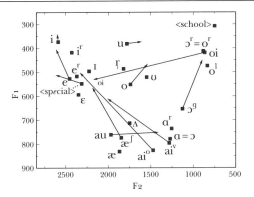

NOTE: She shows fronting of /o/. She also exhibits upgliding /æ/ and /ɛ/ before /ʃ/ and upgliding /ɔ/ before /g/. Her /ai/ shows strong glides. (reading passage supplemented by conversation; NCSU)

SPEAKER 24
Male, Born 1953, from Ironton, Ohio
(recorded in 1994)

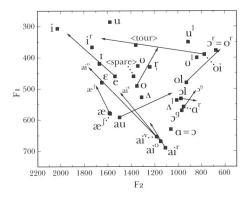

NOTE: His /ʌl/ and /ɔl/ are barely distinct. His /er/ nucleus (in *spare*) is central, but still distinct from the nucleus in *spur*. His /aiʳ/, as in *tire*, is monophthongal (e.g., [tʰaːɹ]). (reading passage; UT)

Pennsylvania. Some younger Ohioans merge /ur/ with /ɔr = or/ in contexts not affected by the *surely/Shirley* merger (e.g., *tour = tore*). Finally, the merger of /ɪ/ and /ɛ/ before nasals is fairly common in some areas (Hartman 1966; Thomas 1996).

Of the subregions of central and southern Ohio, the most northerly is a band that stretches across the north-central part of the state from Canton through Mansfield to Findlay and Lima. This area, sometimes called the "Backbone Region," had a heavy predominance of Pennsylvania settlers (Wilhelm 1982). The settlers represented a mix of Scotch-Irish from southwestern and south-central Pennsylvania and Germans from eastern Pennsylvania (Thomas and Boberg in preparation). In terms of vowels, this area is characterized by resistance to innovations. The distinction between /ɑ/ and /ɔ/ seems largely to be retained in this area. The fronting of the nuclei of /o/ and /au/ occurred later in this area than in the regions just to the south: apparently they first became common with the "Baby Boom" generation. Speakers 17–20, from the vicinity of Findlay, represent this area.

SPEAKER 25
Male, Born 1892, from Mt. Vernon, Ohio
(DARE OH 074; recorded in 1968)

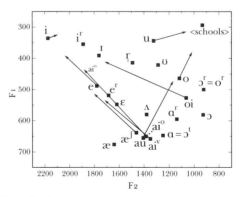

NOTE: His /o/ and /au/ nuclei are not fronted. He shows a partial merger of /ɑ/ with /ɔ/. His /oi/ and /ɔr = or/ nuclei are mid. (reading passage and conversation; NCSU)

SPEAKER 26
Female, Born 1946, from Fredericktown, Ohio
(mother of speaker 27; recorded in 1993)

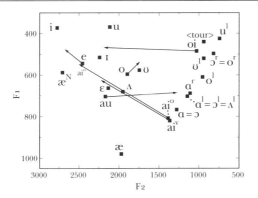

NOTE: She merges /ɑ/ with /ɔ/ and /ʌl/ with /ɔl/. Her /au/ nucleus is front and somewhat raised, but her /æ/ is lowered. Her /ar/ nucleus may be rounded. (reading passage; UT)

SPEAKER 27
Female, Born 1973, from Fredericktown, Ohio
(daughter of speaker 26; recorded in 1992 and 1993)

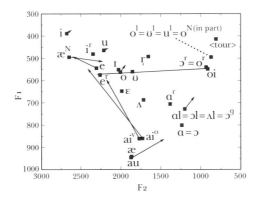

NOTE: Her /o/ nucleus is front. Her /ol/, /ʊl/, and /ul/ are all merged; "/oᴺ/ (in part)" refers to the vowel in *home, don't, won't,* and *only.* Her /æ/ and her /au/ nucleus are lowered. (reading passage; UT)

The Cincinnati metropolitan area has its own peculiarities, too. As described by Strassel and Boberg (1996) and Boberg and Strassel (2000), older natives of Cincinnati retain a distinction between /æ/ and /æː/, with /æː/ being raised as in New York City and Philadelphia. The phonetic distribution of /æ/ and /æː/ differs somewhat from either New York or Philadelphia, however. Strassel and Boberg noted that the distinction is lost among young Cincinnatians and that the distinction between /ɑ/ and /ɔ/ also shows signs of eroding. Speaker 21, from a suburb of Cincinnati, represents this metropolitan center.

Some parts of the southern edge of the state that were settled predominantly from Virginia and Kentucky may show certain South- ern vowel features (see Frazer 1978). Fronting of /au/ nuclei was established earliest in these areas. In some areas along the Ohio River across from Kentucky, traces of r-lessness (mostly in un- stressed syllables), weak-gliding /ai/ (realized as [aːæ]), and the split of /æ/ and /æː/ (with /æː/ realized as [æɛæ]) occur among older natives. Many natives, old and young, show rounding of the nucleus of /ɑr/ to [ɒ]. Monophthongal /ai/ persists before /r/ among younger

SPEAKER 28
Male, Born 1974, from Bladensburg, Ohio
(recorded in 1992)

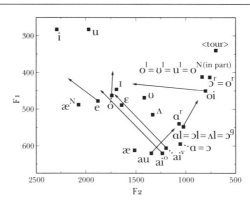

NOTE: His /o/ nucleus is front. His /ol/, /ʊl/, and /ul/ are all merged. His /au/ nucleus is central. (reading passage; UT)

SPEAKER 29
Male, Born 1908, from Columbus, Ohio
(recorded in 1984)

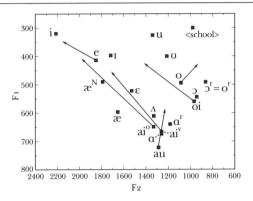

NOTE: His /ɑ/ and /ɔ/ are distinct, but only in morphemes in which no unstressed syllable follows (e.g., *daughter* has /ɑ/). His /au/ and /o/ nuclei are back. (conversation; UT)

SPEAKER 30
Female, Born ca. 1970, from Columbus, Ohio
(recorded in 1985)

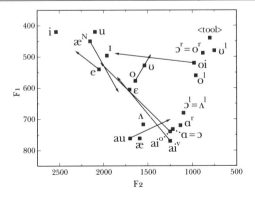

NOTE: She merges /ɑ/ with /ɔ/ and /ʌl/ with /ɔl/. Her /au/ and /o/ nuclei are fronted. Her /oi/ and /ɔr = or/ nuclei are raised, and her /æ/ is lowered. (reading passage; UT)

speakers. By and large, however, the speech of this area is very similar to that of central Ohio. Speakers 22–24 represent this area.

Central Ohio, the featured area in this chapter, was settled mostly by people from south-central and southwestern Pennsylvania and the Blue Ridge region of Virginia, with a significant admixture of upstate New Yorkers but relatively few Pennsylvania Germans. It is represented by speakers 25–49. Of these speakers, only a few, none of them young, maintain the /ɑ/-/ɔ/ distinction. The most striking diachronic change is the frontward movement of /o/. The three oldest speakers (25, 29, and 31) show a backed variant, [ou], but forms with central nuclei, [ɵu ~ əu], appear among speakers born in 1910 or later. Many of the youngest speakers show a further fronting to [øʉ ~ eʉ]. As in many other parts of the country, the fronting does not affect /o/ before /l/. In fact, with vocalization of /l/ in syllable codas, /ol/ sequences can become a monophthongal [oː] (e.g., *pole* [pʰoː]). Two of the three oldest speakers (25 and 29) show central /au/ nuclei, but speakers born immediately after them show fronted nuclei. Because the glide of /ai/ is lowered, the resulting form is [æɔ ~ æɒ]. Some of the young

SPEAKER 31
Female, Born 1900, from Johnstown, Ohio
(recorded in 1993)

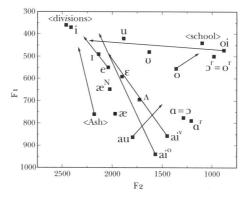

NOTE: Her /o/ is back, and she merges /ɑ/ and /ɔ/. She shows upgliding front vowels before alveopalatal fricatives, as well as /ɔr/ in *wash* (not shown). (conversation; UT)

SPEAKER 32
Female, Born 1910, from Johnstown, Ohio
(mother of speaker 36; recorded in 1993)

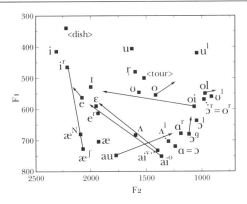

NOTE: She merges /ɑ/ and /ɔ/ but shows no pre-/l/ mergers. She shows upgliding front vowels before alveopalatal fricatives. (reading passage; UT)

SPEAKER 33
Male, Born 1917
(lived in Utica, Ohio, until age 6 but spent the rest of his life in Johnstown, 14 miles away; recorded in 1993)

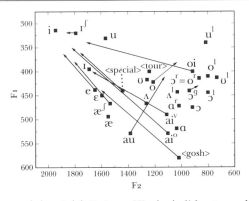

NOTE: He keeps /ɑ/ and /ɔ/ distinct. His /au/ glides toward [u ~ ʉ], not toward [ɔ] (the usual central Ohio form). His front vowels and /ɑ/ show upglides before alveopalatal fricatives, and he has [oə] ~ /ɔr/ in *wash* (not shown). (reading passage; UT)

speakers show the subsequent retraction of the /au/ nucleus that was described above. Several of the young speakers, especially females, show a retraction of /æ/ toward [a]. A few of the young speakers from Johnstown show fronting of the /ai/ nucleus, with the extreme forms being [æe ~ æi]. I have discussed the central Ohio dialect in more detail in Thomas (1989/93, 1996). Speakers 47–49, when they were interviewed, belonged to a clique of eight friends of which speaker 49 was apparently the leader.

There are a few other subareas not covered here. The Marietta-Athens area, which was originally a New England colony, was apparently always set off dialectally from surrounding areas. Clark's (1972) study of the speech of Marietta found that this speech island is losing its distinctiveness, though the study was based on only five speakers. Eastern Ohio, from Youngstown to Steubenville, may show continuing influence from western Pennsylvania. The Dayton area and western Ohio are other possible subareas, though it is doubtful that they differ much from central Ohio (see Boberg and Strassel 2000 on Dayton).

SPEAKER 34
Male, Born 1921, from Johnstown, Ohio
(recorded in 1993)

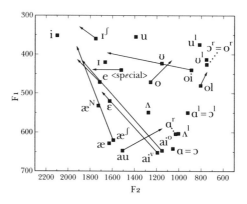

NOTE: He merges /ɑ/ and /ɔ/ but shows no pre-/l/ mergers. His front vowels show upglides before alveopalatal fricatives. (reading passage; UT)

SPEAKER 35

Male, Born 1922, from Johnstown, Ohio
(father of speaker 38; recorded in 1993)

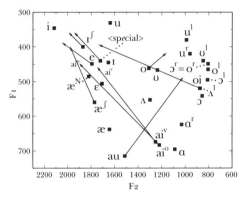

NOTE: He keeps /ɑ/ and /ɔ/ distinct and shows no pre-/l/ mergers. His /au/
shows unusually high glides. His front vowels show upglides before
alveopalatal fricatives. (reading passage; UT)

SPEAKER 36

Female, Born 1933
(lived in Sugar Grove, Ohio, ages 3–11, but in Johnstown the rest of her
life; daughter of speaker 32 and mother of speaker 43; recorded in 1993)

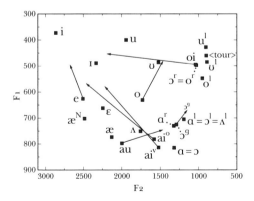

NOTE: She merges /ɑ/ with /ɔ/ and /ʌl/ with /ɔl/. (reading passage; UT)

SPEAKER 37
Female, Born 1935, from Johnstown, Ohio
(mother of speaker 39; recorded in 1993)

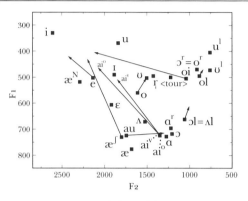

NOTE: Though she distinguished /ɑ/ and /ɔ/ in minimal pairs, it is not clear that she did in the reading passage (on which the plot is based). Her /æ/ shows an upglide before /ʃ/. She merges /ʌl/ with /ɔl/. (reading passage; UT)

SPEAKER 38
Male, born 1950, from Johnstown, Ohio
(college-educated; son of speaker 35 and father of speaker 44; recorded in 1993)

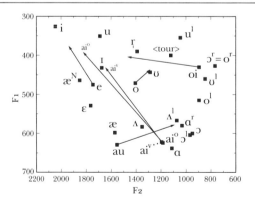

NOTE: He keeps /ɑ/ and /ɔ/ distinct and shows no pre-/l/ mergers. (reading passage; UT)

SPEAKER 39
Female, Born 1956, from Johnstown, Ohio
(wife of speaker 40 and mother of speaker 48; recorded in 1993)

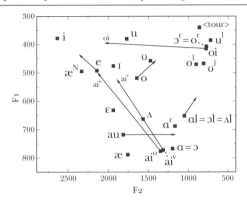

NOTE: She merges /ɑ/ with /ɔ/ and /ʌl/ with /ɔl/. (reading passage; UT)

SPEAKER 40
Male, Born 1956, from Croton, Ohio
(adult life in Johnstown, 7 miles away; husband of speaker 39
and father of speaker 48; recorded in 1993)

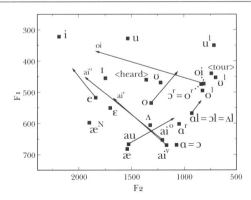

NOTE: He merges /ɑ/ with /ɔ/ and /ʌl/ with /ɔl/. (reading passage; UT)

SPEAKER 41

Male, Born 1959, from Johnstown, Ohio
(husband of speaker 42 and father of speaker 49; recorded in 1994)

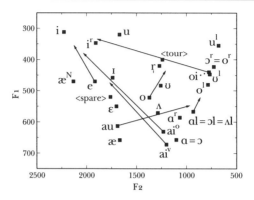

NOTE: He shows mergers of /ɑ/ with /ɔ/ and of /ʌl/ with /ɔl/. (reading passage; UT)

SPEAKER 42

Female, Born 1959, from Johnstown, Ohio
(wife of speaker 41 and mother of speaker 49; recorded in 1994)

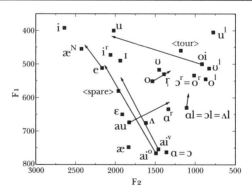

NOTE: She merges /ɑ/ with /ɔ/ and /ʌl/ with /ɔl/. (reading passage; UT)

SPEAKER 43
Female, Born 1963, from Johnstown, Ohio
(daughter of speaker 36; recorded in 1993)

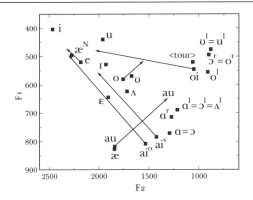

NOTE: She merges /ɑ/ with /ɔ/, /ʌl/ with /ɔl/, and /ʊl/ with /ul/. Her /o/ nucleus is somewhat front. (reading passage; UT)

SPEAKER 44
Male, Born 1981, from Johnstown, Ohio
(son of speaker 38; recorded in 1993)

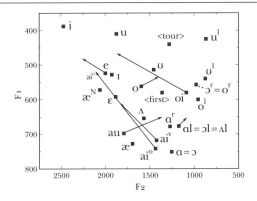

NOTE: He keeps /ol/, /ʊl/, and /ul/ distinct. His /o/ nucleus is central. (reading passage; UT)

SPEAKER 45
Male, Born 1982, from Johnstown, Ohio
(recorded in 1994)

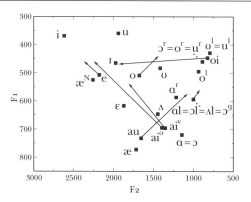

NOTE: He merges /ʊl/ with /ul/ but keeps /ol/ distinct. His nonpostpalatal /ur/ is merged with /ɔr = or/. His /o/ nucleus is somewhat front. (reading passage; UT)

SPEAKER 46
Male, born 1982, from Johnstown, Ohio
(recorded in 1994)

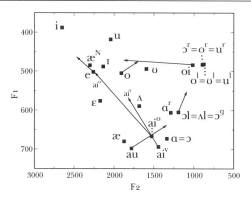

NOTE: His /ol/, /ʊl/, and /ul/ are all merged, and his nonpostpalatal /ur/ is merged with /ɔr = or/. His /o/ nucleus is front. (reading passage; UT)

SPEAKER 47
Female, Born 1982, from Johnstown, Ohio
(daughter of speakers 39 and 40; recorded in 1993)

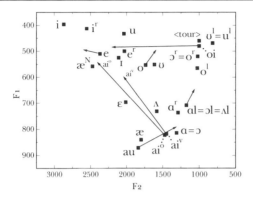

NOTE: She merges /ʊl/ and /ul/ but keeps /ol/ distinct. Her /o/ nucleus is not especially fronted. (reading passage; UT)

SPEAKER 48
Female, born 1981, from Johnstown, Ohio
(daughter of speakers 41 and 42; recorded in 1994)

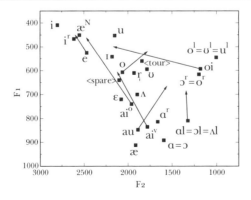

NOTE: Her /ol/, /ʊl/, and /ul/ are all merged. Her /o/ and /ai/ nuclei are front, and her /æ/ is lowered. Her /ʌl = ɔl/ diphthong (with vocalized /l/) glides inward, e.g., *gulls* [gɒʌz], *salt* [sɒʌɾt]. (reading passage; UT)

SPEAKER 49
Female, Born 1982, from Johnstown, Ohio
(recorded in 1994)

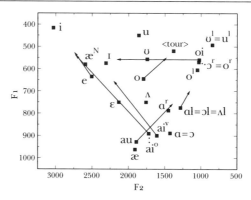

NOTE: Her /ʊl/ and /ul/ are merged, but /ol/ remains distinct. Her /o/ onset is central and her /æ/ is lowered. When she was reinterviewed in 1999, her /o/ had become fronted like that of most of her friends, even though she was the social leader. (reading passage; UT)

CALIFORNIA (speaker 50). Speaker 50 is included mainly to illustrate the similarities between Western speech and that of central and southern Ohio. Anglo speech within California seems to show little clear-cut geographical variation, though published evidence is scarce. DeCamp (1959) noted the presence of r-lessness in San Francisco—the rest of the state is heavily r-ful—and Labov (1991) noted that some speakers in the San Francisco and Los Angeles areas retain the distinction between /ɑ/ and /ɔ/, which is lost in the rest of the state. Metcalf's (1972a) study of southern California speech described the spread of two mergers, that of /ɔ/ and /ɑ/ to [ɑ] and that of /ɪ/ and /ɛ/ before nasals, and a shift of /au/ from [aʊ] to [au]. Godinez (1984) and Godinez and Maddieson (1985) compared the vowels of Anglo and Chicano natives of Los Angeles acoustically, finding that the Anglos tended to have lower /ɪ/, /ɛ/, and /æ/, fronter /u/, and more backed /ɑ/ than the Chicanos. Johnson (1974) reported shifting of /ɔ/ toward [ɑ] and raising of /æ/ and /ɛ/ in west Los Angeles, but also noted that the last two shifts were most prominent before nasals. A few recent studies of speakers largely from the San Francisco Bay area have described recent vowel shifts. Moonwomon (1987) discussed the ongoing merger of /ɔ/ with /ɑ/. Luthin (1987) noted several other shifts: /u/, /ʊ/, /o/, and /ʌ/ are being fronted and /ɪ/, /ɛ/, and /æ/ are being lowered. DeCamp's (1959) earlier study of San Francisco had not found any of the shifts that Luthin described. Labov, Ash, and Boberg (1997) found fronting of /u/ to be characteristic of the West, however. Guenter, Lewis, and Urban (1999) and Guenter (2000) determined that Californians had difficulty associating vowels before /r/, /l/, and /ŋ/ with vowel phonemes (e.g., most did not associate /er/ with /e/ or /ɛ/, nor did most associate /ɪŋ/ with either /ɪ/ or /i/). Guenter (2000) also found that many Californians merge /ʌl/, as in *gull*, with /ol/, as in *goal*, with the resulting vowel closer to [o]. He provided formant values and summary plots for 14 Californians from all parts of the state, though without discussing vowel shifting. Hagiwara (1995) listed formant values and showed plots for 15 southern Californians, also without discussing shifting patterns.

SPEAKER 50

Female, Born 1944, from Sacramento, California

(recorded in 1989)

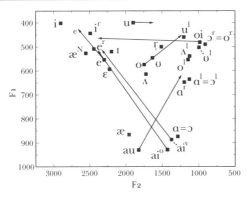

NOTE: Her /o/, /ʊ/, and /u/ nuclei are central. She merges /ɔ/ with /ɑ/ and perhaps /ʌl/ with /ol/. The gap in F1 values between her low and mid vowels is due to the nasality of her voice. (reading passage; NCSU)

4. WHITES FROM THE SOUTHEAST

THE SOUTHEAST REPRESENTS an area of great dialectal diversity, and even though many of the features that used to define different dialects in this region are disappearing (see, e.g., La Ban 1971; O'Cain 1977; Wolfram and Schilling-Estes 1995; Schilling-Estes 1997), much diversity remains and some new features have appeared. The development of /ɔ/ and /æː/ exemplifies the retention and the change. Early in the twentieth century, as suggested by the maps in Kurath and McDavid (1961), both of these vowels showed upgliding diphthongal forms ([ɔo] and [æɛ], respectively) in the Piedmont and mountain regions of the Southeast. Although upgliding /æː/ is now mostly restricted to older speakers and thus is dying out, upgliding /ɔ/ remains a characteristic feature of Southern dialects.

Another old pattern of Southern dialects that persists today is the dialectal division between areas where the plantation culture once predominated and areas where it did not. In former plantation areas, whites show a high degree of *r*-lessness and positional variation of /ai/ in which /ai/ has strong glides before voiceless consonants, as in *tight*, and is monophthongal or has weak glides in other contexts. In nonplantation areas, particularly the mountains and the Piney Woods belt of northern Florida and the southern parts of Georgia, Alabama, and Mississippi, *r*-fulness predominates and /ai/ tends to be monophthongal or weak-gliding in all phonetic contexts.

The "Southern drawl" has long been associated with the speech of this region (see, e.g., Wise 1933b; Sledd 1966; Bailey 1968; Feagin 1987; Wetzell 2000). Among other things, it involves the lengthening and breaking of some stressed vowels. As a result, /oi/ can be realized as [ɔoi], /au/ as [æɛʋ], /æ/ as [æɛæ], /ɛ/ as [eiə], /er/ as [ɛiə], and so on. In the Pamlico Sound region, /ai/ may even occur as [ɐɑˀɛ]. Such breaking seems more prevalent for speakers born before 1960 than for those born later.

A newer pattern that characterizes the speech of this region is the "Southern shift" (see Labov, Yaeger, and Steiner 1972; Feagin 1986; Labov 1991, 1994; Labov and Ash 1997; Fridland 1998, 2000). As noted briefly in chapter 1, besides monophthongization of /ai/, the Southern shift includes centralization and lowering of the nuclei of /e/ and /o/ (and, less often, widening of /i/ and /u/); fronting of /u/, /ʊ/, and /o/; and fronting of /ɪ/ and /ɛ/ to positions along the edge of the vowel envelope. These developments may be seen in the plots for many of the speakers featured here. The fronting of /u/ and the fronting of /au/ to [æɔ] are old features throughout the South, as Kurath and McDavid (1961) demonstrate. One recent shift that characterizes the Southeast is the fronting of the glide of /o/ (discussed in detail in §2.1.10), so that /o/ is produced as [ɜü].

The area of primary focus in this chapter is eastern North Carolina. Except where noted otherwise, the North Carolinians (as well as the Bahamian) were interviewed for the North Carolina Language and Life Project, which operates out of North Carolina State University. Descriptions of each regional dialect covered follow.

WHITE BAHAMIAN ENGLISH (speaker 51). Although Holm (1980) wrote that most white Bahamians came from Bermuda, directly from the British Isles, or from the northern United States in the Loyalist exodus during the American Revolution, white Bahamian English shares many features with white Southern vernaculars. A possible reason is that many of the Loyalist settlers may have initially fled from the South to New York (Childs, Reaser, and Wolfram forthcoming). White Bahamian speech resembles the speech of Pamlico Sound in showing front-gliding /au/ ([aø]), backed /ai/ nuclei ([ɑːˀe]), central /o/ and /u/, and raised monophthongal /ɔ/ ([o]). However, it differs from the Pamlico Sound dialect but resembles the South Carolina Low Country dialect in being heavily r-less and (among the oldest speakers) in having the merger of /ir/, as in *fear*, with /er/, as in *fair*. Wells (1982, 590) states that stressed syllabic /r/ is realized as [əi] in black Bahamian English, but the Abaco Island whites interviewed for the North Caro-

SPEAKER 51

Female, Born 1912, from Cherokee Sound, Abaco Island, Bahamas
(recorded in 1997)

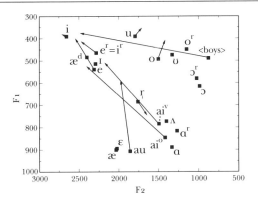

NOTE: She shows the white Bahamian features noted in the text. Her /ɛ/ is lowered and possibly merged with /æ/. Her stressed syllabic /r/ is *r*-ful; otherwise she is *r*-less. (conversation; NCSU)

lina Language and Life Project were consistently *r*-ful in that context. A fuller treatment of the vowels of Abaco whites is given in Childs, Reaser, and Wolfram (forthcoming).

DELMARVA AND CHESAPEAKE BAY ISLANDS (speaker 52). In spite of its distinctiveness and importance as a relic area, dialectal studies of this region are sparse. The main descriptions of vowels are Greet's (1933) study of the Delmarva Peninsula, Shores's (1984, 1985, 2000) descriptions of Tangier Island, Virginia, vowels, Schilling-Estes's (1997) and Schilling-Estes and Wolfram's (1999) studies of Smith Island, Maryland, and, of course, Kurath and McDavid (1961). Greet (1933) noted that /o/, /ʊ/, and /u/ are fronted, as speaker 52 also shows, though his subjects were college students born in the twentieth century and Kurath and McDavid's (1961) nineteenth-century informants have backed /o/. /i/ may be quite diphthongal; Shores (1984) described it as [əi:] on Tangier Island. Greet described /ɪ/, /ɛ/, and /æ/ as being shifted upward, though speaker 52 shows no sign of such raising. /ɔ/ is monophthongal and often somewhat raised, though Schilling-Estes (1997) found it being unrounded and lowered to [ɑ] on Smith Island. She also found lowering of /ɪ/, backing of /ɛ/ and /æ/, and fronting of /ɑ/ and /ʌ/ there. /au/ tends to be a front-gliding [aø] in the region, as with speaker 52; Schilling-Estes (1997) noted that some younger Smith Islanders have the glide unrounded, resulting in [aɛ]. The nucleus of /ai/ is often backed, and the glide may show some weakening, though Schilling-Estes found raising of the /ai/ nucleus before voiceless consonants (Canadian raising) on Smith Island. The nucleus of /ɑr/ is usually rounded, and Kurath and McDavid found that /ɑr/ was merged with /ɔr/, though this merger may be old-fashioned now. /er/ is lowered to [æɹ], though Shores (1984) stated that after palatals (e.g., *chair, care*) it may be merged with syllabic /r/. Shores (1984) noted that /æ/ is replaced with /e/ before /ʃ/, /g/, and /ŋk/ on Tangier Island, and he (1985) stated that /ɔl/, as in *Paul,* may be merged with /ʊl/, as in *pull. R*-fulness predominates in this region.

SPEAKER 52

Male, Born 1911, from Tylerton, Smith Island, Maryland

(recorded in 1983)

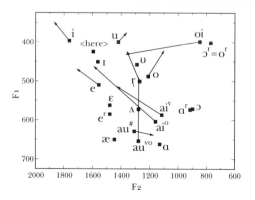

NOTE: His /au/ is realized as [aø] before obstruents and as [aɑ] word-finally; his /aiᵒ/ is produced as [ʌe ~ ɑe] and his /aiᵛ/ as [ʌɛ ~ ɑɛ]. His /er/ nucleus is lowered, and his /ɑr/ nucleus is rounded. He is completely *r*-ful. (conversation; NCSU)

EASTERN VIRGINIA (speakers 53–56). The most distinctive feature of the speech of the Tidewater and Piedmont sections of Virginia is its allophonic variation of /ai/ and /au/. As in many other parts of the South, /ai/ is strongly diphthongal before voiceless consonants and is monophthongal or weak-gliding in other contexts. The main difference is that some (but not all) speakers have a raised nucleus before voiceless obstruents, resulting in [ɐi]. /au/ traditionally showed higher nuclei before voiceless obstruents, too (see speakers 53–55). As noted in §2.1.15, [ɜü] and similar forms occur before voiceless consonants and [æɔ] in other contexts. Though Reeves (1869) noted an unusual pronunciation of *house* in Virginia, Primer (1890) was the first to recognize the two allophones of /au/, and Shewmake (1920, 1925) first stated that the voicing of the following consonant conditioned it. Further discussion about /ai/ and /au/ in Virginia is found in Greet (1931), Lowman (1936), Shewmake (1943, 1945), Tresidder (1941, 1943), Kurath and McDavid (1961), and Frazer (1994). Lowman (1936) described

SPEAKER 53

Male, Born 1846, from Nansemond (now Suffolk), Virginia
(college-educated at Harvard; adult life in Bristol, Virginia;
recording date unknown, ca. 1938)

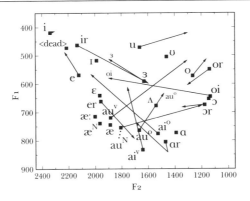

NOTE: His /auᵛ/, based on 3 tokens of *thousand*, patterns with /auᵒ/ (the apparent difference is due to the longer duration of /auᵛ/ and the fronting effect of [θ]). His /ɑr/ nucleus is unrounded. He is almost completely *r*-less. (public address; NCSU)

SPEAKER 54
Male, Born 1897, from Bertrand, Virginia
(college-educated; featured in Ayres and Greet 1930;
recorded in 1927 or 1928)

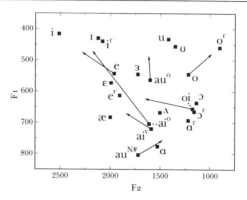

NOTE: His /auᵒ/ nucleus is much higher than his /auᴺ#/ nucleus. His /o/ is back. His /ɑr/ nucleus is rounded; he keeps /ɔr/ distinct from /or/ but perhaps not from /ɑr/. He is completely *r*-less. (reading passage; UT and NCSU)

SPEAKER 55
Female, Born 1940, from Irvington, Virginia
(recorded in 1991)

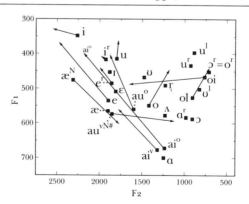

NOTE: Her /auᵒ/ is front-gliding, [ɜ̈ü]. Her /auᵛ/ shows a weak glide. Her /o/ nucleus is central, her /ɔ/ monophthongal, and her /æ/ raised. Her /ɑr/ nucleus is rounded; she merges /ɔr/ with /or/ and is mostly *r*-ful. (reading passage; UT and NCSU)

SPEAKER 56

Female, Born 1972, from Hanover County, Virginia

(college student when recorded in 1991)

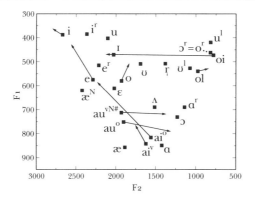

NOTE: Her /auᵒ/ is realized as [æɒ]. Her /aiⱽ/ is usually monophthongal, as is her /ɔ/. Her /o/ has a front nucleus but glides backward. Her /ɑr/ nucleus is rounded; she merges /ɔr/ with /or/ and is completely *r*-ful. (reading passage; UT and NCSU)

what is probably an older pattern from some rural areas in which the raised variant of /au/ was found in all contexts except before or after /n/ (see also speaker 53). The allophonic variation of /au/ is recessive, as speaker 56 shows.

Fronting of /u/ has long been present. However, the fronting of /o/ is not as robust in eastern Virginia as in neighboring North Carolina and Maryland, though speakers 55 and 56 exhibit it, and front-gliding /o/ does not seem to be common. Eastern Virginia speech was traditionally highly *r*-less, as with speakers 53–55, but many younger natives, such as speaker 56, have become *r*-ful. Kurath and McDavid (1961) report a merger of /ɑr/, /ɔ/, and /ɔr/ among some *r*-less Tidewater informants (possibly shown by speaker 54), though this merger is undoubtedly old-fashioned today.

THE LOW COUNTRY OF SOUTH CAROLINA AND GEORGIA (speaker 57). This region once had one of the most distinctive dialects in the South. Primer's (1887) early study of Charleston, South Carolina, speech and more systematic descriptions by McDavid (1955, 1958) and Kurath and McDavid (1961) provide a list of characteristic features of the traditional dialect of this region. /e/ and /o/ were monophthongal in free position and variably ingliding or monophthongal in checked position. Speaker 57 shows monophthongs in checked position, but other speakers showed robust inglides similar to those of Jamaican English (speaker 137). /æ/ and /æ:/ were not distinguished, and *pa*, *ma*, and *-alm* words often had /æ/. Some speakers showed retracted variants of /æ/ approaching [a] in certain words and rounding of /ɑ/ to [ɒ]. /ɔ/ was monophthongal and perhaps slightly raised. /ai/ and /au/ showed "Canadian raising" (see §2.1.13 and §2.1.15), much like eastern Virginia, but /ai/ showed strong glides before voiced obstruents and word-finally and /au/ was not fronted. Thus /au/ was [ʌu] before voiceless obstruents and [ao] in other contexts. Speaker 57 shows the typical /ai/ and /au/ realizations. The accent was highly *r*-less (see McDavid 1948), with stressed syllabic /r/ realized as [ɚ] (e.g., *first* [fɚɪst]). /ir/ and /er/ were merged to [eə], but /ɔr/ and /or/ remained distinct. O'Cain's (1977) survey of Charleston revealed that the

SPEAKER 57
Male, Born 1894, from Cross, South Carolina
(*DARE* SC 019; recorded in 1966)

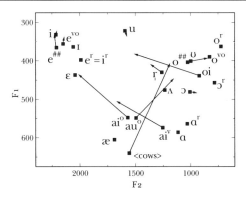

NOTE: /e##/ and /o##/ refer to word-final, prepausal contexts. He shows typical Low Country features except that his checked /e/ and /o/ are monophthongal, not ingliding, and his stressed syllabic /r/ is *r*-ful. Otherwise he is mostly *r*-less. (conversation; NCSU)

dialect was losing much of its distinctiveness because Canadian raising and the /ir/-/er/ merger were disappearing, upgliding /e/ and /o/ were replacing the monophthongal and ingliding forms, and the merger of /ɪ/ and /e/ before nasals had infiltrated. However, Labov, Ash, and Boberg (forthcoming) have found that the nucleus of /e/ remains higher in this region than in other parts of the South. Hopkins (1975) found that the /ir/-/er/ merger and ingliding /e/ and /o/ had become identified with Jewish and Irish Catholic speech in Savannah, Georgia, and thus were stigmatized.

THE GULF COASTAL PLAIN AND PIEDMONT (speakers 58–62). As *LAGS* indicates clearly, this region shows significant dialectal diversity. It describes four cultural zones, each with its own speech features. The Piedmont includes the north-central parts of Georgia and Alabama and is characterized by a high degree of *r*-lessness, with stressed syllabic /r/ realized as [ɜi ~ əi] in old-fashioned speech. It shows the plantation pattern of /ai/ with full glides before voiceless consonants and weak or no glides in other con-

SPEAKER 58
Female, Born 1890, from Moultrie, Georgia
(adult life in Montgomery, Alabama; mother of speakers 59 and 60;
recorded in 1981)

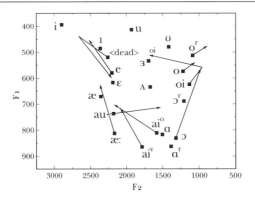

NOTE: Her /oi/ is a triphthongal [ɔɨ]. She produces /æ:/ as [æe]. Her /ɔ/ is realized as [ɑo]. Her /æ/ is raised. Her /ɑr/ nucleus is unrounded; she keeps /ɔr/ and /or/ distinct. She is completely *r*-less. (conversation; UT)

texts. The Plains comprise a narrow band just south of the Piedmont that includes Montgomery, Alabama, of which speakers 59–
62 are natives. Its vowels are generally similar to those of the
Piedmont. South of the Plains lie the Piney Woods, a rural region
composed of northern Florida and the southern parts of Georgia,
Alabama, and Mississippi except for the coast. Speaker 58 is a
native of the Piney Woods region. Pederson (1996) notes that the
speech of this region resembles that of the southern Appalachians
in being relatively *r*-ful (though speaker 58 is an exception), in
commonly having /æ:/ realized as [æɛ], in showing monophthongal
or weak-gliding /ai/ in all contexts, and in showing weak-gliding
[æə] ([æɑ]?) forms of /au/. Finally, the Coast consists of communities along the shores of the Gulf of Mexico, and its vowels are more
like those of the Piedmont.

Numerous other studies of the vowels of this region have been
conducted as well. Among the most important vowel studies are
the following. McMillan's (1946) description of variation in the
standard dialect of the Talladega, Alabama, area set the stage for
later studies. Foley (1972) conducted a linguistic atlas-style survey

SPEAKER 59

Female, Born 1914, from Montgomery, Alabama
(daughter of speaker 58 and sister of speaker 60; recorded in 1981)

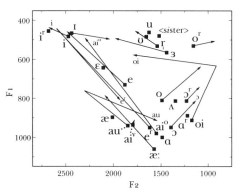

NOTE: Her /au/, /oi/, and /er/ are triphthongal, with /er/ realized as [ajæ].
Her /ʌ/ is backed. Her /ɑr/ nucleus is rounded, and she keeps /ɔr/ and /or/
distinct. *R*-ful and *r*-less tokens of /ɽ ~ ɜ/ are shown separately. She is
mostly *r*-less. (conversation; UT and NCSU)

SPEAKER 60
Female, Born 1929, from Montgomery, Alabama
(daughter of speaker 58, sister of speaker 59, mother of speaker 61,
and grandmother of speaker 62; recorded in 1981)

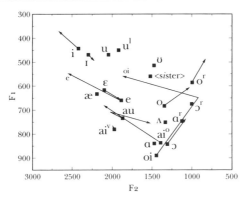

NOTE: Her /au/ and /oi/ are triphthongal, with /oi/ realized as [ɑoɨ]. Her /ʌ/ is backed. Her /ɑr/ nucleus is rounded; she keeps /ɔr/ and /or/ distinct. She is mostly *r*-less. (conversation; UT)

SPEAKER 61
Female, Born 1953, from Montgomery, Alabama
(daughter of speaker 60 and aunt of speaker 62; college-educated;
recorded in 1981)

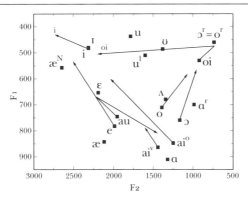

NOTE: Her /au/ and /oi/ are triphthongal. Her /e/ and /i/ nuclei are lowered. Her /o/ and /ʌ/ nuclei are somewhat back. Her /ɑr/ nucleus is rounded, and she merges /ɔr/ with /or/. She is variably *r*-less. (conversation; UT)

SPEAKER 62
Female, Born 1971, from Montgomery, Alabama
(granddaughter of speaker 60 and niece of speaker 61;
college student when recorded in 1990)

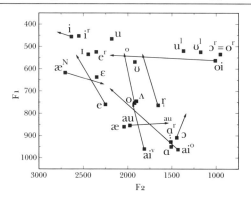

NOTE: Triphthongs are absent. Her /o/ is front-gliding, with a front nucleus, and her /ʌ/ is also fronted. Her /ɑr/ nucleus is unrounded; she merges /ɔr/ with /or/. She is completely r-ful. (reading passage; UT and NCSU)

of Tuscaloosa County, Alabama. He found typical Southern vowel variants. He noted some variation between full and weak glides for /ai/ before voiceless consonants, as well as for /oi/ in all contexts. Crane's (1977) study of /ai/ in Tuscaloosa found that variants with strong glides were associated with older speakers from higher socioeconomic classes, though the social distribution was wider for strong-gliding forms before voiceless consonants than for strong-gliding forms in other contexts. Labov, Yaeger, and Steiner (1972) included acoustic analyses of speakers from Atlanta, Georgia, that showed that Southern shift features were more prevalent among the younger speakers. Feagin's (1986) acoustic analysis of seven speakers from Anniston, Alabama, found evidence of all of the components of the Southern shift, especially the fronting of /u/, /ʊ/, and /o/. Labov and Ash (1997) conducted acoustic analyses of speakers from Birmingham, Alabama, and also found all components of the Southern shift. They also conducted an experiment to determine how well subjects from Birmingham, Chicago, and

Philadelphia could identify Birmingham vowels and found that all groups had some difficulty, even the Birmingham listeners, especially for isolated words.

THE SOUTHERN APPALACHIANS (speakers 63–66). This region includes southern West Virginia, western Virginia, eastern Kentucky, western North Carolina, eastern Tennessee, the northern edge of Georgia, and the northern third of Alabama. Descriptions of the vowels of this region, which seems to be fairly uniform dialectally, are found in Hall (1942), Kurath and McDavid (1961), Wolfram and Christian (1976), Pederson (1983), and *LAGS* (1986–92). In general, /ai/ is monophthongal [aː] in all phonetic contexts, though speakers born in the mid-nineteenth century, such as speaker 63, still retained full diphthongs. /oi/, in contrast, normally shows strong glides. /au/ may also show weak glides, becoming [æɑ]. /e/ and /o/ may have mildly to strongly lowered nuclei, often with some centralization of /e/, and are thus realized as [ɜi ~ ai] and [ʌu ~ ɐu], respectively. Fronting of /o/ to [ɜʉ ~ æʉ ~ ɜü] is a relatively new

SPEAKER 63
Male, Born 1859, from Gatlinburg, Tennessee
(used by Hall 1942; courtesy of Michael Montgomery;
recorded in 1937 or 1938)

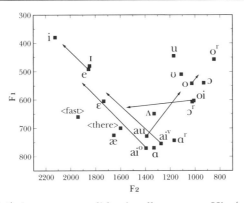

NOTE: His /ai/ shows strong glides in all contexts. His /au/ nucleus is central. His /er/ nucleus (in *there*) is low. He keeps /ɔr/ and /or/ distinct and is mostly *r*-ful. (conversation; UT)

SPEAKER 64

Female, Born 1908, from Robbinsville, North Carolina
(recorded in 1997)

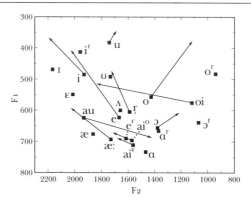

NOTE: Her /ai/ is monophthongal in all contexts. Her /au/ nucleus is fronted. She realizes /æ:/ as [aɛ]. Her /e/, /o/, and /i/ nuclei are lowered. Her /er/ is realized as [aɹ]. She keeps /ɔr/ and /or/ distinct and is almost completely r-ful. (conversation; NCSU)

SPEAKER 65

Female, Born 1948, from Robbinsville, North Carolina
(wife of speaker 66; recorded in 1996)

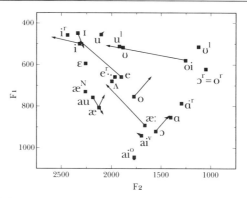

NOTE: Her /ai/ is monophthongal in all contexts. She produces /æ:/ as [aɛ]. Her /e/ and /er/ nuclei are central. Her /ɑr/ nucleus is rounded; she merges /ɔr/ with /or/. She is completely r-ful. (reading passage; NCSU)

SPEAKER 66
Male, Born 1950, from Robbinsville, North Carolina
(husband of speaker 65; recorded in 1996)

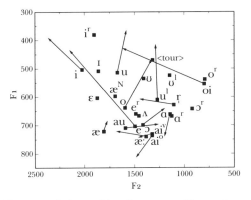

NOTE: His /ai/ is monophthongal in all contexts. He produces /æː/ as [aæ]. His /o/, /e/, and /er/ nuclei are central and lowered. He keeps /ɔr/ and /or/ distinct and is completely *r*-ful. (reading passage; NCSU)

development. The distinction between /æ/ and /æː/ has persisted longer than in most parts of the South. /æː/ is commonly realized as upgliding [æɛ] and may even be retracted to [aɛ ~ aæ], as with speakers 65 and 66. Forms of /er/ that are lowered to [æɹ] or centralized to [ɜɹ] have also persisted longer here than elsewhere. The merger of /ɑ/ and /ɔ/ apparently predominates now in West Virginia and eastern Kentucky, but not farther south (Labov, Ash, and Boberg forthcoming). The entire region is quite *r*-ful.

THE NORTH CAROLINA COASTAL PLAIN AND PIEDMONT (speakers 67–78). Included here are all parts of eastern North Carolina except the Pamlico Sound area, which is covered in a separate section below. Eastern North Carolina shows several distinguishable dialect regions and is one of the most dialectally diverse areas in the United States. Nevertheless, many of the local variations are disappearing and the dialectal divisions are much less apparent for younger speakers than for older speakers.

The lower Cape Fear valley, excepting the Wilmington area, has some features in common with the southern Appalachians. /ai/

tends to be monophthongal in all contexts in this dialect, and the nucleus of /e/ is correspondingly lowered. However, unlike the southern Appalachians, fronted /o/ reached this area at an early date. Strongly lowered /er/ is not as common, either. *R*-lessness is variable. The lower Cape Fear valley is represented by two speakers from Robeson County (speakers 67 and 68).

The dialect of Wilmington (speakers 69 and 70) resembles that of eastern Virginia. Older natives, such as speaker 69, show Canadian raising of /au/, and most natives show full /ai/ glides before voiceless consonants. Front-gliding /o/, however, has spread into the city (see Thomas 1989 and speaker 70). Like eastern Virginia, Wilmington is traditionally *r*-less except for stressed syllabic /r/.

The region that includes most of the North Carolina Piedmont, represented by speakers 71–74, has few features unique to it. Most, but not all, natives have strong /ai/ glides before voiceless obstruents. Front-gliding /o/, shown by speakers 72–74, reached this region later than the coastal plain but earlier than the Appala-

SPEAKER 67

Male, Born 1915, from Proctorville, Robeson County, North Carolina
(recorded in 1996)

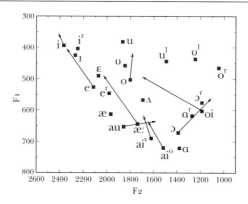

NOTE: His /ai/ is nearly monophthongal in all contexts, but his /e/ and /o/ nuclei are hardly lowered. /æː/ occurs in *last* and *half*. His /ɪ/ is fronted. He keeps /ɔr/ and /or/ distinct and is variably *r*-less. (conversation; NCSU)

SPEAKER 68

Female, Born 1978, from Fairmont, Robeson County, North Carolina
(recorded in 1996)

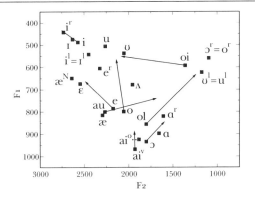

NOTE: Her /ai/ is monophthongal in all contexts. Her /e/ and /o/ nuclei are lowered, and her /ɪ/ and /ɛ/ are fronted. She merges /ul/ with /ʊl/ and /il/ with /ɪl/. She also merges /ɔr/ with /or/. She is completely *r*-ful. (reading passage; NCSU)

SPEAKER 69

Female, Born 1893, from Wilmington, North Carolina
(college-educated aristocrat; recorded in 1973)

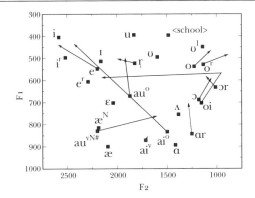

NOTE: She produces /auᵒ/ as [ɜ̈ü] and /auⱽᴺ#/ as [æɒ]. Her /aiᵒ/ glide has a clear steady state. Her /aiⱽ/ is monophthongal. Her /o/ is back. She keeps /ɔr/ and /or/ distinct and is *r*-less except for stressed syllabic /r/. (conversation; NCSU)

chians. Lowering of the nuclei of /e/ and /o/ is moderate. The
degree of r-lessness varies, but younger whites are generally r-ful
(see Levine and Crockett 1966; Anshen 1970). The speech of
some parts of the coastal plain, especially in the Tar and Neuse
valleys, is quite similar, though fronting of /o/ and moderate lowering of /e/ reached those areas earlier.

The dialect of the counties bordering Virginia, represented by
speakers 75–78, is essentially an extension of the eastern Virginia
dialect. Older speakers (speaker 75; see also speaker 146) show
Canadian raising of /au/; in Warren County, most natives born
before 1930 have it, but most born after 1930 do not. Strong glides
of /ai/ are nearly universal before voiceless consonants, and the
fronting of /o/ has been slow and is correlated as much with gender
as with age (McCullough 1996). This area was traditionally the
most r-less part of the state (Eliason 1956; Kurath and McDavid
1961), and it continues to be so, though McCullough (1996)
found that women tend to be much more r-ful than men in Person
County.

SPEAKER 70

Male, Born 1957, from Wilmington, North Carolina

(recorded in 1973)

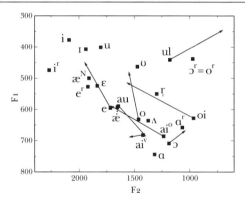

NOTE: He produces /au/ as [æ^ɑ] in all contexts. His /aiᵒ/ shows strong
glides and a backed nucleus; his /aiᵛ/ is variably monophthongal. His /o/ is
front-gliding with a central nucleus. His /æ/ is raised, and his /ɪ/ is fronted.
He is mostly r-less. (conversation and reading passage; TAMU and NCSU)

SPEAKER 71

Male, Born 1954, from Goldston, North Carolina

(recorded in 1996)

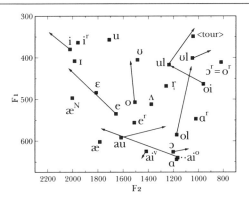

NOTE: His /aiᵛ/ is monophthongal. His /o/ is front-gliding with a central nucleus, and his /ɪ/ is fronted. He produces /er/ as [ɜɹ]. His /ɑr/ nucleus is rounded, and he merges /ɔr/ with /or/. He is almost completely *r*-ful. (reading passage and conversation; NCSU)

SPEAKER 72

Female, Born 1903, from Raleigh, North Carolina

(*DARE* NC 007; recorded in 1966)

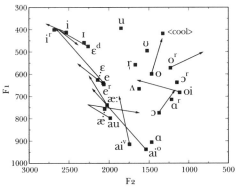

NOTE: Her /aiᵛ/ shows a prolonged nucleus and a very short glide. She produces /æ:/ as [æɛ]. Her /er/ is realized as [ɛɛɹ ~ ɛeə]. Her /ɑr/ nucleus is rounded. She keeps /ɔr/ and /or/ distinct and is variably *r*-less. (conversation; NCSU)

SPEAKER 73
Female, Born 1967, from Raleigh, North Carolina
(college-educated; recorded in 1989)

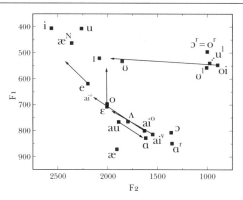

NOTE: Her /aiᵛ/ normally shows a clear glide. Her /o/ is front-gliding, with an exceptionally fronted nucleus. Her /ɔ/ is monophthongal. Her /ɑr/ nucleus is unrounded. She merges /ɔr/ with /or/ and is completely *r*-ful. (reading passage; TAMU)

SPEAKER 74
Female, Born 1982, from Raleigh, North Carolina
(recorded in 1997)

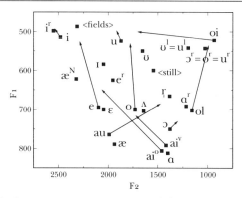

NOTE: Her /aiᵛ/ shows a weak glide. Her /o/ is front-gliding and has a central nucleus. Her /u/ also glides frontward. She merges /ʊl/ with /ul/ but keeps /ɪl/ and /il/ distinct (her twin sister shows the opposite pattern). Her /ɑr/ nucleus is rounded. She merges /ɔr/, /or/, and /ur/ together and is completely *r*-ful. (reading passage; NCSU)

SPEAKER 75
Male, Born 1920, from Hurdle Mills, Person County, North Carolina
(husband of speaker 76; recorded in 1996)

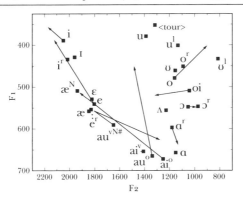

NOTE: He produces /auᵒ/ as [aʉ] and /auⱽᴺ#/ as [æɐ]. His /oi/ has a very weak glide. His /o/ is back. He keeps /ɔr/ and /or/ distinct. He is completely *r*-less except for stressed syllabic /r/, which varies. (reading passage; NCSU)

SPEAKER 76
Female, Born 1922, from Hurdle Mills, Person County, North Carolina
(wife of speaker 75; recorded in 1996)

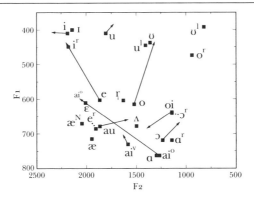

NOTE: She lacks a special /auᵒ/ allophone. Her /oi/ has a very weak glide. Her /o/ nucleus is central. Her /er/ nucleus is low, and she keeps /ɔr/ and /or/ distinct. She is completely *r*-less except for stressed syllabic /r/. (reading passage; NCSU)

SPEAKER 77

Male, Born 1971, from near Leasburg, Person County, North Carolina
(recorded in 1996)

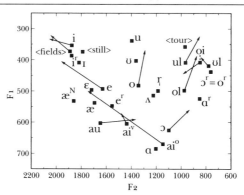

NOTE: His /oi/ has a very weak glide. His /o/ nucleus is central. His /ɑr/ nucleus is rounded and raised, and he merges /ɔr/ with /or/. He is almost completely *r*-less except for stressed syllabic /r/. (reading passage; NCSU)

SPEAKER 78

Female, Born 1982, from Inez, Warren County, North Carolina
(recorded in 1995)

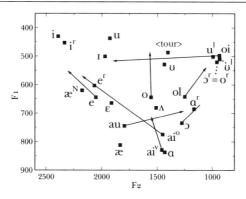

NOTE: Her /oi/ has a strong glide. Her /aiᵛ/ varies between monophthongal and weak-gliding forms. Her /o/ is front-gliding and has a central nucleus. She merges /ɔr/ with /or/ and is completely *r*-ful. (conversation and reading passage; NCSU)

PAMLICO SOUND (speakers 79–87). The dialect of the region around Pamlico Sound, including the entire Outer Banks and all of the mainland counties bordering the sound, has long been recognized as distinctive: Dough (1982) cites remarks by Wiley (1866), Cobb (1910), and Chater (1926) about it. Scholarly inquiries into the vowels of this dialect include several studies of Ocracoke (Morgan 1960; Howren 1962; Wolfram and Schilling-Estes 1995, 1996; Wolfram, Hazen, and Tamburro 1997; Wolfram et al. 1997; Wolfram, Hazen, and Schilling-Estes 1999; Schilling-Estes and Wolfram 1999), Carteret County (Jaffe 1973; Cheek 1995; Wolfram, Cheek, and Hammond 1996), and mainland Hyde County (Wolfram, Thomas, and Green 2000; Wolfram and Thomas forthcoming). The dialect has some features in common with those of the Delmarva region, which is not surprising considering that Delmarva was a primary source of early settlers around Pamlico Sound (R. S. Spencer, Jr., pers. comm., 2000), and both areas remained isolated until recently. The most stereotypical feature of the Pamlico Sound

SPEAKER 79
Male, Born 1896, from Sladesville, North Carolina
(courtesy of the Hyde County Historical and Genealogical Society;
recorded in 1981)

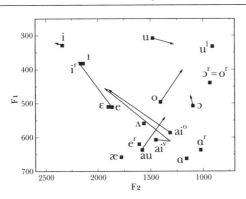

NOTE: He produces /au/ as [aɵ], with the glide only slightly fronted. His /ai/ is variably triphthongal, and the nucleus may be somewhat central. His /e/ and /o/ nuclei are moderately lowered. (conversation; NCSU)

dialect is the backing of the /ai/ nucleus, resulting in [ɑˀːe ~ ɑˀːɛ] or sometimes [ɒːɛ] or [ɐɑˀɛ]. Also commonly recognized by outsiders is the front-gliding /au/, realized as [æɵ ~ aɵ] (old-fashioned) or [aø ~ aɛ] (newer). /ɔ/ is monophthongal and raised, approaching [o]. /o/ is fronted to varying degrees and the nuclei of /e/ and /o/ are moderately lowered, resulting in [ɛi] and [ɜʉ], respectively. /er/ is lowered to [æɹ] or even [aɹ], while /ar/ is backed and variably rounded. Differences occur among different communities within the region. The speech of Ocracoke (speakers 83–86) differs from that of mainland Hyde County (speakers 79–82) in having back-gliding instead of front-gliding /o/, in having preserved the /ɔr/-/or/ distinction longer, and in the presence (for some speakers) of a back-gliding allophone of /au/ in word-final position. The speaker from Harkers Island (speaker 87) shows yet other variations, such as her realization of /i/ as a wide [əi] diphthong. Younger speakers in the Pamlico Sound region, exemplified by speaker 82, have lost all of the traditional vowel variants except for those of /o/ and /e/.

SPEAKER 80

Female, Born 1902, from Engelhard, North Carolina

(recorded in 1997)

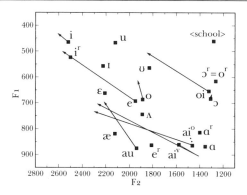

NOTE: She produces /au/ as [aɛ], with an unrounded glide. Her /ai/, especially before voiced obstruents, tends to be triphthongal, roughly [ɐɑɛ]. Her /e/ nucleus is somewhat central. (conversation; NCSU)

SPEAKER 81

Male, Born 1910, from Swan Quarter, North Carolina

(recorded in 1997)

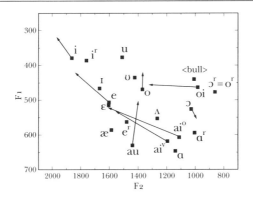

NOTE: He produces /au/ as [aœ], with a rounded glide. (conversation; NCSU)

SPEAKER 82

Female, Born 1979, from Swan Quarter, North Carolina

(recorded in 1997)

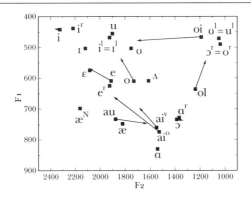

NOTE: She produces /au/ as [æɒ]. Her /ai/ (both /aiᵛ/ and /aiᵒ/) shows weak glides and does not have a backed nucleus. Her /o/ nucleus is front. Her /ɪ/ and /ɛ/ are fronted. She merges /il/ with /ɪl/ and /ul/ with /ʊl/. Her /er/ nucleus is hardly lowered. (reading passage supplemented with conversation; NCSU)

SPEAKER 83
Male, Born 1884, from Ocracoke, North Carolina
(*DARE* NC 027; recorded in 1966)

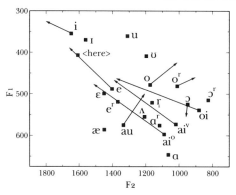

NOTE: He produces /au/ as [æɵ], with a rounded glide. His /ɑr/ nucleus is somewhat central, and he keeps /ɔr/ and /or/ distinct. (conversation; NCSU)

SPEAKER 84
Male, Born 1913, from Ocracoke, North Carolina
(recorded in 1993)

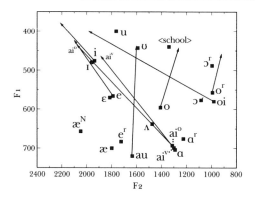

NOTE: He produces /au/ as [aʉ], with a rounded glide. His /e/ and /o/ nuclei are moderately lowered. He keeps /ɔr/ and /or/ distinct. (conversation; UT)

SPEAKER 85
Female, Born 1922, from Ocracoke, North Carolina
(spent much of her adult life in Wilmington, Delaware,
and retired to Ocracoke; recorded in 1993)

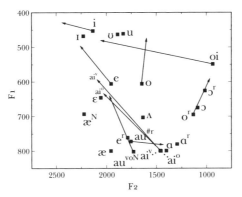

NOTE: She produces /au^voN/ as [aɛ], with an unrounded glide. Her /ai/, produced as [ɑɛ ~ ɑe], differs only in having a more backed nucleus. Her /au^#r/ has a low, back glide. She keeps /ɔr/ and /or/ distinct. (conversation; NCSU)

SPEAKER 86
Male, Born 1953, from Ocracoke, North Carolina
(recorded in 1993)

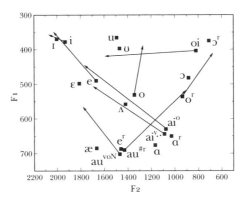

NOTE: He produces /au^voN/ as [aɛ], with an unrounded glide. He produces /au^#r/ as [aɔ]. His /ai/ nuclei may show some rounding, with /ai/ thus produced as [ɒe ~ ɒɛ]. He keeps /ɔr/ and /or/ distinct. (conversation; UT)

SPEAKER 87
Female, Born 1912, from Harkers Island, North Carolina
(recorded in 1994)

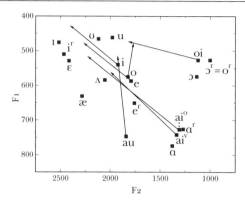

NOTE: Her /au/ is produced as [aü], with a rounded glide. Her /i/ is strongly diphthongal, with a central nucleus, and is barely distinct from /e/, which also has a central nucleus. Her /ɪ/ and /ɛ/ are very front, and her /æ/ is raised. Her /o/ is generally back-gliding. (conversation; NCSU)

5. WHITE ANGLOS FROM THE SOUTH-CENTRAL STATES

In this region, I include Louisiana, Texas, Oklahoma, and Arkansas. Texas as a whole is the area of greatest focus here. One speaker from Louisiana and four from Oklahoma are included for comparison. A Confederate veteran from Arkansas is featured to shed light on what the speech of many of the Arkansas natives who settled northern Texas may have been like. Another speaker from a community in Brazil consisting of the descendants of ex-Confederates who left the South after the Civil War is also included in order to illuminate what the speech of plantation regions of Texas may have been like in the nineteenth century. Short descriptions of these dialects (except those of Arkansas) follow.

SOUTHERN LOUISIANA (speaker 88). With its strong French presence, this region is widely known to have its own distinctive dialect of English. In spite of its reputation, however, studies of the vowels of this dialect are rather sparse. The two most extensive studies of southern Louisiana vowels are Rubrecht's (1971) analysis of *DARE* interviews and *LAGS* (1986–92). Rubrecht found that several vowel variables set French (southern) Louisiana off from Anglo (northern) Louisiana. Among them was the fact that /i/, /e/, /ɔ/, /o/, and /u/ tended to be monophthongal in the French section but not in the Anglo section. *LAGS* noted a high rate of *r*-lessness in southern Louisiana and a correspondingly high frequency of [ɜi] for stressed syllabic /r/, as in *first* [fɜist]. *LAGS* found that the nucleus of /ɑr/ was generally backed and often rounded, but that the nucleus of /or/ was occasionally unrounded. It also reported that /ai/ tended to have full glides and that the nucleus of /au/ was seldom fronted. In fact, southern Louisiana had the lowest incidence of fronted /au/ of any region covered by the atlas. However, Dubois and Horvath (1998, 2000) found a fairly high incidence of monophthongal /ai/ in the Cajun English of St. Landry Parish in southern Louisiana.

SPEAKER 88
Male, Born 1915, from New Orleans, Louisiana
(*DARE* LA 042; recorded in 1968)

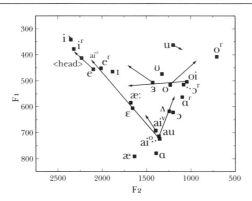

NOTE: His /æ:/ is monophthongal but raised and very close to his /ε/. His /ʌ/ is backed and rounded. His /aiᵛ/ is monophthongal. His /ɑr/ and /ɔr/ nuclei are very close to each other. He is completely *r*-less. (conversation; NCSU)

SPEAKER 89
Male, Born 1847, from White County, Arkansas
(courtesy of Maurice Crane of Michigan State University;
recorded in 1938)

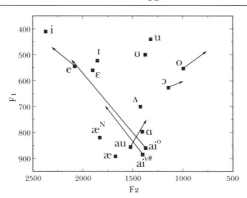

NOTE: His /aiᵒ/ shows strong glides; his /aiᵛ#/ weak glides. His /ɔ/ is raised and upgliding. The apparent lowering of /æ/ may be an artifact of the small number of tokens. He is variably *r*-less. (conversation; UT)

OKLAHOMA (speakers 90–93). The most systematic investigation of Oklahoma vowels of which results have been published comes from the Survey of Oklahoma Dialects (see Bailey et al. 1993, 1996; Bailey, Tillery, and Wikle 1997; Tillery 1997). Oklahoma is dialectally quite similar to Texas (see below), though the northern part shows some influence from Kansas. Most of the same developments, such as unrounding of /ɔ/ (a correlate of the /ɑ/-/ɔ/ merger) and laxing of /u/, /i/, and /e/ before /l/ (correlates of the /ul/-/ʊl/, /il/-/ɪl/, and /el/-/ɛl/ mergers, respectively) occur there, though the social conditioning may differ. A difference in social conditioning may affect /ai/. It is not clear whether the fact that speakers 90 and 91 produce weak-gliding /ai/ while speakers 92 and 93 exhibit /ai/ with strong glides reflects a diachronic difference or a gender difference.

SPEAKER 90

Male, Born 1917, from Yale, Oklahoma

(recorded in 1993)

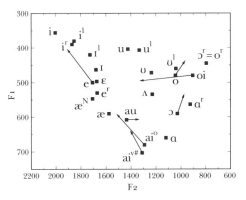

NOTE: His /ai/ varies between showing weak glides or being monophthongal. His /e/ and /o/ nuclei are not lowered. His /ɔ/ is upgliding. His /æ/ is somewhat raised. His /ɑr/ nucleus is rounded, and he merges /ɔr/ with /or/. (reading passage; UT)

SPEAKER 91
Male, Born 1937, from Yale, Oklahoma
(recorded in 1993)

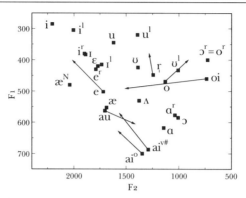

NOTE: His /ai/ shows weak glides. His /o/ is back, and his /ɔ/ is monophthongal. He merged /ɔ/ with /ɑ/ in minimal pairs, but not in the reading
passage. His /ul/ is central, and his /æ/ and /ɛ/ are raised. His /ɑr/ onset is
rounded. (reading passage; UT)

SPEAKER 92
Female, Born 1960, from Yale, Oklahoma
(recorded in 1993)

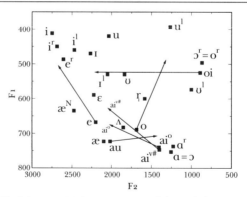

NOTE: Her /ai/ glides are fairly strong. Her /e/ and /o/ nuclei are lowered.
She merges /ɔ/ with /ɑ/, but shows no pre-/l/ mergers. Her /ul/ is backed,
and her /ɑr/ nucleus is unrounded. (reading passage; UT)

SPEAKER 93
Female, Born 1975, from Yale, Oklahoma
(recorded in 1993)

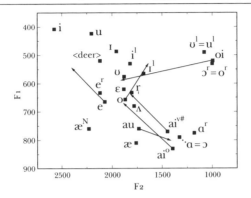

NOTE: Her /ai/ glides are fairly strong. Her /e/ and /o/ nuclei are somewhat lowered. Her /o/ nucleus is fronted. She merges /ɔ/ with /ɑ/ and /ul/ with /ʊl/, but /il/ and /ɪl/ remain barely distinct. Her /ar/ nucleus is generally unrounded. (reading passage; UT)

BRAZILIAN EX-CONFEDERATES (speaker 94). As explained in more detail by Medeiros (1982), Montgomery and Melo (1990), and Bailey and Smith (1992), a group of former Confederates emigrated to Brazil after the Civil War and founded communities such as Americana there. The largest numbers came from Texas (including speaker 94's parents), Alabama, and Georgia. They are heavily *r*-less and have [ɜi] for stressed syllabic /r/. They also show little glide weakening of /ai/ and lack the merger of /ɪ/ and /ɛ/ before nasals, as in *pin* and *pen*. Montgomery and Melo (1990) and Bailey and Smith (1992) suggest that these features reflect mid-nineteenth-century Southern speech norms. However, both studies caution that Portuguese influence is possible. The strong /ai/ glides, as well as the nearly monophthongal /e/ and /o/ that speaker 94 shows, might conceivably have been influenced by Portuguese.

SPEAKER 94
Female, Born 1905, from Americana, São Paolo, Brazil
(bilingual in English and Portuguese and daughter of ex-Confederates
from Texas who moved to Brazil after the Civil War; recorded in 1989)

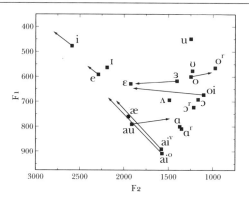

NOTE: Her /e/ and /o/ are variably monophthongal. She keeps /ɔr/ and /or/
distinct. She is completely r-less. (conversation; UT)

TEXAS (speakers 95–135). Texas has a history of extensive dialectal
inquiry, including several studies that included vowel variation
(see Stanley 1936; Klipple 1945; Norman 1956; Wheatley and
Stanley 1959; McDowell and McRae 1972; Walsh and Mote 1974;
Hamilton 1977; and, of course, *LAGS* 1986–92; see also studies of
Mexican American English in Texas listed in chap. 7). More recently, the Phonological Survey of Texas (PST) has investigated
Texas vowels using a systematic telephone survey and other proce-
dures. The methods of PST are discussed in Bailey and Bernstein
(1989) and Bailey and Dyer (1992) and the results in Bailey,
Wikle, and Sand (1991a, 1991b); Bailey et al. (1991, 1996);
Bernstein (1993); Thomas (1997); Thomas and Bailey (1992);
and Tillery (1997).

Texans often think of their state as being dialectally divided
into eastern and western portions. However, vocalic differences
between the eastern and western parts are not clear-cut. The most
obvious difference relating to vowels is that older natives of the
eastern and Gulf coast regions (which were settled by people from

SPEAKER 95
Male, Born 1878
(childhood partly in Barksdale, Texas, and partly in nearby Leakey;
courtesy of the Benson American History Center at the University of
Texas at Austin; recorded in 1979)

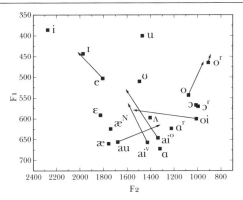

NOTE: His /aiᵒ/ shows weak glides, and his /aiᵛ/ is variably monophthongal.
His /ɔ/ is monophthongal. He keeps /ɔr/ and /or/ distinct. He is variably
r-less. (conversation; UT)

SPEAKER 96
Female, Born 1886, from Oglesby, Texas
(recorded in 1987)

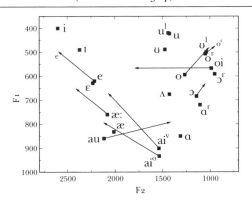

NOTE: Her /ai/ shows some glide weakening. Her /ɔ/ is upgliding. Her /ɑr/
nucleus is rounded, but she keeps /ɔr/ and /or/ distinct. She is mostly *r*-ful.
(conversation; UT)

the Gulf states) are more *r*-less than those from other parts of the state. Even so, a small degree of *r*-lessness once occurred in the northern and central sections, which were settled by people from Tennessee, Arkansas, and Germany. This difference has nearly disappeared as *r*-fulness has become predominant throughout Texas among Anglos (non-Hispanic whites) as well as Mexican Americans. Another former difference has to do with the merger of /ɑ/ and /ɔ/, which was once confined to the Panhandle (as with speakers 107 and 114). It appears to have spread to the Dallas–Fort Worth "Metroplex" (see Bailey, Wikle, and Sand 1991a and speaker 116) shortly after World War II, but since 1960 has spread across most of the state, with only a few areas in the southeastern corner resisting it (as with speakers 118 and 119; see Tillery 1989; Bernstein 1993). Thus, Texas as a whole shows little truly regional differentiation in vowels. The main difference among Anglos is now between those from rural areas and small cities and those from large metropolitan centers, as discussed below.

SPEAKER 97

Male, Born 1894, from Chappell Hill, Texas

(recorded in 1987)

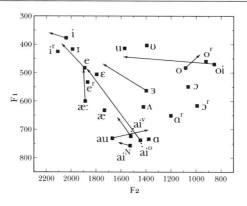

NOTE: His /aiᵒ/ shows strong glides, but his /aiᵛ/ is practically monophthongal. His /ɔ/ is monophthongal. His /ɜ/ shows a fronting glide (e.g., *first* [fʌest]). He keeps /ɔr/ and /or/ distinct. He is completely *r*-less. (conversation; UT)

Female, Born 1895, from Independence, Texas
(German American; Independence was a German settlement;
recorded in 1987)

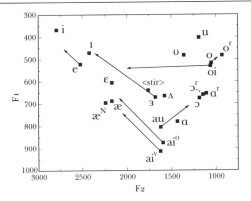

NOTE: Her /au/ nucleus is central, and her /o/ is nearly monophthongal, possibly from German influence. Her /ɜ/ shows a fronting glide. She distinguishes /ar/ from /ɔr/ by the greater length of /ar/. She is completely *r*-less. (conversation; UT)

Female, Born 1899, from Canyon, Texas
(college-educated; recorded in 1991)

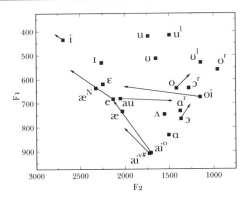

NOTE: Her /aiᵒ/ shows stronger glides than her /aiᵛ/. Her /ɔ/ is upgliding. Her /e/ nucleus is slightly lowered. Her /ar/ nucleus is rounded; she keeps /ɔr/ and /or/ distinct. She is mostly *r*-ful. (reading passage; UT)

The positional variation in which /ai/ shows strong glides before voiceless consonants (e.g., *sight*) and weak glides in other
contexts is not as common in Texas as in regions to the east,
especially for Texans born after World War I. Monophthongization
or glide weakening of /ai/ in all phonetic contexts is more common. A number of apparent diachronic trends are visible in the
plots for the Texans featured here. /u/ and the nucleus of /o/
become increasingly fronted, and the nuclei of both /o/ and /e/
show a lowering trend. However, /o/ rarely glides to the front in
Texas, even when the nucleus is fronted. Pre-/l/ mergers appear
among the youngest generation: the merger of /ul/ and /ʊl/ (e.g.,
fool = *full*) is most common, followed by the merger /il/ and /ɪl/ (e.g.,
feel = *fill*). The merger of /el/ and /ɛl/ (e.g., *fail* = *fell*; shown only for
speaker 135) is somewhat less common. The alignment of /ɑr/, /ɔr/,
and /or/ also shows change: Texans born before World War I keep
all three distinct; those born between the world wars may keep all

SPEAKER 100
Female, Born 1903, from Gilmer, Texas
(recorded in 1989)

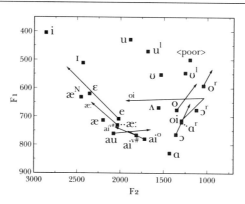

NOTE: Her /ai/ shows very weak glides in all environments. Her /oi/ is
triphthongal, and her /e/ and /o/ nuclei are lowered. Her /æː/ is realized as
[æɛ] but is distinct from /e/, which is realized as [æi]. Her /ɔ/ is upgliding.
Her /ɑr/ nucleus is rounded; she keeps /ɔr/ and /or/ distinct. She is *r*-less
except for stressed syllabic /r/. (reading passage; UT)

SPEAKER 101
Female, Born 1906, from Houston, Texas
(college-educated; recorded in 1989)

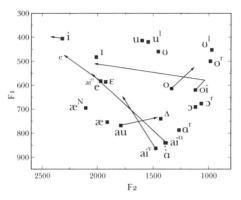

NOTE: Her /ai/ shows strong glides in all environments. Her /e/ and /o/ nuclei are not lowered. Her /ɔ/ is monophthongal. She keeps /ɔr/ and /or/ distinct and is mostly *r*-less. (reading passage; UT)

SPEAKER 102
Female, Born 1907, from the Brazos Bottoms of Burleson County, Texas
(adult life spent ten miles away in "Springville"; recorded ca. 1988)

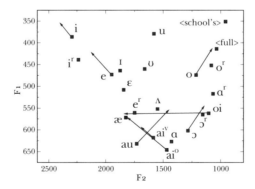

NOTE: Her /ai\u1d5b/ is monophthongal, and her /ai\u1d52/ shows weak glides. Her /e/ and /o/ nuclei are not lowered. Her /ɔ/ is upgliding. Her /ɑr/ is distinguished from her /ɔr/ by greater length. She keeps /ɔr/ and /or/ distinct. She is variably *r*-less. (conversation; NCSU)

three distinct, may merge /ɑr/ and /ɔr/ together, or may merge /ɔr/ and /or/ together; and those born since World War II consistently merge /ɔr/ and /or/ but keep /ɑr/ distinct (Thomas and Bailey 1992).

Recently, a dialectal split has developed between Anglos from the largest metropolitan areas—Houston, the Dallas–Fort Worth "Metroplex," San Antonio, Austin, and El Paso—and those from the rest of the state (Thomas 1997). Most young Anglos from the metropolitan centers, such as speakers 128–33 and 135, no longer show such typically Southern vowel variants as monophthongal /ai/ or lowered nuclei of /e/ and /o/. Young Anglos from the rural areas and small cities that make up the rest of the state, such as speakers 118–27, retain the Southern variants and may show them to a greater degree than older Texans.

SPEAKER 103

Male, Born 1909, from Wise County, Texas, near Stony
(featured in Ayres and Greet 1930; recorded in 1927 or 1928)

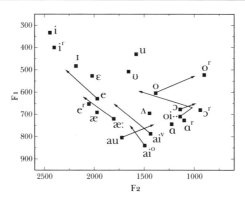

NOTE: His /ai/ shows weak glides in all environments. His /oi/ is triphthongal. His /e/ and /o/ nuclei are not lowered. His /ɔ/ is upgliding. He is mostly r-ful. (reading passage; UT and NCSU)

SPEAKER 104
Male, Born ca. 1915, from Henderson, Texas
(recorded in 1989)

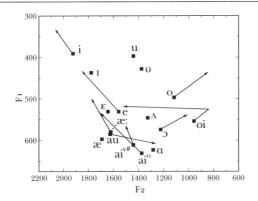

NOTE: His /aiᵒ/ shows more or less full glides; his /aïᵛ#/ is monophthongal. His /oi/ is triphthongal. His /ɔ/ is upgliding. He is mostly *r*-less. (conversation; UT)

SPEAKER 105
Female, Born 1916, from Tyler, Texas
(mother of speaker 112; recorded in 1989)

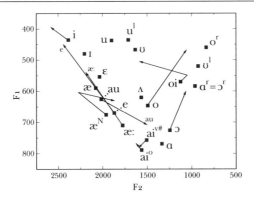

NOTE: Her /ai/ is monophthongal in all contexts. Her /e/ and /o/ nuclei are lowered. Her /æ:/, realized as [æe], is distinct from /e/, which is realized as [æi]. Her /ɔ/ is upgliding. She merges /ar/ with /ɔr/ but keeps /or/ distinct. She is completely *r*-ful. (reading passage; UT)

SPEAKER 106
Female, Born 1923, from Clifton, Texas
(recorded in 1989)

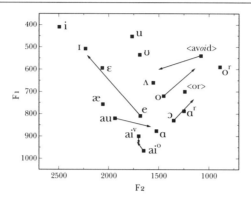

NOTE: Her /ai/ is monophthongal in all contexts, and her /e/ and /o/ nuclei are lowered. Her /ɔr/ (in *or*) is apparently distinct from her /or/. She is completely *r*-ful. (conversation; UT)

SPEAKER 107
Female, Born 1926, from Perryton, Texas
(mother of speaker 114; recorded in 1991)

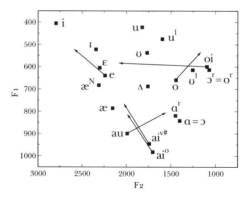

NOTE: Her /ai/ shows weak glides in all contexts. Her /e/ and /o/ nuclei are not much lowered. She merges /ɔ/ with /a/, as is typical of the Texas panhandle. She also merges /ɔr/ with /or/. She is completely *r*-ful. (reading passage; UT)

SPEAKER 108
Female, Born 1930, from Dallas, Texas
(mother of speaker 116; recorded in 1989)

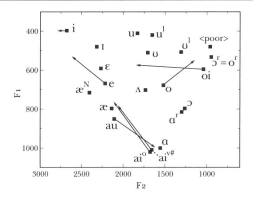

NOTE: Her /ai/ shows somewhat weak glides. Her /ɔ/ is monophthongal. Her /ɑr/ nucleus is rounded; she merges /ɔr/ with /or/. (reading passage; UT)

SPEAKER 109
Male, Born 1934, from Dallas, Texas
(recorded in 1991)

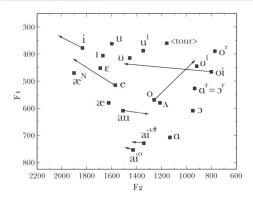

NOTE: His /ai/ is monophthongal in all contexts. His /e/ and /o/ nuclei are only moderately lowered. His /ɔ/ is monophthongal. His /æ/ and /e/ are raised. He merges /ɑr/ with /ɔr/ but keeps /or/ distinct. (reading passage; UT)

SPEAKER 110
Male, Born 1937, from Garland, Texas
(father of speaker 124; recorded in 1990 and 1993)

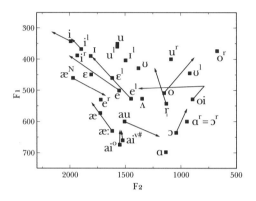

NOTE: His /ai/ is monophthongal in all contexts and fronted to [æ]. His /oi/ is triphthongal. His /e/ and /o/ onsets are slightly lowered. His /ɔ/ is upgliding. He merges /ɑr/ with /ɔr/ and keeps /or/ distinct. (reading passage; UT)

SPEAKER 111
Female, Born 1939, from Houston, Texas
(recorded in 1989)

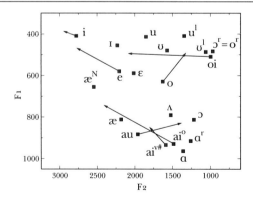

NOTE: Her /aiᵒ/ shows strong glides; her /aiᵛ#/ shows very weak glides. Her /e/ and /o/ nuclei are not much lowered. Her /ɔ/ is monophthongal. She merges /ɔr/ with /or/. (reading passage; UT)

SPEAKER 112
Female, Born 1939, from Troup, Texas
(daughter of speaker 105 and mother of speaker 117; recorded in 1989)

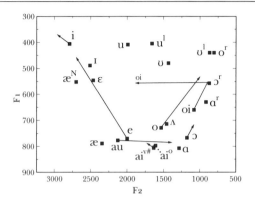

NOTE: Her /ai/ is monophthongal in all contexts, and her /e/ and /o/ nuclei are lowered. Her /ɔ/ is upgliding, and her /ɑr/, /ɔr/, and /or/ are all distinct. (reading passage; UT)

SPEAKER 113
Female, Born 1944, from Honey Grove, Texas
(mother of speaker 125; recorded in 1990)

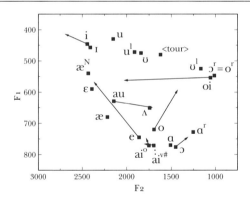

NOTE: Her /ai/ is monophthongal in all contexts, and her /e/ and /o/ nuclei are lowered. Her /o/ nucleus is somewhat fronted; her /ɔ/ is low but upgliding. She merges /ɔr/ with /or/. (reading passage; UT)

SPEAKER 114
Male, Born 1950, from Dumas, Texas
(son of speaker 107 and father of speaker 126; recorded in 1991)

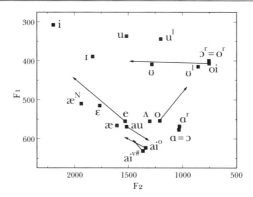

NOTE: His /ai/ is monophthongal in all contexts, and his /e/ and /o/ nuclei are lowered. He merges /ɔ/ with /ɑ/ and /ɔr/ with /or/. (reading passage; UT)

SPEAKER 115
Female, Born 1951, from Elkhart, Texas
(recorded in 1989)

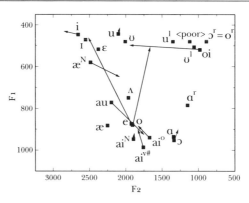

NOTE: Her /ai/ is monophthongal in all contexts, and her /e/ and /o/ nuclei are strongly lowered. Her /ɔ/ is low and barely upgliding. She merges /ɔr/ with /or/. (reading passage; UT)

SPEAKER 116

Female, Born 1955, from Grand Prairie, Texas
(daughter of speaker 108 and mother of speaker 131; recorded in 1989)

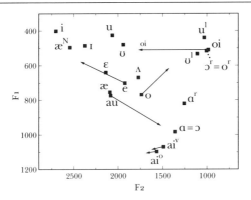

NOTE: Her /ai/ is monophthongal in all contexts, and her /e/ and /o/ nuclei are moderately lowered. She merges /ɔ/ with /ɑ/ and /ɔr/ with /or/. (reading passage; UT)

SPEAKER 117

Female, Born 1961, from Kilgore, Texas
(daughter of speaker 112; recorded in 1989)

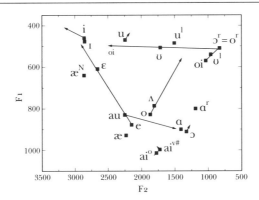

NOTE: Her /ai/ is monophthongal in all contexts, and her /oi/ is triphthongal. Her /e/ and /o/ nuclei are lowered. Her /ɔ/ is low and barely upgliding. She merges /ɔr/ with /or/. (reading passage; UT)

SPEAKER 118
Female, Born 1971, from Silsbee, Texas
(recorded in 1989)

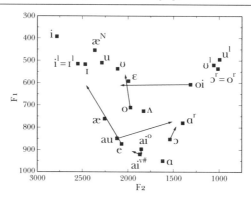

NOTE: Her /ai/ is monophthongal in all contexts, and her /e/ nucleus is lowered. Her /o/ is front-gliding, with a somewhat front nucleus. Her /ɔ/ is upgliding. She merges /il/ with /ɪl/ but keeps /ul/ barely distinct from /ʊl/. (reading passage; TAMU)

SPEAKER 119
Male, Born 1971, from Silsbee, Texas
(recorded in 1989)

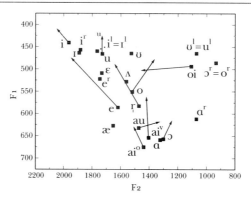

NOTE: His /ai/ is monophthongal or weak-gliding in all contexts, and his /e/ and /o/ nuclei are lowered. His /o/ nucleus is fronted; his /ɔ/ is low and upgliding. His /ɛ/ is raised. His stressed syllabic /r/ shows a strong upglide (i.e., [ɚɹ]). (reading passage; NCSU)

SPEAKER 120
Female, Born 1973, from Snyder, Texas
(recorded in 1989)

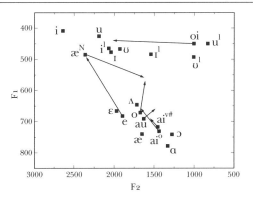

NOTE: Her /aiᵛ#/ is monophthongal, but her /aiᵒ/ may show weak glides. Her /e/ and /o/ nuclei are lowered. Her /ɔ/ is monophthongal and barely distinct from /ɑ/. She has no pre-/l/ mergers. (reading passage; UT)

SPEAKER 121
Female, Born 1972, from Kilgore, Texas
(recorded in 1989)

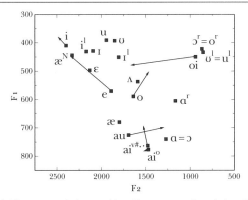

NOTE: Her /ai/ is monophthongal in all contexts; her /e/ and /o/ nuclei are moderately lowered. Her /e/ is raised. She merges /ɔ/ with /ɑ/ and /ʊl/ with /ul/ but keeps /il/ and /ɪl/ distinct. Her /ɑr/ nucleus is rounded and raised. (reading passage; UT)

SPEAKER 122
Female, Born 1973, from Kilgore, Texas
(recorded in 1989)

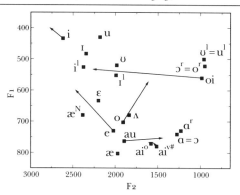

NOTE: Her /ai/ is monophthongal in all contexts, and her /e/ and /o/ nuclei are lowered. Her /o/ nucleus is fronted. She merges /ɑ/ with /ɔ/ and /ʊl/ with /ul/ but keeps /ɪl/ and /il/ distinct. Her /ɑr/ nucleus is apparently unrounded. (reading passage; UT)

SPEAKER 123
Male, Born 1974, from Kilgore, Texas
(recorded in 1989)

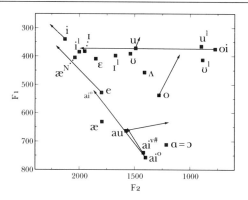

NOTE: His /aiᵒ/ shows strong glides, and his /aiᵛ#/ is variably monophthongal. His /e/ and /o/ nuclei are somewhat lowered. His /ɛ/ is raised. He merges /ɔ/ with /ɑ/ but shows no pre-/l/ mergers. (reading passage; UT)

SPEAKER 124

Female, Born 1973, from Royse City, Texas
(daughter of speaker 110; recorded in 1990)

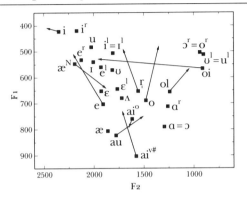

NOTE: Her /aiᵒ/ is monophthongal, but her /aiᵛ#/ may show weak glides. Her /e/ and /o/ nuclei are moderately lowered. She shows mergers of /ɔ/ and /ɑ/, of /ʊl/ and /ul/, of /ɪl/ and /il/, and, unlike her father, of /ɔr/ and /or/. (reading passage; UT)

SPEAKER 125

Female, Born 1973, from Royse City, Texas
(daughter of speaker 113; recorded in 1990)

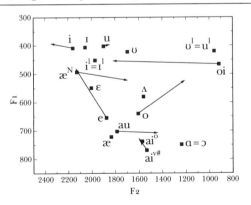

NOTE: Her /ai/ is monophthongal in all contexts. Her /e/ and /o/ nuclei are lowered. She shows mergers of /ɔ/ and /ɑ/, of /ʊl/ and /ul/, and of /ɪl/ and /il/. (reading passage; UT)

SPEAKER 126
Female, Born 1972, from Perryton, Texas
(daughter of speaker 114; recorded in 1991)

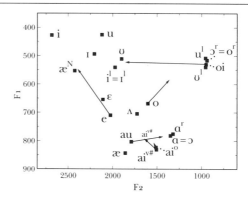

NOTE: Her /aiᵒ/ is monophthongal; her /aiᵛ#/ may show weak glides. Her /e/ and /o/ nuclei are moderately lowered. She merges /ɔ/ with /ɑ/ and /ɪl/ with /il/, but keeps /ʊl/ and /ul/ barely distinct. (reading passage; UT)

SPEAKER 127
Female, Born 1976, from Perryton, Texas
(recorded in 1991)

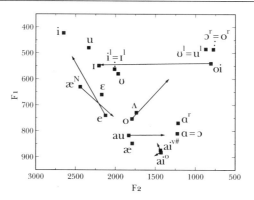

NOTE: Her /ai/ is monophthongal in all contexts. Her /e/ and /o/ nuclei are lowered. Her /o/ nucleus is fronted. She shows mergers of /ɔ/ and /ɑ/, of /ʊl/ and /ul/, and of /ɪl/ and /il/. (reading passage; UT)

SPEAKER 128
Female, Born 1974, from Richardson, Texas
(recorded in 1989)

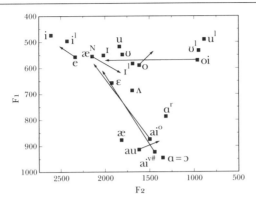

NOTE: Her /o/ nucleus, /u/, and /ʊ/ are all central. She merges /ɔ/ with /ɑ/ but shows no pre-/l/ mergers. Her /ɑr/ is raised to [ɐɹ]. (reading passage; UT)

SPEAKER 129
Female, Born 1974, from Plano, Texas
(recorded in 1989)

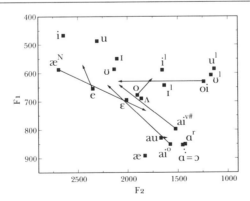

NOTE: Her /u/ and /ʊ/ are fronted; her /o/ nucleus is central. Her /au/ is nearly monophthongal. She merges /ɔ/ with /ɑ/ but keeps the pairs /ul/ and /ʊl/ and /il/ and /ɪl/ barely distinct. (reading passage; UT)

SPEAKER 130
Male, Born 1972, from Carrollton, Texas
(college student when recorded in 1991)

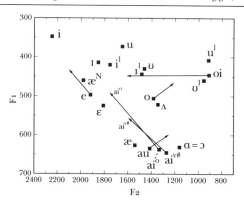

NOTE: His /o/ nucleus, /u/, and /ʊ/ are all central. He merges /ɔ/ with /ɑ/ but shows no pre-/l/ mergers. (reading passage; UT)

SPEAKER 131
Female, Born 1980, from DeSoto, Texas
(daughter of speaker 116; recorded in 1989)

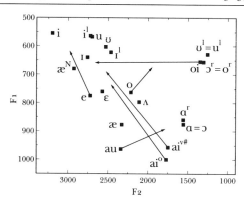

NOTE: Her /u/ and /ʊ/ are front, but her /o/ nucleus is central. She merges /ɔ/ with /ɑ/ and /ul/ with /ʊl/, but keeps /il/ and /ɪl/ distinct. (reading passage; UT)

SPEAKER 132
Female, Born 1970, from Houston, Texas
(first-semester college student when recorded in 1989)

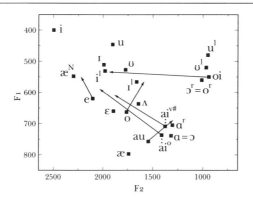

NOTE: Her /o/ nucleus, /u/, and /ʊ/ are all fronted. She merges /ɔ/ with /ɑ/ but shows no pre-/l/ mergers. Her /il/ onset tends to be centralized and close to realization of /ɪ/, as also appears for several other speakers (e.g., speakers 120 and 130). (reading passage; UT)

SPEAKER 133
Female, Born 1974, from El Paso, Texas
(recorded in 1989)

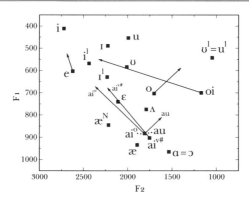

NOTE: Her /u/ and /ʊ/ are front-central; her /o/ nucleus is central. She merges /ɔ/ with /ɑ/ and /ul/ with /ʊl/, but keeps /il/ and /ɪl/ distinct. (reading passage; UT)

SPEAKER 134
Male, Born 1974, from Leander, Texas
(recorded in 1991)

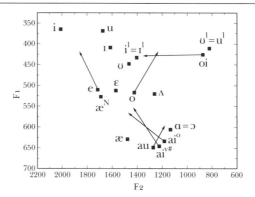

NOTE: His /ai/ shows weak glides. His /u/ is front, but his /o/ nucleus is central. He shows mergers of /ɔ/ and /ɑ/, of /ul/ and /ʊl/, and of /il/ and /ɪl/. (reading passage; UT)

SPEAKER 135
Female, Born 1974, from Leander, Texas
(recorded in 1991)

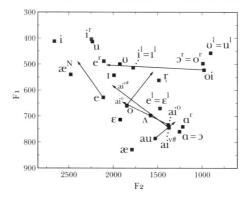

NOTE: Her /ai/ shows strong glides. Her /o/ nucleus, /u/, and /ʊ/ are all front. She shows mergers of /ɔ/ and /ɑ/, of /ul/ and /ʊl/, of /il/ and /ɪl/, and of /el/ and /ɛl/. (reading passage; UT)

6. AFRICAN AMERICANS

THIS CHAPTER FEATURES three speakers of Caribbean Anglophone creoles and 33 African Americans. Regrettably, there is only one African American from a Northern state (speaker 157), but the coverage of Southern African American English is more comprehensive. Five of the ex-slaves who are featured in Bailey, Maynor, and Cukor-Avila (1991) are included here as speakers 139–43. In spite of the huge amount of research conducted on African American Vernacular English (AAVE) since the 1960s—more than on any other dialect of American English—little inquiry has been directed toward vowel variation in AAVE. Most scholarly attention paid to AAVE has been devoted to morphosyntactic variation and to a few consonantal variables, namely *r*-lessness, final consonant cluster simplification, deletion of certain other final consonants, devoicing of final stops, mutations of /θ/ and /ð/, and mutation of /str/ (as in *street*) to /skr/. The only vowel variable in AAVE that has received much notice is glide weakening or monophthongization of /ai/ (e.g., Ash and Myhill 1986; Deser 1990), which is described below.

CARIBBEAN CREOLES AND GULLAH (speakers 136–39). The three speakers of Caribbean creoles and the single Gullah speaker included here certainly do not depict the entire range of variation in these varieties, but they are included here for comparison with African American vowels. Caribbean creoles are quite diverse. Not only does each Anglophone nation have its own local speech traits, but each has its own creole continuum, too. As a result there is a myriad of different varieties. I will not attempt to describe these varieties in detail here. A summary of literature on the phonology of Caribbean English and Anglophone creoles is provided in Wells (1982). Some of these varieties have been studied far more than others, and no acoustic studies have been conducted aside from Veatch's (1991) and Patrick's (1996) analyses, each of two Jamaicans; analyses of three black Bahamians in Childs, Reaser, and Wolfram (forthcoming); and the analyses included here (two of which are also shown in Thomas and Bailey 1998), so much remains to be done.

The three Caribbean natives featured in this chapter are a basilectal speaker from Guyana, a mesolectal speaker from Kingston, Jamaica, and an upper-mesolectal speaker from Grenada. Although they show obvious differences from each other, all three also differ from the African Americans who follow them here. /o/ and /e/ are not upgliding. Speakers 136 and 138 exhibit monophthongal forms of /o/ and /e/. The Jamaican (speaker 137) shows ingliding or downgliding forms ([uə] and [ie], respectively) of those vowels. These are the forms that Cassidy and LePage (1967) depict as [uo] and [ie], though Veatch (1991) argues that they tend to be more ingliding than downgliding. As noted in chapters 2 and 4, similar forms occur in old-fashioned white speech of the Low Country of South Carolina and Georgia (Kurath and McDavid 1961). Monophthongal /o/ and /e/ occur in the oldest African American speech (see below). /æ/ is produced as [a], quite unlike the [ɛ] forms predominant in African American speech. /æ/ may be merged with

SPEAKER 136
Female, Born ca. 1933, from "Cane Walk," Guyana
(basilectal speaker; courtesy of John Rickford; recorded in 1975 or 1976)

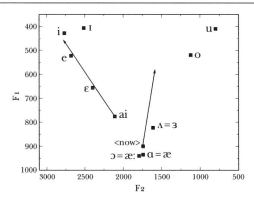

NOTE: She shows monophthongal /e/ and /o/ and mergers of /ɑ/ and /æ/ as [a], of /ʌ/ and /ɜ/ as [ɔ], and of /aː/ and /ɔ/ as [aː]. The high nuclear F1 in *now* may be an artifact of nasality. She is completely *r*-less. (conversation; UT)

/ɑ/ in Caribbean varieties, as with speakers 136 and 137. /æ:/ may be distinct from /æ/, as with speaker 137, and may even be merged with /ɔ/ to [aː], as with speaker 136. /ʌ/ tends to be more or less backed; this backing also occurs in some African American English. Unlike in most African American speech, /ai/ is realized with a strong glide except in black Bahamian speech, where it may be monophthongal before voiced consonants (Childs, Reaser, and Wolfram forthcoming). /oi/ may be merged with /ai/, though the distinction can be maintained by production of /oi/ as [wai] (Veatch 1991). /au/ is usually realized as [ɔu] ~ [ʌu]. While the distinction between /ɔr/ and /or/ is often maintained, the distinction between /ir/ and /er/ is frequently lost, as with speaker 137. This merger is another feature that ties the Caribbean to the Low Country of South Carolina and Georgia. Finally, like AAVE, most Caribbean varieties except for that of Barbados are *r*-less, though some, such as Jamaican English, show variable *r*-fulness.

The Gullah speaker (speaker 139) shares features with both Caribbean creoles and African American English. His /e/ and /o/

SPEAKER 137
Male, Born 1944, from Kingston, Jamaica
(mesolectal speaker; courtesy of Peter Patrick; recorded in 1989)

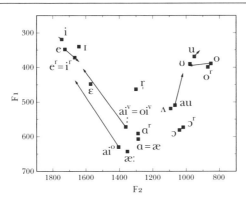

NOTE: He shows a typical Jamaican vowel configuration, with ingliding /e/ and /o/. His stressed syllabic /r/ is usually *r*-ful; otherwise he is mostly *r*-less. (conversation; NCSU)

SPEAKER 138
Male, Born 1918, from St. George's, Grenada
(upper-mesolectal speaker; courtesy of Larry Beason; recorded ca. 1992)

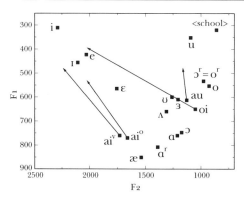

NOTE: His /e/ and /o/ are monophthongal. /ʌ/, /ɜ/, and/or /ʊ/ may be merged (it is unclear from the data). He is completely r-less. (conversation; UT)

SPEAKER 139
Male, Born 1844, from Skidaway Island, Georgia
(mesolectal Gullah speaker; recorded in 1935)

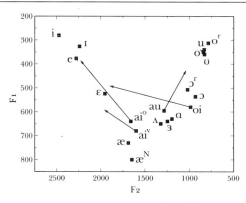

NOTE: His /e/ and /o/ are monophthongal. His /aiʸ/ shows weak glides; his /æ/ is low; his /ɔr/ and /or/ are distinct. He is completely r-less. (conversation; UT)

are monophthongal, his /æ/ is low and [a]-like, and his /au/ is produced as [ʌu], like /au/ in Caribbean speech. However, his /ai/ shows glide weakening before voiced consonants and his /ɑ/ is clearly distinct from his /æ/.

AFRICAN AMERICAN SPEECH (speakers 140–71). The vowels of African Americans show a surprising degree of uniformity over much of the country. This uniformity is undoubtedly linked to the relative recentness of the "Great Migration" of African Americans out of the South to Northern and Western cities: the migration did not become a mass movement until the boll weevil infestation of 1915 disrupted cotton production in the South and World War I created labor shortages in the North (Wesley 1927; Ellison 1974; Grossman 1989). A consequence of the Great Migration is that the center of African American culture has shifted to urban centers, and this shift apparently applies to language as well as other aspects of culture. Rural Southern features are giving way to norms typical of urban African American speech.

SPEAKER 140
Male, Born 1848, from Charlottesville, Virginia
(recorded in 1944)

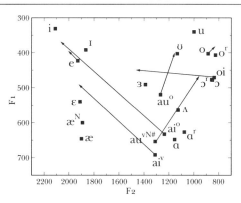

NOTE: His /e/ and /o/ are variably monophthongal. He shows Canadian raising of /au/, with [ʌu] and [ɑo] as the allophones. He keeps /ɔr/ and /or/ distinct. He is completely *r*-less. (conversation; UT)

As Dorrill (1986a) found, African Americans in some parts of the South Atlantic states do show features typical of local white vernaculars, such as mid /au/ nuclei before voiceless consonants (e.g., in *house* and *out*) in Virginia. African Americans in Louisiana and Appalachia undoubtedly show local features, too. For the most part, such assimilation to Southern white vernaculars seems to be old-fashioned in African American speech, and younger African Americans are moving toward nationwide norms for African Americans. Wolfram, Thomas, and Green (2000) and Wolfram and Thomas (forthcoming) examined the AAVE of Hyde County, North Carolina. In this coastal community, the local AAVE shows a considerable degree of assimilation to the local white vernacular, especially for vowels. Speakers 152–56, from Hyde County, depict this assimilation. The study found that, although African Americans appeared to be diverging from white usage for certain morphosyntactic variables and for *r*-lessness, they were undergoing the same vowel developments as whites: backed /ai/ nuclei, fronted /au/ glides, and lowered /er/ nuclei were disappearing, but

SPEAKER 141
Male, Born 1856, from Dallas County, Alabama
(recorded in 1941)

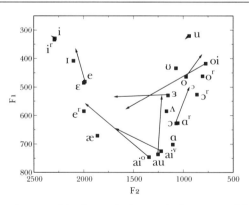

NOTE: His vowels resemble the typical twentieth-century African American configuration except that he has [ɜi] in *first.* He is completely *r*-less. (conversation; NCSU)

SPEAKER 142
Female, Born ca. 1855, from Hempstead, Texas
(recorded in 1941)

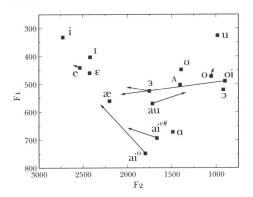

NOTE: Her /o/ is monophthongal; her /e/ variably so. Her /aiᵛ#/ shows weak glides. She is completely *r*-less, with [ɜɪ] in *first*. (conversation; TAMU)

SPEAKER 143
Female, Born 1859, from Tyler, Texas
(recorded in 1974)

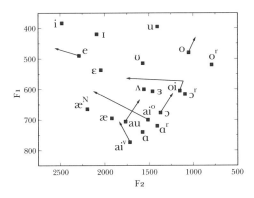

NOTE: Her /o/ is variably monophthongal, but her /e/ is diphthongal. Her /aiᵛ/ is variably monophthongal, and her /oi/ variably triphthongal. She keeps /ɔr/ and /or/ distinct. She is completely *r*-less. (conversation; UT)

fronted /o/ and monophthongal /ɔ/ were being maintained. The overall pattern, then, was that the speech of young African Americans in Hyde County was becoming more like that of African Americans elsewhere, but was still distinct.

The shift away from the rural South has led to a pattern in which African Americans are concentrated in inner-city areas and a few African American suburbs (e.g., in Prince Georges County, Maryland) and thus have less contact with whites than rural African Americans in the South had. The result, as Graff, Labov, and Harris (1986), Labov and Harris (1986), and Labov (1987, 1991) note, mostly on the basis of research in Philadelphia (though with comparisons to other Northern cities), is that African American vowels no longer tend to be affected by sound changes occurring in white vernaculars. Gordon (2000) found the same pattern in Gary, Indiana, and noted that two innovations—the /il/-/ɪl/ and /el/-/ɛl/ mergers—occurred only in African American speech. Hall (1976) and Thomas (1989) reported a similar African American resistance to a sound change that occurred in white speech—the fronting of /o/—in southeastern Georgia and Wilmington, North

SPEAKER 144

Female, Born 1905, from Wilmington, North Carolina
(courtesy of Ronald R. Butters; recorded in 1973)

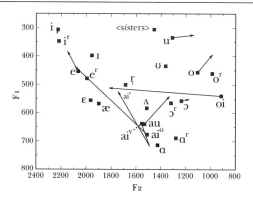

NOTE: Her vowels are typical of AAVE in most respects. Her /aiʸ/ is somewhat triphthongal, realized as [ɐaɛ]. She distinguishes /ɔr/ from /or/ and is r-less except for stressed syllabic /r/. (conversation; NCSU)

SPEAKER 145
Male, Born 1955, from Wilmington, North Carolina
(courtesy of Ronald R. Butters; recorded in 1973)

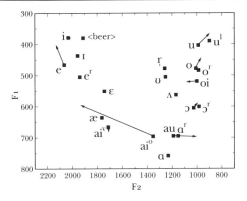

NOTE: He shows a monophthongal /aiᵛ/ and a nearly monophthongal /au/ and /oi/. He is the youngest speaker in this collection to distinguish /ɔr/ and /or/. He is *r*-less except for stressed syllabic /r/. (conversation; NCSU)

SPEAKER 146
Male, Born 1930, from Inez, Warren County, North Carolina
(recorded in 1995)

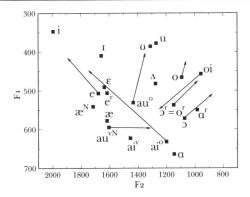

NOTE: He shows Canadian raising of /au/, with [ɜʉ] and [æɒ] as the allophones. His /aiᵛ/ is monophthongal, his /oi/ downgliding, and his /ɔ/ upgliding. He shows a rounded /ɑr/ nucleus, and he merges /ɔr/ and /or/. (conversation; NCSU)

Carolina, respectively. There is some conflicting evidence, however. In Thomas (1989/93) I found that African Americans in Columbus, Ohio, showed some accommodation to sound changes in the white community, including the fronting of /o/. Likewise, Deser (1990) found that Detroit African Americans showed what appeared to be assimilation to the Detroit white vernacular for three variables: preadolescent African Americans whose parents were born in Detroit showed more raising of /æ/, less glide-weakening or monophthongization of /ai/, and shorter vowel durations than those with at least one parent from the South. Nevertheless, teenagers showed some tendency to revert to more Southern-like forms. Though Deser acknowledged that her sample was small, her results are certainly suggestive.

In general the African American avoidance of sound changes that have occurred in white vernaculars holds true in the South. Several variants set African American vowels off from those of white Southern vernaculars. These trends are discussed in more detail in Thomas and Bailey (1998) and Bailey and Thomas (1998).

SPEAKER 147

Female, Born 1985, from Liberia, Warren County, North Carolina
(recorded in 1996)

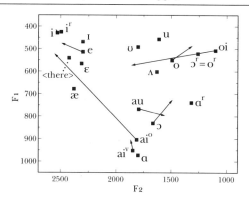

NOTE: Her /ai^v/ is monophthongal, her /au/ nucleus somewhat raised. She shows upgliding /ɔ/. She is r-less except for stressed syllabic /r/. (conversation; NCSU)

SPEAKER 148
Female, Born 1927, from Red Springs, Robeson County, North Carolina
(recorded in 1994)

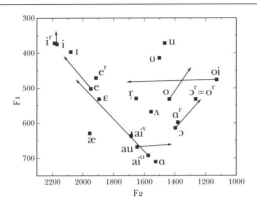

NOTE: Her /aiᵛ/ is monophthongal, and her /ɔ/ upgliding. She has merged /ɔr/ and /or/ and is mostly *r*-less. (conversation; NCSU)

SPEAKER 149
Female, Born 1974, from Maxton, Robeson County, North Carolina
(recorded in 1994)

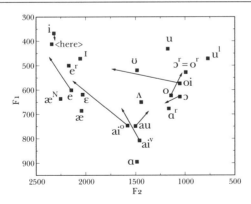

NOTE: Her /aiᵛ/ shows weak glides, as does her /au/. Her /ɔ/ is somewhat ingliding. She is mostly *r*-less. (conversation; NCSU)

/o/, /ʊ/, and /u/ usually remain backed (see Hall 1976; Thomas 1989, as noted above). The nucleus of /au/ is not fronted to [æ] for the majority of African Americans; /au/ is most often realized as [aɔ], but may occasionally be a monophthongal [a] ~ [ɑ], especially before voiceless consonants. Graff, Labov, and Harris (1986) and Labov and Harris (1986) discuss the failure of /au/ and /o/ to be fronted in Philadelphia AAVE, but this tendency occurs across the South as well. Records from *LAMSAS* (cited in Dorrill 1986a) and from *LAGS*, as well as Bernstein's (1993) Texas study, all describe the low frequency of fronted /au/ in Southern AAVE. The *LAGS* records also indicate that monophthongal or ingliding /au/, [aː] ~ [aə], is more frequent among African Americans than among whites in the Gulf states. Other vowels also show distinctive patterns in African American English. /æ/ is usually raised to [ɛ]; /ɛ/ and /ɪ/ correspondingly tend to be shifted upward, and they tend to be very fronted as well. This pattern for /æ/, /ɛ/, and /ɪ/ also occurs in Southern white vernaculars (Labov 1991), but it is not receding in African American English as it seems to be in Southern white

SPEAKER 150
Female, Born 1904, from Ocracoke, North Carolina
(sister of speaker 151; recorded in 1995)

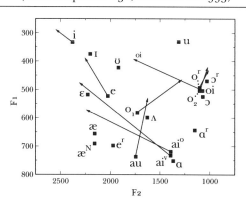

NOTE: She shows a strange mixture of Pamlico Sound and AAVE features, with central-gliding /au/, low /er/ nuclei, and /o/ split into two lexically determined classes, one backed and the other central. She is mostly *r*-less. (conversation; NCSU)

SPEAKER 151

Female, Born 1915

(Ocracoke, North Carolina, until age 14, then in Washington, North
Carolina; much of her adult life in New Haven, Connecticut; sister of
speaker 150; recorded in 1996)

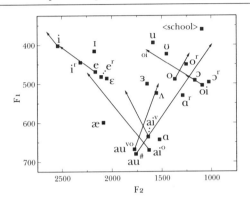

NOTE: Her vowels are more AAVE-like than her sister's. She is almost
completely *r*-less. (conversation; NCSU)

SPEAKER 152

Female, Born in 1906, from Engelhard, Hyde County, North Carolina
(recorded in 1997)

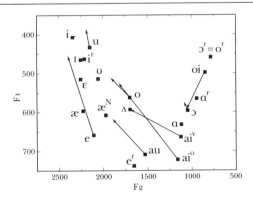

NOTE: She shows a clearly Pamlico Sound vowel configuration. Her /au/ is
realized as [aɛ]. She is mostly *r*-ful. (conversation; NCSU)

English. Backed forms of /ʌ/ are common but not universal in African American English. /ɔ/ varies among African Americans: some have an upgliding form like that of most Southern whites, while others produce /ɔ/ as a monophthong. The merger of /ɑ/ and /ɔ/ is considerably less frequent among African Americans than among other ethnic groups (see Bernstein 1993). Dorrill (1986a, 1986b), who examined *LAMSAS* records from Maryland, Virginia, and North Carolina, found that monophthongal forms of /e/, /o/, /ɔ/, /i/, and /u/ were more frequent among African American speakers than among white speakers. His speakers, of course, were born in the nineteenth century. Thomas (1989) and Thomas and Bailey (1998) found that African Americans born before World War I often show monophthongal forms of /e/ and /o/, but those born after World War I seldom do.

Two features that most African Americans share with Southern whites are glide weakening or monophthongization of /ai/ and the merger of /ɪ/ and /ɛ/ before nasals, as in *pin* and *pen*. In AAVE as well as certain white Southern vernaculars (as described in chap. 4), /ai/

SPEAKER 153

Female, Born 1909, from Swan Quarter, Hyde County, North Carolina
(recorded in 1997)

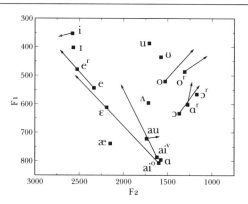

NOTE: She shows an AAVE-like configuration, with upgliding /ɔ/ and back-gliding /au/, though her /aiᵛ/ shows strong glides. She is *r*-less except for stressed syllabic /r/. (conversation; NCSU)

Male, Born 1910, from Engelhard, Hyde County, North Carolina
(father of speaker 155 and great-grandfather of speaker 156;
recorded in 1997)

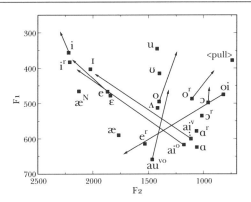

NOTE: He shows a Pamlico Sound configuration. His /au/ is realized as
[aə]. He is almost completely *r*-ful. (conversation; NCSU)

SPEAKER 155
Female, Born 1935, from Engelhard, Hyde County, North Carolina
(daughter of speaker 154; recorded in 1997)

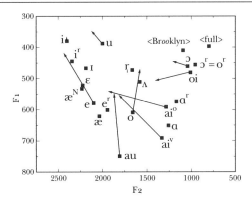

NOTE: She shows a Pamlico Sound configuration. The apparent raising of
/aiᵒ/ is an artifact of the consonantal context of the words measured. She is
mostly *r*-ful. (conversation; NCSU)

shows strong glides before voiceless consonants, but is monophthongal or shows weak glides (i.e., is realized as [aː] ~ [aːæ]) in
other phonetic contexts. Thus, *tight* is [tʰaet] ~ [tʰait] while *tide* is
[tʰaːd] ~ [tʰaːæd] and *tie* is [tʰaː] ~ [tʰaːæ]. This configuration predominates in African American speech across the South and undoubtedly in many other parts of the United States. Weak-
gliding /ai/ before voiceless consonants is quite unusual in Southern African American speech, as both *LAGS* data and Bernstein's
(1993) Texas data show. However, Anderson and Milroy (1999)
and Anderson (forthcoming) encountered it, along with fronting
of /u/ and /ʊ/, among African Americans in Detroit. They attributed
the unusual situation in Detroit to the fact that African Americans
live alongside Appalachian whites and both groups are in conflict
with Northern whites. Some African Americans, especially from
higher socioeconomic backgrounds, appear to avoid weak-gliding
/ai/ in any phonetic context. An additional feature that AAVE
shares with white vernaculars is the replacement of [ɪ] in unstressed syllables (e.g., the second syllable of *happy*) with [i] (Den-

SPEAKER 156

Female, Born 1981, from Engelhard, North Carolina
(great-granddaughter of speaker 154; recorded in 1997)

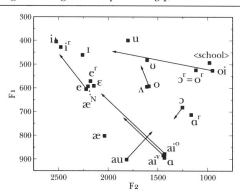

NOTE: She has lost many Pamlico Sound features: her /aiʸ/ may have weak
glides, and her /au/ is back-gliding. However, her /o/ is front-gliding, with
a central nucleus. She is mostly *r*-ful. (conversation; NCSU)

SPEAKER 157

Female, Born ca. 1970, from Columbus, Ohio
(recorded in 1985)

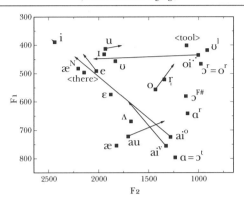

NOTE: She shows some features of the local white dialect, including fronted nuclei of /u/, /ʊ/, /o/, and /au/, a partial merger of /ɑ/ and /ɔ/, and complete *r*-fulness. However, she shows rounded /ɑr/ nuclei and raised /ɔ^{F#}/, which are common in African American English but not in the local white dialect. (reading passage; NCSU)

SPEAKER 158

Male, Born 1954, from Memphis, Tennessee
(college-educated; recorded in 1993)

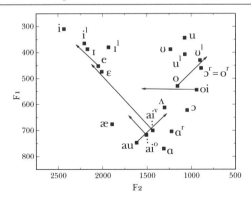

NOTE: He shows a typical African American configuration. His /ɔ/ is monophthongal, and he merges /ɔr/ and /or/. He is variably *r*-less. (reading passage; UT)

ning 1989), though this shift has happened later in AAVE than in most white varieties.

One important feature that typifies AAVE is *r*-lessness. AAVE is probably the most *r*-less variety of American English. It tends to be more *r*-less than neighboring white vernaculars not only in the North (e.g., Wolfram 1969; Labov and Harris 1986) but in the South, too (e.g., *LAGS* 1986–92; Bernstein 1993; Wolfram, Thomas, and Green 2000). Although African Americans born before World War I tend to be *r*-less even for stressed syllabic /r/, as in *first*, the pattern that seems to be emerging in Southern AAVE is that stressed syllabic /r/ is *r*-ful, but other syllable rhymes, as in *other*, *here*, and *four*, are *r*-less. In old-fashioned AAVE (as in some old-fashioned Southern white speech), /or/ may be produced as [ou ~ oː] (e.g., *four* [fou ~ foː]), which would make *four* and *foe* nearly or completely homophonous, but this situation appears to be less common among young African Americans. On the other hand, the merger of /ɔr/ and /or/ has taken hold in contemporary AAVE just as in white vernaculars.

SPEAKER 159
Male, Born 1972, from Memphis, Tennessee
(college student when interviewed; recorded in 1993)

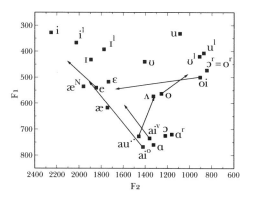

NOTE: He also shows a typical African American configuration. His /ɔ/ is monophthongal. He is mostly *r*-ful. (reading passage; UT)

SPEAKER 160
Male, Born 1892, from Ganado, Texas
(recorded ca. 1985)

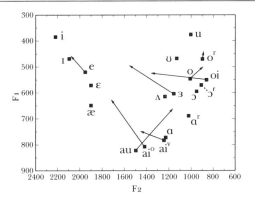

NOTE: His /e/ and /o/ are generally upgliding, but his /ɔ/ is monophthongal. He keeps /ɔr/ and /or/ distinct. He is completely *r*-less. (conversation; UT)

SPEAKER 161
Male, Born 1912, from "Springville," Texas
(recorded ca. 1988)

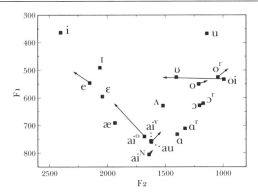

NOTE: His /o/ is variably monophthongal, but his /e/ is usually diphthongal. His /au/ is variably, and his /ɔ/ is consistently, monophthongal. He keeps /ɔr/ and /or/ distinct. He is mostly *r*-less. (conversation; UT)

SPEAKER 162
Male, born 1920, from "Springville," Texas
(recorded ca. 1988)

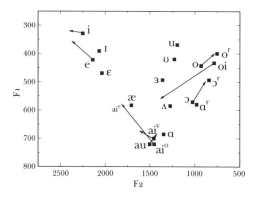

NOTE: His /e/ and /o/ are consistently diphthongal. His /oi/ is downgliding, [oɐ], and his /ɔ/ is upgliding. His /ɑr/ nucleus is rounded; he keeps /ɔr/ and /or/ distinct. He is completely r-less. (conversation; UT)

SPEAKER 163
Male, Born 1922, from Midway, Texas
(recorded ca. 1985)

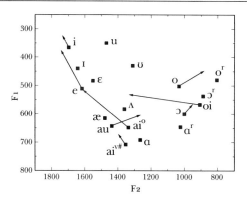

NOTE: His /e/ and /o/ are diphthongal. Unusually for an African American, he shows fronted /u/ and /au/ nuclei. He keeps /ɔr/ and /or/ distinct. He is mostly r-less. (conversation; UT)

SPEAKER 164
Female, Born 1937, from Bryan, Texas
(recorded ca. 1988)

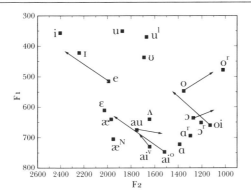

NOTE: She shows upgliding /ɔ/. Her /u/ is fronted. She keeps /ɔr/ and /or/ distinct and is mostly *r*-less. (conversation; UT)

SPEAKER 165
Female, Born 1946, from Houston, Texas
(recorded ca. 1988)

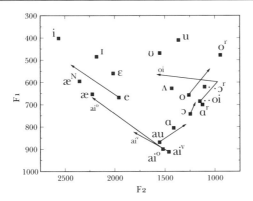

NOTE: Her /oi/ is triphthongal, and her /ɔ/ upgliding. Her /ar/ nucleus is rounded; she keeps /ɔr/ and /or/ distinct. She is mostly *r*-less. (conversation; UT)

SPEAKER 166
Female, Born 1961, from "Springville," Texas
(recorded ca. 1988)

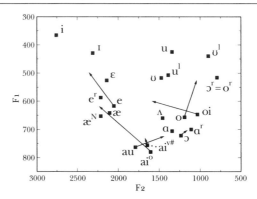

NOTE: Her /aiᵛ#/ is monophthongal. Her /e/ and /o/ nuclei are lowered. Her /ɔ/ is usually monophthongal. She merges /ɔr/ and /or/ and is mostly *r*-less. (reading passage; UT)

SPEAKER 167
Female, Born 1961, from Austin, Texas
(college-educated; recorded in 1992)

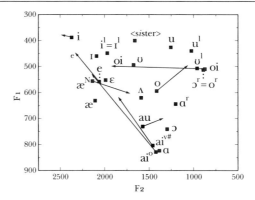

NOTE: Her /aiᵛ#/ shows weak glides. Her /o/ nucleus is somewhat central, and her /ɔ/ is monophthongal. She shows mergers of /ɔr/ and /or/ and of /il/ and /ɪl/, but not of /ʊl/ and /ul/. She is mostly *r*-ful. (reading passage; UT)

SPEAKER 168
Male, Born 1969, from Silsbee, Texas
(recorded in 1989)

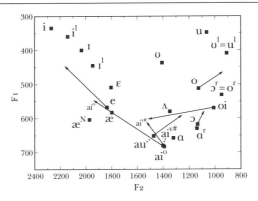

NOTE: His /ɔ/ is monophthongal. He merges /ul/ and /ʊl/. He is *r*-less except for stressed syllabic /r/. (reading passage; UT)

SPEAKER 169
Female, Born 1970, from Silsbee, Texas
(recorded in 1989)

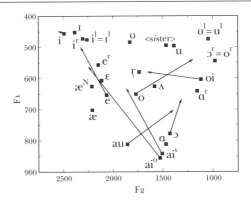

NOTE: Her /aiʸ/ shows strong glides. Her /o/ nucleus is unusually fronted; speaker 168 is more typical of Silsbee African Americans. Her /ɔ/ is upgliding. She is mostly *r*-less. (reading passage; NCSU)

SPEAKER 170
Male, Born 1972, from Kilgore, Texas
(recorded in 1989)

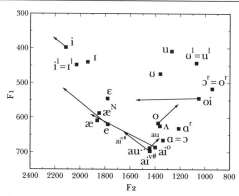

NOTE: His /ai^v#/ shows weak glides, his /au/ is nearly monophthongal, and his /e/ and /o/ nuclei are somewhat lowered. He shows mergers of /ɑ/ and /ɔ/, of /il/ and /ɪl/, and of /ul/ and /ʊl/. He is mostly r-ful. (reading passage; UT)

SPEAKER 171
Female, Born 1972, from Dallas, Texas
(recorded in 1987)

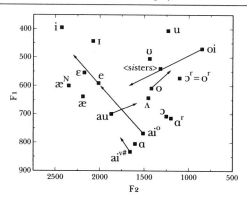

NOTE: Her /au/ nucleus is fronted. Her /oi/ is downgliding, and her /ɔ/ monophthongal. She is mostly r-less. (conversation; UT)

7. MEXICAN AMERICANS

ALTHOUGH HISPANICS WILL SOON BE the largest minority in the United States, dialectal variation in their speech has attracted far less scholarly attention than that of African Americans. Nonetheless, there have been numerous impressionistic descriptions of the vowels of Hispanic English, mostly for Mexican Americans and Puerto Ricans. Impressionistic discussions of the vowels of Mexican American English from Texas are found in Sawyer (1959, 1964), McDowell and McRae (1972), Thompson (1975), Hamilton (1977), Merrill (1987), and Galindo (1988); from California in Castro-Gingrás (1972), Metcalf (1972b), and García (1984); from Arizona in Register (1977); from Indiana in Hartford (1978) and Gordon (2000); and from Illinois in Frazer (1996). Impressionistic studies of the vowels of Puerto Rican English in the Northeast include Ma and Herasimchuk (1971) and Poplack (1979). However, there have been very few acoustic studies of vowels thus far, all of Mexican American English with California natives (Godinez 1984; Godinez and Maddieson 1985; Veatch 1991; Fought 1999) or Texas natives (Thomas 1993, 2000).

Mexican Americans have developed a dialect that shows Spanish influence, but is firmly established as a variety of English (see Bills 1977; Wald 1984; Penfield and Ornstein-Galicia 1985; Santa Ana A. 1993). Several vowel variants typify it. /u/, /ʊ/, and /o/ usually remain as back vowels (though see Fought 1999). The nucleus of /au/ is usually not fronted. Prenasal /æ/, as in *hand*, is generally not raised, as it is in most Anglo varieties (Thomas 1993; Gordon 2000, 134). Features of Anglo vernaculars, such as lowering of the nuclei of /e/ and /o/, tend not to appear. /e/ and /o/ may be monophthongal, though many speakers—including most of those featured here—consistently show upgliding diphthongal forms of these vowels. It is often reported that Mexican American English does not distinguish between /i/ and /ɪ/, between /e/ and /ɛ/, or between /u/ and /ʊ/ (e.g., Castro-Gingrás 1972; Galindo 1988; Ornstein 1975; Penfield and Ornstein-Galicia 1985; González 1988), but those mergers seem mainly to occur for speakers who learned English as a second language, not for those who learned English as young children. Another reported feature is lowering of /ʌ/ to [ɑ] or [ɔ], which Castro-Gingrás (1972), Hartford (1978), and Frazer (1996) found among some of their subjects. In Thomas (2000), I found that Mexican Americans from Laredo do not produce higher, fronter /ai/ glides before /t/ than before /d/ to the extent that Anglos from central Ohio do and do not perceive the difference in glides the same way.

In not fronting /u/, /ʊ/, /o/, or /au/ and in not showing certain other features of Anglo vernaculars, Mexican American English resembles African American Vernacular English. It differs, however, in being heavily *r*-ful, in exhibiting /ai/ with strong glides in all phonetic contexts, in not having /æ/ raised as much, and in showing a high incidence of mergers: both the merger of /ɑ/ and /ɔ/ and various pre-/l/ mergers are common among Mexican Americans, at least in Texas (Tillery 1989, 1997; Bernstein 1993) and Arizona (Register 1977), and the merger of /ɔr/ and /or/ occurs in the speech of all the Chicanos featured here. In Texas, Mexican Ameri-

SPEAKER 172
Female, Born ca. 1920, from Cuero, Texas
(recorded in 1988)

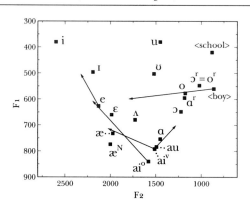

NOTE: Her /au/ nucleus is backed. Her /o/ is monophthongal, though her /e/ is consistently upgliding. She keeps /ɔ/ and /ɑ/ distinct. Her /ar/ nucleus is rounded. (conversation; UT)

SPEAKER 173
Male, Born 1936, from Edinburg, Texas
(most of adult life in San Antonio; college-educated; husband of
speaker 177 and father of speaker 184; recorded in 1992)

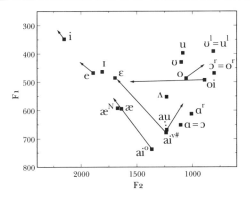

NOTE: His /e/ and /o/ are usually upgliding. His /æ/ is somewhat raised. He
merges /ɔ/ with /ɑ/ and /ul/ with /ʊl/. (reading passage; UT)

SPEAKER 174
Male, Born 1946, from Donna, Texas
(recorded in 1989)

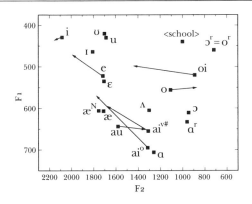

NOTE: His /au/ nucleus, /u/, and /ʊ/ are fronted. His /æ/ is somewhat raised.
He keeps /ɔ/ and /ɑ/ distinct. His /ɑr/ nucleus is usually rounded. (conversation; UT)

cans who merge /ɑ/ and /ɔ/ have the resulting vowel more fronted than Anglos with the merger. Correspondingly, they do not show lowering or retraction of /æ/, as some young Anglos do. The acoustic data presented in Godinez (1984), Godinez and Maddieson (1985), and Veatch (1991) indicate that Mexican Americans in California also show more fronted values of the merged /ɑ = ɔ/ than Anglos there and do not show lowering or retraction of /æ/. Moreover, they show higher variants of /ɪ/ and /ɛ/ than California Anglos.

Speakers 172–84 represent what seems to be the mainstream of Mexican American English in Texas. Many of them are from southern Texas, where a large majority of the residents are Hispanic and nearly 90% of the Hispanics are Mexican American. In that demographic setting, Spanish influence in the dialect would be expected to persist. Speaker 185, who lived until age 2 in Mexico, represents the recent tide of migration to the Southeast from Mexico, Guatemala, and Honduras. Speakers 186–88 are middle-class Mexican Americans from Texas who have assimilated

SPEAKER 175

Female, Born 1950, from Cotulla, Texas

(student at junior college when recorded in 1989)

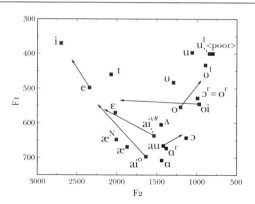

NOTE: Her /au/ nucleus is backed. She keeps /ɔ/ and /ɑ/ distinct as well as /ul/ and /ʊl/. Her /ɑr/ nucleus is unrounded. (reading passage; UT)

SPEAKER 176
Female, Born 1959, from Laredo, Texas
(student at junior college when recorded in 1989)

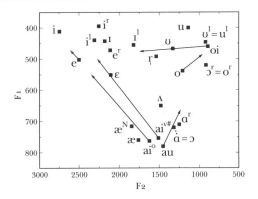

NOTE: She merges /ɔ/ with /ɑ/ and /ul/ with /ʊl/. Her /ar/ nucleus is generally unrounded. (reading passage; UT)

SPEAKER 177
Female, Born 1961, from San Antonio, Texas
(wife of speaker 173 and mother of speaker 184; recorded in 1992)

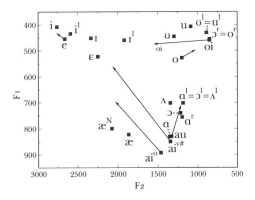

NOTE: Her /au/ nucleus is backed. She keeps /ɔ/ and /ɑ/ distinct as well as /il/ and /ɪl/, but merges /ul/ with /ʊl/ and /ʌl/ with /ɔl/. Her /ar/ nucleus shows some rounding. (reading passage; UT)

some features of Anglo vernaculars, such as the fronting of /o/ and /u/, but not necessarily all features. Fought (1999) found that fronting of /u/ among Chicanos in Los Angeles was correlated primarily with nonmembership in gangs and secondarily with middle-class status.

All of the speakers featured here learned English as children. Most of them are probably fluent in Spanish as well. Unfortunately, knowledge of Spanish was not ascertained in the surveys from which some of the recordings came. Speakers 172, 173, 177, 179, 184, 185, and 188 are known to be fluent in Spanish; information on the other speakers is lacking. Speakers 173 and 177 reported that they were Spanish-dominant as children, while their son, speaker 184, reported that he was English-dominant. Speaker 185 said that she spoke mostly Spanish at home but mostly English with her friends.

SPEAKER 178
Female, Born 1966, from McAllen, Texas
(recorded in 1989)

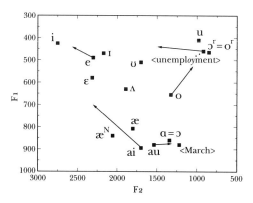

NOTE: She merges /ɔ/ with /ɑ/. Her /ɑr/ nucleus (in *March*) is apparently unrounded. (conversation; UT)

SPEAKER 179
Female, Born 1970, from "Springville," Texas
(recorded ca. 1988)

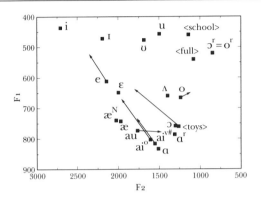

NOTE: Her /au/ nucleus is somewhat fronted. She keeps /ɔ/ and /ɑ/ distinct. Her /ɑr/ nucleus shows some rounding. (conversation; UT)

SPEAKER 180
Male, Born 1970, from Bovina, Texas
(recorded in 1989)

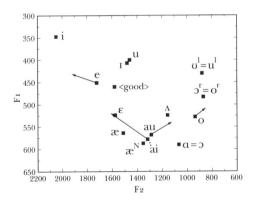

NOTE: He merges /ɔ/ with /ɑ/ and /ul/ with /ʊl/. His /u/ is apparently somewhat fronted (but possibly skewed by the small number of tokens). (conversation; UT)

SPEAKER 181

Female, Born 1971, from Laredo, Texas

(student at junior college when recorded in 1989)

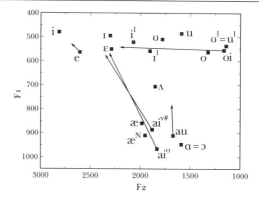

NOTE: Her /o/ is monophthongal, and her /e/ is variably monophthongal. She merges /ɔ/ with /ɑ/ and /ul/ with /ʊl/; she keeps /il/ and /ɪl/ distinct. (reading passage; UT)

SPEAKER 182

Male, Born 1972, from El Paso, Texas

(recorded in 1989)

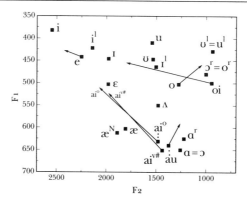

NOTE: He merges /ɔ/ with /ɑ/ and /ul/ and /ʊl/ but keeps /il/ and /ɪl/ distinct. His /ɑr/ nucleus is generally unrounded. (reading passage; UT)

SPEAKER 183
Male, Born 1973, from Snyder, Texas
(recorded in 1989)

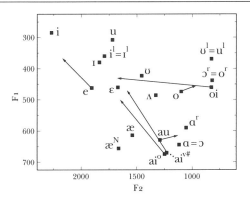

NOTE: His /u/ and, to some extent, his /ʊ/ are fronted. He merges /ɔ/ with /ɑ/, /ul/ with /ʊl/, and /il/ with /ɪl/. His /ɑr/ nucleus may show some rounding. (reading passage; UT)

SPEAKER 184
Male, Born 1978, from San Antonio, Texas
(son of speakers 173 and 177; recorded in 1992)

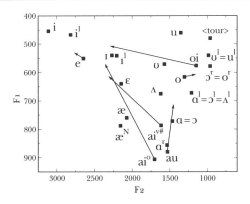

NOTE: His /au/ nucleus is backed. He merges /ɔ/ with /ɑ/, /ul/ with /ʊl/, and /ʌl/ with /ɔl/, but keeps /il/ and /ɪl/ distinct. His /ɑr/ nucleus is unrounded. (reading passage; UT)

SPEAKER 185
Female, Born 1986, from Siler City, North Carolina
(recorded in 1996)

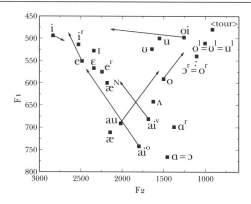

NOTE: Her /au/ nucleus is fronted. She shows mergers of /ɔ/ with /ɑ/ and of /ol/, /ʊl/, and /ul/. Her /ɑr/ nucleus may show some rounding. (reading passage supplemented with conversation; NCSU)

SPEAKER 186
Female, Born 1967, from San Antonio, Texas
(college student when recorded in 1989)

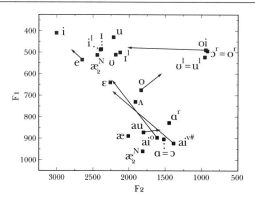

NOTE: Her /u/ and /ʊ/ are front, her /o/ nucleus is central, and her /au/ nucleus is somewhat fronted. Her /æ^N/ is split into two classes, one raised and one lowered. She merges /ɔ/ with /ɑ/ and /ul/ with /ʊl/ but keeps /il/ and /ɪl/ distinct. (reading passage; UT)

SPEAKER 187
Male, Born 1968, from Laredo, Texas
(student at junior college when recorded in 1989)

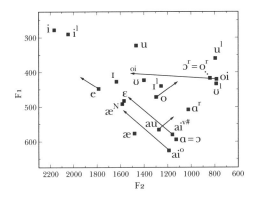

NOTE: His /o/ nucleus, /u/, and /ʊ/ are central. His /æ^N/ is somewhat raised.
He merges /ɔ/ with /ɑ/ but shows no pre-/l/ mergers. His /ɑr/ nucleus is
rounded. (reading passage; UT)

SPEAKER 188
Female, Born 1969, from Corpus Christi, Texas
(college-educated; recorded in 1991)

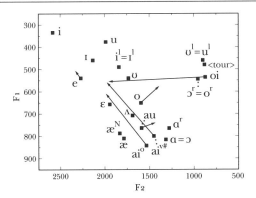

NOTE: Her /u/ and /ʊ/ are front; her /o/ nucleus is central, and her /ʌ/
rather front. Her /æ^N/ is not raised. She merges /ɔ/ with /ɑ/, /ul/ with /ʊl/,
and /il/ with /ɪl/. Her /ɑr/ nucleus is not usually rounded. (reading passage;
UT)

8. NATIVE AMERICANS

THIS CHAPTER PROVIDES a small sampling of the English of Native Americans. Two of the groups that are most prominent in North Carolina, the Lumbees and the Cherokees, are represented here, with a Navajo from New Mexico for comparison. These speakers show varying degrees of assimilation to the dialects of whites and African Americans that are found where they live. Naturally, numerous factors—including the structure of the original language, a speaker's language dominance and competence in each language, the rate of the community's shift to English, and the specific white contact dialect—shape specific varieties of Native American English.

LUMBEES (speakers 189 and 190). The Lumbees are concentrated most heavily in Robeson County, North Carolina, and have been monolingual in English as long as there is any historical mention of

SPEAKER 189
Lumbee Male, Born 1919, from Prospect Community,
Robeson County, North Carolina
(recorded in 1994)

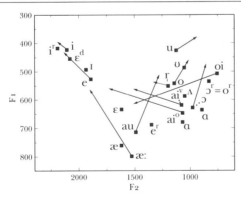

NOTE: He realizes /ai/ as [ɒɛ], with a rounded nucleus. He produces /æ:/ as an [ae] diphthong. His /o/ and /u/ are more or less back. He is mostly r-less. (conversation; NCSU)

SPEAKER 190
Lumbee Female, Born 1980, from Lumberton,
Robeson County, North Carolina
(recorded in 1995)

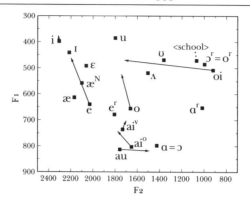

NOTE: Her /æ/, /ɛ/, and /ʌ/ are all raised, and her /ɪ/ is fronted. She appears to merge /ɑ/ with /ɔ/. Her /er/ nucleus is lowered and retracted. She is variably r-less. (conversation; NCSU)

them. Older Lumbees, such as speaker 189, often show backed /ai/ nuclei and fronted /au/ glides, like whites from the Pamlico Sound region. However, they also show upgliding /æː/ and /ɔ/ and backed /o/ and /ʌ/, like whites from inland parts of the state. Younger Lumbees, such as speaker 190, generally show monophthongal /ai/, back-gliding /au/, fronted /o/, and no trace of upgliding /æː/, much like young whites from Robeson County (see speaker 68). However, they are more r-less than whites. See Wolfram and Dannenberg (1999).

CHEROKEES (speaker 191). The Cherokees are divided into the Eastern Band, which lives in the mountains of North Carolina, and the Western Band, which lives in Oklahoma. As with most Native American groups, their original language has been studied more than their English. Anderson (1999) investigated the /ai/ and /oi/ realizations of the Snowbird Cherokees in North Carolina and found that they showed monophthongal realizations ([aː] and [oː], respectively), except when the sound was prepausal or fol-

SPEAKER 191
Cherokee Male, Born 1953, from Snowbird Community,
Graham County, North Carolina
(speaks Cherokee fluently; recorded in 1996)

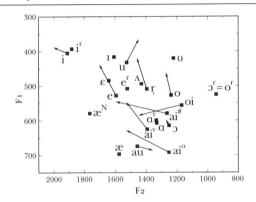

NOTE: His /ai/ is more diphthongal than that of whites from Graham
County (speakers 64–66). His /ʌ/ is raised. (conversation; NCSU)

lowed by a vowel, in which case it was diphthongal. Whites in the
area showed monophthongal /ai/ and diphthongal /oi/ in all contexts. Speaker 191 is one of her subjects. The Cherokees in the
Snowbird Community have retained the Cherokee language to a
greater degree than other Eastern Band Cherokees have.

NAVAJOS (speaker 192). Relatively little is written about the English
of Navajos and even less about Navajo English vowels, though a
brief treatment is given in Cook and Sharp (1966). Speaker 192
was not asked whether she spoke Navajo, but she almost certainly
did: she shows several interference features, such as devoicing and
glottalization of final stops and insertion of glottal stops before
word-initial vowels, and Spolsky (1971) reported that most children in Shiprock were Navajo-dominant in 1970. Although speaker
192 shows clearly diphthongal /e/ and /o/, she shows other features
that are probably due to interference, such as her retracted /æ/ and
/ʌ/. Her /ɛ/ is rather low as well. It is uncertain how typical these
features are of Navajo English.

SPEAKER 192
Navajo Female, Born 1976, from Shiprock, New Mexico
(recorded in 1992)

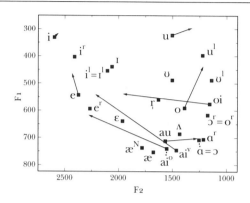

NOTE: Antiformants around 500 Hz, 1000 Hz, and 2000 Hz (perhaps from nasality) distorted some of her formant readings (e.g., for /ai/ glides). Her /o/ is backed. She merges /il/ with /ɪl/ but not /ul/ with /ʊl/. She is almost completely r-ful. (reading passage; NCSU)

APPENDIX A: LOCATIONS OF SPEAKERS' HOMETOWNS

St. John's

Belmont
Greenwich
Haverhill
Uxbridge
Toronto
North Truro
Meriden
Lino Lakes
New York
Sacramento
Philadelphia
Burgettstown
Charlottesville
Tylerton
Memphis
Irvington
White County
Bertrand
Shiprock
Nansemond
Yale
Hanover County
Gatlinburg
Cross
Skidaway Island
Moultrie
New Orleans
Cherokee Sound
Dallas County
Montgomery
Kingston

NORTH CAROLINA

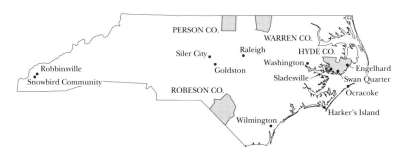

TEXAS

OHIO

APPENDIX B: INTERNATIONAL PHONETIC ALPHABET

CONSONANTS

	Bilabial	Labio-dental	Dental	Alveolar	Post-alveolar	Retroflex	Palatal	Velar
Plosive	p b			t d		ʈ ɖ	c ɟ	k g
Nasal	m	ɱ		n		ɳ	ɲ	ŋ
Trill	ʙ			r				
Tap or flap				ɾ				
Fricative	ɸ β	f v	θ ð	s z	ʃ ʒ	ʂ ʐ	ç ʝ	x ɣ
Lateral fricative				ɬ ɮ				
Approximant		ʋ		ɹ		ɻ	j	ɰ
Lateral approximant				l		ɭ	ʎ	ʟ
Ejective stop	pʼ			tʼ		ʈʼ	cʼ	kʼ
Implosive	ɓ			ɗ			ʄ	ɠ

Where symbols appear in pairs, the one to the right represents a voiced consonant. Shaded areas denote

DIACRITICS

̥	Voiceless	̜	More rounded	ʷ	Labialized	̃	Nasalized
̬	Voiced	̹	Less rounded	ʲ	Palatalized	ⁿ	Nasal release
ʰ	Aspirated	̟	Advanced*	ˠ	Velarized	ˡ	Lateral release
̈	Breathy voiced	̠	Retracted*	̴	Pharyngealized	̚	No audible release
̰	Creaky voiced	̈	Centralized	~	Velarized or pharyngealized		
̼	Linguolabial	̽	Mid centralized		Raised* (ɹ̝ = voiced alreolar fricative)		
̪	Dental	̘	Advanced tongue root				
̺	Apical	̙	Retracted tongue root		Lowered* (β̞ = voiced bilabial approximant)		
̻	Laminal	˞	Rhoticity	̩	Syllabic	̯	Nonsyllabic

Uvular	Pharyn-geal	Glottal
q G		ʔ
N		
R		
χ ʁ	ħ ʕ	h ɦ
q'		
ɢ		

articulations judged impossible.

VOWELS

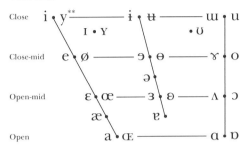

Where symbols appear in pairs, the on to the right represents a rounded vowel.

OTHER SYMBOLS

ʍ	Voiceless labial-velar fricative	⊙	Bilabial click
w	Voiced labial-velar approximant	ǀ	Dental click
ɥ	Voiced labial-palatal approximant	ǃ	(Post)alveolar click
ʜ	Voiceless epiglottal fricative	ǂ	Palatalveolar click
ʢ	Voiced epiglotal plosive	ǁ	Alveolar lateral click
ʡ	Voiced epiglottal fricative	ɺ	Alveolar lateral flap
ɧ	Simultaneous ʃ and x	ɕ ʑ	Alveolo-palatal fricatives

Affricates and double articulations can be represented by two symbols joined by a tie bar if necessary.

k͡p   t͡s

SUPERSEGMENTALS

ˈ	Primary stress
ˌ	Secondard stress
ː	Long
ˑ	Half-long
˘	Extra-short
.	Syllable break
|	Minor (foot) group
‖	Major (foot) group
‿	Linking (absence of a break)
↗	Global rise
↘	Global fall

LEVEL TONES

˵ or ˥	Extra-high
´	˦	High
¯	˧	Mid
`	˩	Low
˷	˩	Extra-low
↓		Downstep
↑		Upstep

CONTOUR TONES

ˇ or ˄	Rising
ˆ	˥	Falling
˘	˧	High rising
˷	˨	Low rising
˜	˦	Rising-falling
		Etc.

NOTES

* For shifting vowels, I use [<>˅˄] instead of the approved [₊˗₊˔] because they are more familiar to most readers.
** In this volume, [ü] is used instead of [y] for close front rounded vowel to avoid possible confusion with the palatal approximant.

REFERENCES

Abel, Ken. 1996. *The Tongue-in-Cheek Guide to Pittsburgh.* Carnegie, Pa.: ABELexpress.

Allen, Harold B. 1976. *The Linguistic Atlas of the Upper Midwest.* Vol. 3, *The Pronunciation.* Minneapolis: Univ. of Minnesota Press.

Anderson, Bridget L. 1999. "Source-Language Transfer and Vowel Accommodation in the Patterning of Cherokee English /ai/ and /oi/." *American Speech* 74: 339–68.

———. Forthcoming. "Dialect Leveling and /ai/ Monophthongization among African American Detroiters." *Journal of Sociolinguistics.*

Anderson, Bridget L., and Lesley Milroy. 1999. "Southern Sound Changes and the Detroit AAVE Vowel System." Paper presented at the 28th Meeting on New Ways of Analyzing Variation in English (NWAVE 28), Toronto, 15 Oct.

Anshen, Frank. 1970. "A Sociolinguistic Analysis of a Sound Change." *Language Sciences* 9: 20–21.

Armour, Malcolm. 1983. "The Social Stratification of (e) in Midlothian, Texas." In Edmondson, 2–21.

Arnold, Jennifer, Renée Blake, Brad Davidson, Scott Schwenter, and Julie Solomon, eds. 1996. *Sociolinguistic Variation: Data, Theory, and Analysis: Selected Papers from NWAV 23 at Stanford.* Stanford, Calif.: Center for the Study of Language and Information, Stanford Univ.

Ash, Sharon. 1982. "The Vocalization of Intervocalic /l/ in Philadelphia." *SECOL Review* 6: 162–75.

———. 1996. "Freedom of Movement: /uw/-Fronting in the Midwest." In Arnold et al., 3–25.

Ash, Sharon, and John Myhill. 1986. "Linguistic Correlates of Inter-Ethnic Contact." In Sankoff, 33–44.

Atal, B. S., and Suzanne L. Hanauer. 1971. "Speech Analysis and Synthesis by Linear Prediction of the Speech Wave." *Journal of the Acoustical Society of America* 50: 637–55.

Avis, Walter S. 1956. "Speech Differences along the Ontario-U.S. Border: III. Pronunciation." *Journal of the Canadian Linguistic Association* 2: 41–59.

———. 1961. "The 'New England Short *o*': A Recessive Phoneme." *Language* 37: 544–58.

———. 1972. "The Phonemic Segments of an Edmonton Idiolect." In *Studies in Linguistics in Honor of Raven I. McDavid, Jr.,* ed. Lawrence M. Davis, 239–50. University: Univ. of Alabama Press.

Ayres, Harry Morgan, and W. Cabell Greet. 1930. "American Speech Records at Columbia University." *American Speech* 5: 333–58.

Bailey, Charles-James N. 1968. "Segmental Length in Southern States English: An Instrumental Phonetic Investigation of a Standard Dialect in South Carolina." PEGS Paper No. 20. ERIC/PEGS. Washington, DC: Center for Applied Linguistics.

———. 1975. "Further Investigations on Unmarked Rule Order." *International Journal of American Linguistics* 41: 73–78.

———. 1985. "Toward Principles Governing the Progress and Patterning of Phonetological Development." In *Developmental Mechanisms of Language*, ed. Charles-James N. Bailey and Roy Harris, 1–49. Language and Communication Library 6. New York: Pergamon.

Bailey, Guy, and Cynthia Bernstein. 1989. "Methodology for a Phonological Survey of Texas." *Journal of English Linguistics* 22: 6–16.

Bailey, Guy, and Margie Dyer. 1992. "An Approach to Sampling in Dialectology." *American Speech* 67: 1–18.

Bailey, Guy, and Natalie Maynor. 1989. "The Divergence Controversy." *American Speech* 64: 12–39.

Bailey, Guy, Natalie Maynor, and Patricia Cukor-Avila, eds. 1991. *The Emergence of Black English: Texts and Commentary*. Creole Language Library 8. Amsterdam: John Benjamins.

Bailey, Guy, and Clyde Smith. 1992. "Southern English in Brazil, No?" *SECOL Review* 16: 71–89.

Bailey, Guy, and Erik Thomas. 1998. "Some Aspects of African-American Vernacular English Phonology." In *African American English*, ed. Salikoko S. Mufwene, John Rickford, John Baugh, and Guy Bailey, 85–109. London: Routledge.

Bailey, Guy, Jan Tillery, and Tom Wikle. 1997. "Methodology of A Survey of Oklahoma Dialects." *SECOL Review* 21: 1–30.

Bailey, Guy, Tom Wikle, and Lori Sand. 1991a. "The Focus of Linguistic Innovation in Texas." *English World-Wide* 12: 195–214.

———. 1991b. "The Linguistic Landscape of Texas." *North American Culture* 7: 21–48.

Bailey, Guy, Tom Wikle, Jan Tillery, and Lori Sand. 1991. "The Apparent Time Construct." *Language Variation and Change* 3: 241–64.

———. 1993. "Some Patterns of Linguistic Diffusion." *Language Variation and Change* 5: 359–90.

———. 1996. "The Linguistic Consequences of Catastrophic Events: An Example from the American Southwest." In Arnold et al., 435–51.

Bernstein, Cynthia. 1993. "Measuring Social Causes of Phonological Variables." *American Speech* 68: 227–40.

Bernstein, Cynthia, Thomas Nunnally, and Robin Sabino, eds. 1997. *Language Variety in the South Revisited.* Tuscaloosa: Univ. of Alabama Press.

Bills, Garland D. 1977. "Vernacular Chicano English: Dialect or Interference?" *Journal of the Linguistic Association of the Southwest* 2: 30–36.

Bloomfield, Morton W. 1948. "Canadian English and Its Relation to Eighteenth-Century American Speech." *Journal of English and German Philology* 47: 59–67.

Boberg, Charles. 2000. "Geolinguistic Diffusion and the U.S.-Canada Border." *Language Variation and Change* 12: 1–24.

Boberg, Charles, and William Labov. 1998. "The Phonological Status of Western New England." Paper presented at the 27th Meeting on New Ways of Analyzing Variation in English (NWAVE 27), Athens, Ga., 3 Oct.

Boberg, Charles, and Stephanie M. Strassel. 2000. "Short-*a* in Cincinnati." *Journal of English Linguistics* 28: 108–26.

Bowie, David. 1998. "Does Perception Really Lead Production? Evidence from a Series of Related Mergers in Southern Maryland." Paper presented at the 27th Meeting of New Ways of Analyzing Variation in English (NWAVE 27), Athens, Ga., 2 Oct.

Brown, Cynthia. 1982. "A Search for Sound Change: Lowering of Tense Vowels before Liquids in the Pittsburgh Area." Master's thesis, Univ. of Pittsburgh.

Brown, Vivian R. 1991. "Evolution of the Merger of /ɪ/ and /ɛ/ before Nasals in Tennessee." *American Speech* 66: 303–15.

Buckingham, Andrew. 1983. "The Stratification of the Sociolinguistic Variable (e) in the Speech of Residents of Midlothian, Texas." In Edmondson, 22–36.

Callary, Robert E. 1975. "Phonological Change and the Development of an Urban Dialect in Illinois." *Language and Society* 4: 155–69.

Cassidy, Frederic G., and Robert B. LePage, eds. 1967. *Dictionary of Jamaican English.* Cambridge: Cambridge Univ. Press.

Castro-Gingrás, Rosario. 1972. "An Analysis of the Linguistic Characteristics of the English Found in a Set of Mexican-American Child Data." ERIC document ED 111 002.

Chambers, J. K. 1973. "Canadian Raising." *Canadian Journal of Linguistics/ La Revue canadienne de Linguistique* 18: 113–35.

————. 1989. "Canadian Raising: Blocking, Fronting, Etc."*American Speech* 64: 75–88.

————. 1991. "Canada." In Cheshire, 89–107.

Chambers, J. K., and Margaret F. Hardwick. 1986. "Comparative Sociolinguistics of a Sound Change in Canadian English." *English World-Wide* 7: 23–46.

Chater, Melville. 1926. "Motor-Coaching through North Carolina." *National Geographic* 44: 475–523.

Cheek, Davina Adrianne. 1995. "Harkers Island /ɔ/ and the Southern Norm: A Microcosm of Languages in Contact." Master's thesis, North Carolina State Univ.

Cheshire, Jenny, ed. 1991. *English around the World: Sociolinguistic Perspectives*. Cambridge: Cambridge Univ. Press.

Childs, Becky, Jeffrey Reaser, and Walt Wolfram. Forthcoming. "Defining Ethnic Varieties in the Bahamas: Phonological Accommodation in Black and White Enclave Communities." In *Eastern Caribbean Creoles and Englishes*, ed. Michael Aceto. Amsterdam: John Benjamins.

Clark, Thomas L. 1972. *Marietta, Ohio: The Continuing Erosion of a Speech Island*. Publication of the American Dialect Society 57. University: Univ. of Alabama Press.

Clarke, Sandra. 1991. "Phonological Variation and Recent Language Change in St. John's English." In Cheshire, 108–22.

————, ed. 1993. *Focus on Canada*. Varieties of English around the World 11. Amsterdam: John Benjamins.

Clarke, Sandra, Ford Elms, and Amani Youssef. 1995. "The Third Dialect of English: Some Canadian Evidence." *Language Variation and Change* 7: 209–28.

Cobb, Collier. 1910. "Early English Survivals on Hatteras Island." *University of North Carolina Magazine* 40.1: 3–10.

Colbourne, B. Wade. 1982. "A Sociolinguistic Study of Long Island, Notre Dame Bay, Newfoundland." Master's thesis, Memorial Univ. of Newfoundland.

Cook, Mary Jane, and Margaret Amy Sharp. 1966. "Problems of Navajo Speakers in Learning English." *Language Learning* 16: 21–29.

Cook, Stanley Joseph. 1969. "Language Change and the Emergence of an Urban Dialect in Utah." Ph.D. diss., Univ. of Utah.

Crane, L. Ben. 1977. "The Social Stratification of /aɪ/ among White Speakers in Tuscaloosa, Alabama." In *Papers in Language Variation: SAMLA-ADS Collection*, ed. David L. Shores and Carole P. Hines, 189–200. University: Univ. of Alabama Press.

Dailey-O'Cain, Jennifer. 1997. "Canadian Raising in a Midwestern U.S. City." *Language Variation and Change* 9: 107–20.

D'Arcy, Alexandra. 1999. "The Linguistic Oddball Phenomenon in St. John's, Newfoundland." Paper presented at the 10th International Conference on Methods in Dialectology, St. John's, Newfoundland, 3 Aug.

DARE. Dictionary of American Regional English. 1985–. Vol. 1 (A–C), ed. Frederic G. Cassidy. Vols. 2 (D–H) and 3 (I–O), ed. Frederic G. Cassidy and Joan Houston Hall. 3 vols. to date. Cambridge, Mass.: Belknap Press of Harvard Univ. Press.

DeCamp, David. 1959. "The Pronunciation of English in San Francisco, Part II." *Orbis* 8: 54–77.

Denning, Keith M. 1989. "Convergence with Divergence: A Sound Change in Vernacular Black English." *Language Variation and Change* 1: 145–67.

Denning, Keith M., Sharon Inkelas, Faye C. McNair-Knox, and John C. Rickford, eds. 1987. *Variation in Language: NWAV-XV at Stanford. Proceedings of the Fifteenth Annual Conference on New Ways of Analyzing Variation.* Stanford, Calif.: Dept. of Linguistics, Stanford Univ.

Deser, Toni. 1990. "Dialect Transmission and Variation: An Acoustic Analysis of Vowels in Six Urban Detroit Families." Ph.D. diss., Boston Univ.

de Wolf, Gaelan Dodds. 1993. "Local Patterns and Markers of Speech in Vancouver English." In Clarke, 269–93.

Dickey, Laura Walsh. 1997. "The Phonology of Liquids." Ph.D. diss., Univ. of Massachusetts at Amherst.

Di Paolo, Marianna. 1992. "Hypercorrection in Response to the Apparent Merger of (ɔ) and (ɑ) in Utah English." *Language and Communication* 12: 267–92.

Di Paolo, Marianna, and Alice Faber. 1990. "Phonation Differences and the Phonetic Content of the Tense-Lax Contrast in Utah English." *Language Variation and Change* 2: 155–204.

Disner, Sandra Ferrari. 1984. "Insights on Vowel Spacing." In *Patterns of Sounds*, ed. Ian Maddieson, 136–55. Cambridge: Cambridge Univ. Press.

Dorrill, George T. 1986a. *Black and White Speech in the South: Evidence from the Linguistic Atlas of the Middle and South Atlantic States.* Bamberger Beiträge zur Englischen Sprachwissenschaft 19. New York: Peter Lang.

———. 1986b. "A Comparison of Stressed Vowels of Black and White Speakers in the South." In *Language Variety in the South: Perspectives in Black and White*, ed. Michael B. Montgomery and Guy Bailey, 149–57. University: Univ. of Alabama Press.

Dough, Wynne C. 1982. "A Preliminary Survey of the Speech of the Northern Outer Banks of North Carolina." Bachelor's thesis, Univ. of North Carolina.

Dubois, Sylvie, and Barbara Horvath. 1998. "From Accent to Marker in Cajun English: A Study of Dialect Formation in Progress." *English World-Wide* 19: 161–88.

———. 2000. "When the Music Changes, You Change Too: Gender and Language Change in Cajun English." *Language Variation and Change* 11: 287–313.

Eckert, Penelope. 1987. "The Relative Values of Variables." In Denning et al., 101–10.

———. 1988. "Adolescent Social Structure and the Spread of Linguistic Change." *Language in Society* 17: 183–207.

———. 1989a. "The Whole Woman: Sex and Gender Differences in Variation." *Language Variation and Change* 1: 245–67.

———. 1989b. *Jocks and Burnouts: Social Categories and Identities in the High School.* New York: Teachers' College Press.

———. 1996. "(ay) Goes to the City: Exploring the Expressive Use of Variation." In Guy et al., 47–68.

———, ed. 1991. *New Ways of Analyzing Sound Change.* Quantitative Analyses of Linguistic Structure 5. New York: Academic.

Edgerton, William B. 1935. "Another Note on the Southern Pronunciation of 'Long *i.*'" *American Speech* 10: 190.

Edmondson, Jerold A., ed. 1983. *Research Papers of the Texas Summer Institute of Linguistics 13. Pilot Studies in Sociolinguistics: Variation, Use, and Attitudes.* Dallas: Summer Institute of Linguistics.

Eliason, Norman E. 1956. *Tarheel Talk: An Historical Study of the English Language in North Carolina to 1860.* Chapel Hill: Univ. of North Carolina Press.

Ellison, Mary. 1974. *The Black Experience: American Blacks since 1865.* New York: Harper and Row.

Esling, John H. 1991. "Sociophonetic Variation in Vancouver." In Cheshire, 123–33.

Esling, John H., and Henry J. Warkentyne. 1993. "Retracting of /æ/ in Vancouver English." In Clarke, 229–46.

Evans, Medford. 1935. "Southern 'Long *i.*'" *American Speech* 10: 188–90.

Faber, Alice. 1992. "Articulatory Variability, Categorical Perception, and the Inevitability of Sound Change." In *Explanation in Historical Linguistics*, ed. Garry W. Davis and Gregory K. Iverson, 59–75. Amsterdam: John Benjamins.

Faber, Alice, and Marianna Di Paolo. 1995. "The Discriminability of Nearly Merged Sounds." *Language Variation and Change* 7: 35–78.

Feagin, Crawford. 1986. "More Evidence for Major Vowel Change in the South." In Sankoff, 83–95.

———. 1987. "A Closer Look at the Southern Drawl: Variation Taken to Extremes." In Denning et al., 137–50.

———. 1996. "Peaks and Glides in Southern States Short-*a*." Guy et al., 135–60.

Fischer, David Hackett. 1989. *Albion's Seed: Four British Folkways in America.* Oxford: Oxford Univ. Press.

Flanigan, Beverly Olson, and Franklin Paul Norris. 2000. "Cross-Dialectal Comprehension as Evidence for Boundary Mapping: Perceptions of the Speech of Southwestern Ohio." *Language Variation and Change* 12: 175–201.

Foley, Lawrence M. 1972. *A Phonological and Lexical Study of the Speech of Tuscaloosa County, Alabama.* Publication of the American Dialect Society 58. University: Univ. of Alabama Press.

Fought, Carmen. 1999. "A Majority Sound Change in a Minority Community: /u/-Fronting in Chicano English." *Journal of Sociolinguistics* 3: 5–23.

Frazer, Timothy C. 1978. "South Midland Pronunciation in the North Central States." *American Speech* 53: 40–48.

———. 1983. "Sound Change and Social Structure in a Rural Community." *Language and Society* 12: 313–28.

———. 1987a. "Attitudes Toward Regional Pronunciation." *Journal of English Linguistics* 20: 89–100.

———. 1987b. *Midland Illinois Dialect Patterns.* Publication of the American Dialect Society 73. University: Univ. of Alabama Press.

———. 1994. "Perception and Gender in Virginia Speech: The Case of /aw/." *American Speech* 69: 145–54.

———. 1996. "Chicano English and Spanish Interference in the Midwestern United States." *American Speech* 71: 72–85.

———, ed. 1993. *"Heartland" English: Variation and Transition in the American Midwest.* Tuscaloosa: Univ. of Alabama Press.

Fridland, Valerie. 1998. "The Southern Vowel Shift: Linguistic and Social Factors." Ph.D. diss., Michigan State Univ.

———. 2000. "The Southern Shift in Memphis, Tennessee." *Language Variation and Change* 11: 267–85.

Galindo, D. Letticia. 1988. "Towards a Description of Chicano English: A Sociolinguistic Perspective." In *Linguistic Change and Contact (Proceedings of the Sixteenth Annual Conference on New Ways of Analyzing Variation in Language)*, ed. Kathleen Ferrara, Becky Brown, Keith Walters, and John Baugh, 113–23. Texas Linguistics Forum 30. Austin: Dept. of Linguistics, Univ. of Texas.

García, Maryellen. 1984. "Parameters of the East Los Angeles Speech Community." In Ornstein-Galicia, 85–98.

Godinez, Manuel, Jr. 1984. "Chicano English Phonology: Norms Versus Interference Phenomena." In Ornstein-Galicia, 42–48.

Godinez, Manuel, Jr., and Ian Maddieson. 1985. "Vowel Differences between Chicano and General Californian English?" *International Journal of the Sociology of Language* 53: 43–58.

González, Gustavo. 1988. "Chicano English." In *Chicano English in the Bilingual Classroom*, ed. Dennis J. Bixler-Márquez and Jacob Ornstein-Galicia, 71–81. American University Studies 6, Foreign Language Instruction 6. New York: Peter Lang.

Gordon, Matthew James. 1997. "Urban Sound Change beyond City Limits: The Spread of the Northern Cities Shift in Michigan." Ph.D. diss., Univ. of Michigan.

———. 2000. "Phonological Correlates of Ethnic Identity: Evidence of Divergence?" *American Speech* 75: 115–36.

———. 2001. *Small-Town Values, Big-City Vowels: A Study of the Northern Cities Shift in Michigan*. Publication of the American Dialect Society 84. Durham, N.C.: Duke Univ. Press.

Graff, David, William Labov, and Wendell A. Harris. 1986. "Testing Listeners' Reactions to Phonological Markers of Ethnic Identity: A New Method for Sociolinguistic Research." In Sankoff, 45–58.

Greet, William Cabell. 1931. "A Phonographic Expedition to Williamsburg, Virginia." *American Speech* 6: 161–72.

———. 1933. "Delmarva Speech." *American Speech* 8: 56–63.

Gregg, Robert J. 1957. "Notes on the Pronunciation of Canadian English as Spoken in Vancouver, British Columbia." *Journal of the Canadian Linguistic Association* 3: 20–26.

———. 1973. "The Diphthongs əi and aɪ in Scottish, Scotch-Irish and Canadian English." *Canadian Journal of Linguistics* 18: 136–45.

Grossman, James R. 1989. *Land of Hope: Chicago, Black Southerners, and the Great Migration*. Chicago: Univ. of Chicago Press.

Guenter, Joshua. 2000. "Vowels of California English before /r/, /l/, and /ŋ/." Ph.D. diss., Univ. of California at Berkeley.

Guenter, Joshua, Julie Lewis, and Margaret Urban. 1999. "A Perceptual Study of Vowels before /r/." In *Proceedings of the 14th International Congress of Phonetic Sciences*, ed. John J. Ohala, Yoko Hasegawa, Manjari Ohala, Daniel Granville, and Ashlee Bailey, 2461–64. Berkeley: Univ. of California Press.

Guy, Gregory R., Crawford Feagin, Deborah Schiffrin, and John Baugh, eds. 1996. *Towards a Social Science of Language: Papers in Honor of William Labov*. Amsterdam Studies in the Theory and History of Linguistic Science, series 4, Current Issues in Linguistic Theory. Amsterdam: John Benjamins.

Habick, Timothy. 1980. "Sound Change in Farmer City: A Sociolinguistic Study Based on Acoustic Data." Ph.D. diss., Univ. of Illinois at Urbana-Champaign.

———. 1993. "Farmer City, Illinois: Sound Systems Shifting South." In Frazer, 97–124.

Hagiwara, Robert. 1995. *Acoustic Realizations of American /r/ as Produced by Women and Men*. UCLA Working Papers in Phonetics 90. Los Angeles: Dept. of Lingusitics, Univ. of California, Los Angeles.

Hall, Joan Houston. 1976. "Rural Southeast Georgia Speech: A Phonological Analysis." Ph.D. diss., Emory Univ.

Hall, Joseph Sargent. 1942. "The Phonetics of Great Smoky Mountain Speech." *American Speech* 17.2.2: 1–110.

Hamilton, Westley H. 1977. "Phonological Variations Observed in San Antonio, Texas." *Journal of the Linguistic Association of the Southwest* 2: 83–93.

Handcock, W. Gordon. 1977. "English Migration to Newfoundland." In *The Peopling of Newfoundland: Essays in Historical Geography*, ed. John J. Mannion, 15–48. Social and Economic Papers 8. St. John's: Institute of Social and Economic Research, Memorial Univ. of Newfoundland.

Hankey, Clyde T. 1972. "Notes on West Penn-Ohio Phonology." In *Studies in Linguistics in Honor of Raven I. McDavid, Jr.*, ed. Lawrence M. Davis, 49–61. University: Univ. of Alabama Press.

Hartford, Beverly S. 1978. "Phonological Differences in the English of Adolescent Female and Male Mexican-Americans." *International Journal of the Sociology of Language* 17: 55–64.

Hartman, James W. 1966. "Pressures for Dialect Change in Hocking County, Ohio." Ph.D. diss., Univ. of Michigan.

———. 1984. "Some Possible Trends in the Pronunciation of Young Americans (Maybe)." *American Speech* 59: 218–25.

———. 1985. "Guide to Pronunciation." In *DARE*, 1: xli–lxi.

Herndobler, Robin. 1993. "Sound Change and Gender in a Working-Class Community." In Frazer, 137–56.

Herold, Ruth. 1990. "Mechanisms of Merger: The Implementation and Distribution of the Low Back Merger in Eastern Pennsylvania." Ph.D. diss., Univ. of Pennsylvania.

———. 1997. "Solving the Actuation Problem: Merger and Immigration in Eastern Pennsylvania." *Language Variation and Change* 9: 165–89.

Hillenbrand, James, Laura A. Getty, Michael J. Clark, and Kimberlee Wheeler. 1995. "Acoustic Characteristics of American English Vowels." *Journal of the Acoustical Society of America* 97: 3099–111.

Hindle, Donald. 1980. "The Social and Structural Conditioning of Phonetic Variation." Ph.D. diss., Univ. of Pennsylvania.

Hoffman, Michol. 1999. "Plasure Not Pleasure: Lax Vowel Lowering in Canadian English." Paper presented at the 10th International Conference on Methods in Dialectology, St. John's, Newfoundland, 3 Aug.

Holm, John. 1980. "African Features in White Bahamian English." *English World-Wide* 1: 45–65.

Hopkins, John Rathbone. 1975. "The White Middle Class Speech of Savannah, Georgia: A Phonological Analysis." Ph.D. diss., Univ. of South Carolina.

House, Arthur S., and Grant Fairbanks. 1953. "The Influence of Consonant Environment upon the Secondary Acoustical Characteristics of Vowels." *Journal of the Acoustical Society of America* 25: 105–13.

Howren, Robert. 1962. "The Speech of Ocracoke, North Carolina." *American Speech* 37: 163–75.

Humphries, Stephanie D. 1999. "The Low Vowels of Chauncey, Ohio." Master's thesis, Ohio Univ.

Hung, Henrietta, John Davison, and J. K. Chambers. 1993. "Comparative Sociolinguistics of (aw)-Fronting." In Clarke, 247–67.

Ito, Rika. 1999. "Diffusion of Urban Sound Change in Rural Michigan: A Case of Northern Cities Shift." Ph.D. diss., Michigan State Univ.

Ito, Rika, and Dennis R. Preston. 1998. "Identity, Discourse, and Language Variation." *Journal of Language and Social Psychology* 17: 465–83.

Jaffe, Hilda. 1973. *The Speech of the Central Coast of North Carolina: The Carteret County Version of the Banks "Brogue."* Publication of the American Dialect Society 60. University: Univ. of Alabama Press.

Johnson, Bruce Lee. 1971. "The Western Pennsylvania Dialect of American English." *Journal of the International Phonetic Association* 1: 69–73.

Johnson, Keith. 1997. *Acoustic and Auditory Phonetics.* Cambridge, Mass.: Blackwell.

Johnson, Lawrence Alfred. 1974. "A Sociolinguistic Study of Selected Vowel Changes in Los Angeles English." Ph.D. diss., Univ. of Southern California.

Johnstone, Barbara, Neeta Bhasin, and Denise Wittkofski. 2000. "'Dahntahn' Pittsburgh: Monophthongal /aw/ and Representations of Localness in Southwestern Pennsylvania." Paper presented at the 29th Meeting of New Ways of Analyzing Variation in English (NWAVE 29), East Lansing, Mich., 6 Oct.

Joos, Martin. 1942. "A Phonological Dilemma in Canadian English." *Language* 18: 141–44.

Kerr, Nora Fields. 1963. "The Pronunciation of the Vowel Nuclei in Baltimore City Speech." Master's thesis, Georgetown Univ.

Kilbury, James. 1983. "Talking about Phonemics: Centralized Diphthongs in a Chicago-Area Idiolect." In *Essays in Honor of Charles F. Hockett,* ed. Frederick B. Agard, Gerald Kelley, Adam Makkai, and Valerie Becker Makkai, 336–41. Leiden: Brill.

King, Robert D. 1972. "A Note on Opacity and Paradigm Regularity." *Linguistic Inquiry* 3: 535–38.

Kingston, John, Neil A. Macmillan, Laura Walsh Dickey, Rachel Thornburn, and Christine Bartels. 1997. "Integrality in the Perception of Tongue Root Position and Voice Quality in Vowels." *Journal of the Acoustical Society of America* 101: 1696–709.

Kinloch, A. Murray. 1983. "The Phonology of Central/Prairie Canadian English." *American Speech* 58: 31–35.

Kirwin, William J. 1993. "The Planting of Anglo-Irish in Newfoundland." In Clarke, 65–84.

Klipple, Florence Carmelita. 1945. "The Speech of Spicewood, Texas." *American Speech* 20: 187–91.

Knack, Rebecca. 1991. "Ethnic Boundaries in Lingusitic Variation." In Eckert, 251–72.

Kretzschmar, William A., Jr., Virginia G. McDavid, Theodore K. Lerud, and Ellen Johnson, eds. 1994. *Handbook of the Linguistic Atlas of the Middle and South Atlantic States.* Chicago: Univ. of Chicago Press.

Kroch, Anthony. 1996. "Dialect and Style in the Speech of Upper Class Philadelphia." In Guy et al., 23–45.

Kurath, Hans, Marcus L. Hansen, Julia Bloch, and Bernard Bloch. 1939. *Handbook of the Linguistic Geography of New England.* Providence, R.I.: Brown Univ. Press and American Council of Learned Societies.

Kurath, Hans, and Raven I. McDavid, Jr. 1961. *The Pronunciation of English in the Atlantic States.* Ann Arbor: Univ. of Michigan Press.

La Ban, Frank K. 1971. "From Cockney to Conch." In *A Various Language: Perspectives on American Dialects,* ed. Juanita V. Williamson and Virginia M. Burke, 301–08. New York: Holt, Rinehart, and Winston.

Labov, William. 1963. "The Social Motivation of a Sound Change." *Word* 19: 273–309.

———. 1966. *The Social Stratification of English in New York City.* Washington, D.C.: Center for Applied Linguistics.

———. 1971. "Methodology." In *A Survey of Linguistic Science,* ed. William Orr Dingwell, 412–97. College Park: Univ. of Maryland Press.

———. 1972. *Sociolinguistic Patterns.* Conduct and Communication 4. Philadelphia: Univ. of Pennsylvania Press.

———. 1980. "The Social Origins of Sound Change." In *Locating Language in Time and Space,* ed. William Labov, 251–65. Qualitative Analyses of Linguistic Structure 1. New York: Academic.

———. 1987. "Are Black and White Vernaculars Diverging?" *American Speech* 62: 5–12, 62–67.

———. 1988. "The Judicial Testing of Linguistic Theory." In *Language in Context: Connecting Observation and Understanding,* ed. Deborah Tannen, 159–82. Norwood, N.J.: Ablex.

———. 1989. "Exact Description of the Speech Community: Short *a* in Philadelphia." In *Language Change and Variation,* ed. Ralph W. Fasold and Deborah Schiffrin, 1–57. Amsterdam Studies in the Theory and History of Linguistic Science, Series 4, Current Issues in Linguistic Theory 52. Amsterdam: John Benjamins.

———. 1991. "The Three Dialects of English." In Eckert, 1–44.

———. 1994. *Principles of Linguistic Change.* Vol. 1, *Internal Factors.* Language in Society 20. Oxford: Blackwell.

Labov, William, and Sharon Ash. 1997. "Understanding Birmingham." In Bernstein, Nunnally, and Sabino, 508–73.

Labov, William, Sharon Ash, and Charles Boberg. 1997. "A National Map of the Regional Dialects of American English." Unpublished MS.

———. Forthcoming. *Phonological Atlas of North American English.* Berlin: Mouton de Gruyter.

Labov, William, and Wendell A. Harris. 1986. "De Facto Segregation of Black and White Vernaculars." In Sankoff, 1–24.

Labov, William, Mark Karen, and Corey Miller. 1991. "Near-Mergers and the Suspension of Phonemic Contrast." *Language Variation and Change* 3: 33–74.

Labov, William, Malcah Yaeger, and Richard Steiner. 1972. *A Quantitative Study of Sound Change in Progress.* Philadelphia: U.S. Regional Survey.

Laferriere, Martha. 1977. "Boston Short *a*: Social Variation as Historical Residue." In *Studies in Language Variation: Semantics, Syntax, Phonology, Pragmatics, Social Situations, Ethnographic Approaches*, ed. Ralph W. Fasold and Roger W. Shuy, 100–107. Washington, D.C.: Georgetown Univ. Press.

———. 1979. "Ethnicity in Phonological Variation and Change." *Language* 55: 603–17.

LAGS. *The Linguistic Atlas of the Gulf States.* 1986–92. Ed. Lee A. Pederson, Susan Leas McDaniel, Guy Bailey, Marvin H. Basset, Carol M. Adams, Caisheng Liao, and Michael Montgomery. 7 vols. Athens: Univ. of Georgia Press.

LAMSAS. *Linguistic Atlas of the Middle and South Atlantic States and Affiliated Projects: Basic Materials.* 1982–86. Ed. Raven I. McDavid, Jr. et al. Chicago Microfilm Manuscripts on Cultural Anthropology, general ed. Norman McQuown. Series 68.360–64, 69.365–69, 71.375–80. Chicago: Joseph Regenstein Library, Univ. of Chicago.

Lance, Donald M. 1994. "Variation in American English." In *American Pronunciation*, by John Samuel Kenyon. 12th ed., ed. Donald M. Lance and Stewart A. Kingsbury, 345–73. Ann Arbor, Mich.: George Wahl.

LANCS. *Linguistic Atlas of the North-Central States: Basic Materials.* 1977. Ed. Raven I. McDavid, Jr., and Richard C. Payne. Manuscript on Cultural Anthropology, series 38, nos. 200–208. Chicago: Univ. of Chicago Press. Microfilm.

LANE. *The Linguistic Atlas of New England.* 1939–43. Ed. Hans Kurath, Marcus L. Hansen, Miles L. Hanley, Guy S. Lowman, and Bernard Bloch. 3 vols. Providence, R.I.: Brown Univ. Press and American Council of Learned Societies.

Lehiste, Ilse, and Gordon E. Peterson. 1961. "Transitions, Glides, and Diphthongs." *Journal of the Acoustical Society of America* 33: 268–77.

Levine, Lewis, and Harry J. Crockett, Jr. 1966. "Speech Variation in a Piedmont Community: Postvocalic *r.*" *Sociological Inquiry* 36: 204–26.

Liljencrants, Johan, and Björn Lindblom. 1972. "Numerical Simulation of Vowel Quality Systems: The Role of Perceptual Contrast." *Language* 48: 839–62.

Lindau, Mona. 1978. "Vowel Features." *Language* 54: 541–63.

———. 1985. "The Story of /r/." In *Phonetic Linguistics: Essays in Honor of Peter Ladefoged*, ed. Victoria A. Fromkin, 157–68. Orlando, Fla.: Academic.

Lindblom, Björn. 1986. "Phonetic Universals in Vowel Systems." In *Experimental Phonology*, ed. John J. Ohala and Jeri J. Jaeger, 13–44. Orlando, Fla.: Academic.

Lowman, Guy S., Jr. 1936. "The Treatment of /au/ in Virginia." In *Proceedings of the Second International Congress on Phonetic Sciences*, ed. Daniel Jones and D. B. Fry, 122–25. Cambridge: Cambridge Univ. Press.

Lusk, Melanie M. 1976. "Phonological Variation in Kansas City: A Sociolinguistic Analysis of Three-Generation Families." Ph.D. diss., Univ. of Kansas.

Luthin, Herbert W. 1987. "The Story of California (ow): The Coming-of-Age of English in California." In Denning et al., 312–24.

Ma, Roxanna, and Eleanor Herasimchuk. 1971. "Dimensions of a Bilingual Neighborhood." In *Bilingualism in the Barrio*, ed. Joshua A. Fishman, Robert L. Cooper, and Roxanna Ma, 347–464. Bloomington: Indiana Univ. Press.

Maclagan, Margaret A., and Elizabeth Gordon. 1996. "Out of the AIR and into the EAR: Another View of the New Zealand Diphthong Merger." *Language Variation and Change* 8: 125–47.

Martinet, André. 1952. "Function, Structure, and Sound Change." *Word* 8: 1–32.

McCullough, Amerylis Jill. 1996. "Some Features of the Person County, North Carolina, Speech." Unpublished MS.

McDavid, Raven I., Jr. 1948. "Postvocalic /-r/ in South Carolina: A Social Analysis." *American Speech* 23: 194–203.

———. 1955. "The Position of the Charleston Dialect." *Publication of the American Dialect Society* 23: 35–50.

———. 1958. "The Dialects of American English." In *The Structure of American English*, ed. W. Nelson Francis, 480–543. New York: Ronald.

McDowell, John, and Susan McRae. 1972. "Differential Response of the Class and Ethnic Components of the Austin Speech Community to Marked Phonological Variables." *Anthropological Linguistics* 14: 228–39.

McElhinny, Bonnie. 1999. "More on the Third Dialect of English: Linguistic Constraints on the Use of Three Phonological Variables in Pittsburgh." *Language Variation and Change* 11: 171–95.

McMillan, James B. 1946. "Phonology of the Standard English of East Central Alabama." Ph.D. diss., Univ. of Chicago.

Medeiros, Regina Del Negri. 1982. "American Brazilian English." *American Speech* 57: 150–52.

Meechan, Marjory. 1999. "American English in a Canadian Context: The Sociolinguistic Structure of Ethnicity." Paper presented at the 10th International Conference on Methods in Dialectology, St. John's, Newfoundland, 3 Aug.

Mendoza-Denton, Norma Catalina, and Melissa Iwai. 1993. "'They Speak More Caucasian': Generational Differences in the Speech of Japanese-Americans." In Queen and Barrett, 58–67.

Merrill, Celia Dale. 1987. "Mexican-American English in McAllen, Texas: Features of Accentedness in the English of Native Spanish Bilinguals." Ph.D. diss., Univ. of Texas at Austin.

Metcalf, Allan A. 1972a. "Directions of Change in Southern California English." *Journal of English Linguistics* 6: 28–34.

———. 1972b. "Mexican-American English in Southern California." *Western Review* 9: 13–21.

Miller, Virginia R. 1953. "Present-Day Use of the Broad *a* in Eastern Massachusetts." *Speech Monographs* 20: 235–46.

Mills, Carl. 1980. "The Sociolinguistics of the [a]-[ɒ] Merger in Pacific Northwest English: A Subjective Reaction Test." *Papers in Linguistics* 13: 345–88.

Mock, Carol C. 1991. "Impact of the Ozark Drawl: Its Role in the Shift of the Diphthong /ey/." In Eckert, 233–50.

Montgomery, Michael B., and Cecil Ataide Melo. 1990. "The Phonology of the Lost Cause: The English of the Confederados in Brazil." *English World-Wide* 11: 195–216.

Moonwomon, Birch. 1987. "Truly Awesome: (ɔ) in California English." In Denning et al., 325–36.

Morgan, Lucia C. 1960. "The Speech of Ocracoke, North Carolina: Some Observations." *Southern Speech Journal* 25: 314–22.

Moulton, William G. 1962. "Dialect Geography and the Concept of Phonological Space." *Word* 18: 23–32.

Murray, Thomas E. 1992. "Social Structure and Phonological Variation on a Midwestern College Campus." *American Speech* 67: 163–74.

Niedzielski, Nancy. 1996. "Acoustic Analysis and Language Attitudes in Detroit." *University of Pennsylvania Working Papers in Linguistics* 3: 73–85.

———. 1999. "The Effect of Social Information on the Perception of Sociolinguistic Variables." *Journal of Language and Social Psychology* 18: 62–85.

Nobbelin, Kent G. 1980. "The Low-Back Vowels of the North-Central States." Ph.D. diss., Illinois Institute of Technology.

Norman, Arthur M. Z. 1956. "A Southeast Texas Dialect Survey." *Orbis* 5: 61–79.

O'Cain, Raymond K. 1977. "A Diachronic View of the Speech of Charleston, South Carolina." In *Papers in Language Variation: SAMLA-ADS Collection*, ed. David L. Shores and Carole P. Hines, 135–50. University: Univ. of Alabama Press.

Ohala, John J. 1974. "Experimental Historical Phonology." In *Historical Linguistics II: Theory and Description in Phonology*, ed. John M. Anderson and Charles Jones, 353–89. Amsterdam: North-Holland.

———. 1981. "The Listener as a Source of Sound Change." In *Papers from the Parasession on Language and Behavior, Chicago Linguistic Society, May 1–2, 1981*, ed. Carrie S. Masek, Roberta A. Hendrick, and Mary Frances Miller, 178–203. Chicago: Chicago Linguistic Society.

———. 1992. "The Costs and Benefits of Phonological Analysis." In *The Linguistics of Literacy*, ed. Pamela Downing, Susan D. Lima, and Michael Noonan, 211–37. Amsterdam: John Benjamins.

Ornstein, Jacob. 1975. "Sociolinguistics and the Study of Spanish and English Language Varieties and Their Use in the U.S. Southwest (with a Proposed Plan of Research)." In *Three Essays on Linguistic Diversity in the Spanish-Speaking World (the U.S. Southwest and the River Plate area)*, ed. Jacob Ornstein, 9–45. The Hague: Mouton.

Ornstein-Galicia, Jacob, ed. 1984. *Form and Function in Chicano English*. Rowley, Mass.: Newberry.

Paddock, Harold. 1981. *A Dialect Survey of Carbonear, Newfoundland*. Publication of the American Dialect Survey 68. University: Univ. of Alabama Press.

———. 1986. *Book of Lectures for Linguistics 2210 by Correspondence. Language in Newfoundland and Labrador: An Introduction to Linguistic Variation*. 3d ed. St. John's: Linguistics Dept., Memorial Univ. of Newfoundland.

Paradis, Carole. 1980. "La Règle de Canadian Raising et L'analyse en Structure Syllabique." *Canadian Journal of Linguistics* 25: 35–45.

Parslow, Robert L. 1967. "The Pronunciation of English in Boston, Massachusetts: Vowels and Consonants." Ph.D. diss., Univ. of Michigan.

Patrick, Peter L. 1996. "The Urbanization of Creole Phonology: Variation and Change in Jamaican." Guy et al., 329–55.

Payne, Arvilla. 1980. "Factors Controlling the Acquisition of the Philadelphia Dialect by Out-of-State Children." In *Locating Language in Time and Space*, ed. William Labov, 143–78. Orlando: Academic.

Pederson, Lee. 1965. *The Pronunciation of English in Metropolitan Chicago*. Publication of the American Dialect Society 44. University: Univ. of Alabama Press.

———. 1983. *East Tennessee Folk Speech*. Bamberger Beiträge zur Englischen Sprachwissenschaft 12. Frankfurt am Main: Peter Lang.

———. 1996. "Piney Woods Southern." In Schneider, 13–23.

Penfield, Joyce, and Jacob L. Ornstein-Galicia. 1985. *Chicano English: An Ethnic Contact Dialect*. Varieties of English around the World 7. Amsterdam: John Benjamins.

Picard, Marc. 1977. "Canadian Raising: The Case against Reordering." *Canadian Journal of Linguistics* 22: 144–55.

Pilch, Herbert. 1955. "The Rise of the American Vowel Pattern." *Word* 11: 57–63.

Poplack, Shana. 1979. "Dialect Acquisition among Puerto Rican Bilinguals." *Language in Society* 7: 89–103.

Porter, Ruth Schell. 1965. *A Dialect Study in Dartmouth, Massachusetts*. Publication of the American Dialect Society 43. University: Univ. of Alabama Press.

Primer, Sylvester. 1887. "Charleston Provincialisms." *Transactions of the Modern Language Association* 3: 84–99.

———. 1890. "Pronunciation near Fredericksburg, Virginia." *Publication of the Modern Language Association* 5: 185–99.

Pringle, Ian, and Enoch Padolsky. 1983. "The Linguistic Survey of the Ottawa Valley." *American Speech* 58: 325–44.

Queen, Robin, and Rusty Barrett, eds. 1993. *Salsa I (Proceedings of the First Annual Symposium about Language and Society—Austin*. Texas Linguistic Forum 33. Austin: Dept. of Linguistics, Univ. of Texas at Austin.

Reeves, Henry. 1869. "Our Provincialisms." *Lippincott's Magazine* 3: 310–21.

Register, Norma A. 1977. "Some Sound Patterns of Chicano English." *Journal of the Linguistic Association of the Southwest* 2: 111–22.

Roberts, Julie. 1997. "Hitting a Moving Target: Acquisition of Sound Change in Progress by Philadelphia Children." *Language Variation and Change* 9: 249–66.

Rubrecht, August Weston. 1971. "Regional Phonological Variants in Louisiana." Ph.D. diss., Univ. of Florida.

Sankoff, David, ed. 1986. *Diversity and Diachrony*. Amsterdam Studies in the Theory and History of Linguistic Science, series 4, Current Issues in Linguistic Theory 53. Amsterdam: John Benjamins.

Santa Anna A., Otto. 1993. "Chicano English and the Nature of the Chicano Language Setting." *Hispanic Journal of Behavioral Sciences* 15: 3–35.

Sawyer, Janet B. 1959. "Aloofness from Spanish Influence in Texas English." *Word* 15: 270–81.

———. 1964. "Social Aspects of Bilingualism in San Antonio, Texas." *Publication of the American Dialect Society* 41: 7–15.

Schilling-Estes, Natalie. 1996. "The Linguistic and Sociolinguistic Status of /ay/ in Outer Banks English." Ph.D. diss., Univ. of North Carolina at Chapel Hill.

———. 1997. "Accommodation Versus Concentration: Dialect Death in Two Post-Insular Island Communities." *American Speech* 72: 12–32.

Schilling-Estes, Natalie, and Walt Wolfram. 1997. "Symbolic Identity and Language Change: A Comparative Analysis of Post-Insular /ay/ and /aw/." *University of Pennsylvania Working Papers in Linguistics* 4: 83–104.

———. 1999. "Alternative Models of Dialect Death: Dissipation Versus Concentration." *Language* 75: 486–521.

Schneider, Edgar W., ed. 1996. *Focus on the USA.* Varieties of English around the World 16. Amsterdam: John Benjamins.

Schnitzer, Marc L. 1972. "The 'Baltimore /o/' and Generative Phonology." *General Linguistics* 12: 86–93.

Schwartz, Jean-Marie, Louis-Jean Boë, Nathalie Vallée, and Christian Abry. 1997. "The Dispersion-Focalization Theory of Vowel Systems." *Journal of Phonetics* 25: 255–86.

Shewmake, Edwin Francis. 1920. "English Pronunciation in Virginia." Ph.D. diss., Univ. of Virginia.

———. 1925. "Laws of Pronunciation in Eastern Virginia." *Modern Language Notes* 40: 489–92.

———. 1943. "Distinctive Virginia Pronunciation." *American Speech* 18: 33–38.

———. 1945. "How to Find [ʌɪ] in Eastern Virginia." *American Speech* 20: 152–53.

Shores, David L. 1984. "The Stressed Vowels of the Speech of Tangier Island, Virginia." *Journal of English Linguistics* 17: 37–56.

———. 1985. "Vowels before /l/ and /r/ in the Tangier Dialect." *Journal of English Linguistics* 18: 124–26.

———. 2000. *Tangier Island: Place, People, and Talk.* Newark: Univ. of Delaware Press.

Sledd, James H. 1966. "Breaking, Umlaut, and the Southern Drawl." *Language* 42: 18–41.

Spolsky, Bernard. 1971. *Navajo Language Maintenance II: Six-Year-Olds in 1970.* Navajo Reading Study Progress Report 13. Albuquerque: Univ. of New Mexico Press.

Stanley, Oma. 1936. "The Speech of East Texas." *American Speech* 11: 1–36, 145–66, 232–55, 327–55.

Stevens, Kenneth N. 1989. "On the Quantal Nature of Speech." *Journal of Phonetics* 17: 3–45.

Strassel, Stephanie M., and Charles Boberg. 1996. "The Reversal of a Sound Change in Cincinnati." *University of Pennsylvania Working Papers in Linguistics* 3: 247–56.

ten Bosch, Louis. 1991. "On the Structure of Vowel Systems." Ph.D. diss., Univ. of Amsterdam.

Thomas, Charles Kenneth. 1958. *An Introduction to the Phonetics of American English.* New York: Ronald.

———. 1961. "The Phonology of New England Speech." *Speech Monographs* 28: 223–32.

Thomas, Erik R. 1989. "The Implications of /o/ Fronting in Wilmington, North Carolina." *American Speech* 64: 327–33.

———. 1989/93. "Vowel Changes in Columbus, Ohio." *Journal of English Linguistics* 22: 205–15.

———. 1991. "The Origin of Canadian Raising in Ontario." *The Canadian Journal of Linguistics/La Revue canadienne de Linguistique* 36: 147–70.

———. 1993. "Why We Need Descriptive Studies: Phonological Variables in Hispanic English." In Queen and Barrett, 42–49.

———. 1995. "Phonetic Factors and Perceptual Reanalyses in Sound Change." Ph.D., diss., Univ. of Texas at Austin.

———. 1996. "A Comparison of Variation Patterns of Variables Among Sixth-Graders in an Ohio Community." In Schneider, 149–68.

———. 1997. "A Rural/Metropolitan Split in the Speech of Texas Anglos." *Language Variation and Change* 9: 309–32.

———. 2000. "Spectral Differences in /ai/ Offsets Conditioned by Voicing of the Following Consonant." *Journal of Phonetics* 28: 1–25.

Thomas, Erik R., and Guy Bailey. 1992. "A Case of Competing Mergers and Their Resolution." *SECOL Review* 16: 179–200.

———. 1998. "Parallels between Vowel Subsystems of African American Vernacular English and Caribbean Anglophone Creoles." *Journal of Pidgin and Creole Languages* 13: 267–96.

Thomas, Erik R., and Charles Boberg. In preparation. "A History of Vowels in Ohio."

Thompson, Roger M. 1975. "Mexican-American English: Social Corre-
    lates of Regional Pronunciation." *American Speech* 50: 18–24.

Tillery, Jan. 1989. "The Merger of the Phonemes /ɔ/ and /ɑ/ in Texas: A
    Sociological and Phonetic Study." Master's thesis, Texas A&M Univ.

———. 1997. "The Role of Social Processes in Language Variation and
    Change." In Bernstein, Nunnally, and Sabino, 434–46.

Trager, George L., and Henry Lee Smith, Jr. 1957. *An Outline of English
    Structure.* 2d ed. Studies in Linguistics: Occasional Papers 3. Washing-
    ton: American Council of Learned Societies.

Tresidder, Argus. 1941. "Notes on Virginia Speech." *American Speech* 16:
    112–20.

———. 1943. "The Sounds of Virginia Speech." *American Speech* 18: 261–
    72.

Trudgill, Peter. 1986. *Dialects in Contact.* Language in Society 10. Oxford:
    Blackwell.

Tucker, R. Whitney. 1944. "Notes on the Philadelphia Dialect." *American
    Speech* 19: 39–42.

Vance, Timothy J. 1987. "'Canadian Raising' in Some Dialects of the
    Northern United States." *American Speech* 62: 195–210.

Veatch, Thomas Clark. 1991. "English Vowels: Their Surface Phonology
    and Phonetic Implementation in Vernacular Dialects." Ph.D. diss.,
    Univ. of Pennsylvania.

Wald, Benji. 1984. "The Status of Chicano English as a Dialect of Ameri-
    can English." In Ornstein-Galicia, 14–31.

Walsh, Harry, and Victor L. Mote. 1974. "A Texas Dialect Feature."
    American Speech 49: 40–53.

Warden, Michael. 1979. "The Phonetic Realization of Diphthongs." In
    Toronto English: Studies in Phonetics to Honor C. D. Rouillard, ed. Pierre
    R. Léon and Philippe Martin, 35–47. Studia Phonetica 14. Montreal:
    Didier.

Warkentyne, Henry J., and John H. Esling. 1995. "The Low Vowels of
    Vancouver English." In *Studies in General and English Phonetics: Essays
    in Honour of Professor J. D. O'Connor,* ed. Jack Windsor Lewis, 395–400.
    London: Routledge.

Wells, J. C. 1982. *Accents of English 3: Beyond the British Isles.* Cambridge:
    Cambridge Univ. Press.

Wesley, Charles H. 1927. *Negro Labor in the United States, 1859–1925: A
    Study in American Economic History.* New York: Vanguard.

Wetmore, Thomas H. 1959. *The Low-Central and Low-Back Vowels in the
    English of the Eastern United States.* Publication of the American Dialect
    Society 32. University: Univ. of Alabama Press.

Whetzell, Brett. 2000. "Rhythm, Dialects, and the Southern Drawl." Master's thesis, North Carolina State Univ.

Wheatley, Katherine E., and Oma Stanley. 1959. "Three Generations of East Texas Speech." *American Speech* 34: 84–94.

Wiley, Calvin Henderson. 1866. *Roanoke: or, Where is Utopia?* Philadelphia: Peterson.

Wilhelm, H. G. H. 1982. *The Origin and Distribution of Settlement Groups: Ohio, 1850*. Athens: Dept. of Geography, Ohio Univ.

Wise, Claude Merton. 1933a. "Southern American Dialect." *American Speech* 8.2: 37–43.

———. 1933b. "The Southern American Drawl." *Le Maitre Phonetique*, third series 48.44: 69–71.

Wolfram, Walt. 1969. *A Linguistic Description of Detroit Negro Speech.* Washington, D.C.: Center for Applied Linguistics.

Wolfram, Walt, Adrianne Cheek, and Hal Hammond. 1996. "Competing Norms and Selective Assimilation: Mixing Outer Banks and Southern /ɔ/." In Arnold et al., 41–67.

Wolfram, Walt, and Donna Christian. 1976. *Appalachian Speech.* Washington, D.C.: Center for Applied Linguistics.

Wolfram, Walt, and Clare Dannenberg. 1999. "Dialect Identity in a Tri-Ethnic Context: The Case of Lumbee American Indian English." *English World-Wide* 20: 179–216.

Wolfram, Walt, Kirk Hazen, and Natalie Schilling-Estes. 1999. *Dialect Change and Maintenance on the Outer Banks.* Publication of the American Dialect Society 81. Tuscaloosa: Univ. of Alabama Press.

Wolfram, Walt, Kirk Hazen, and Jennifer Ruff Tamburro. 1997. "Isolation within Isolation: A Solitary Century of African-American Vernacular English." *Journal of Sociolinguistics* 1: 7–38.

Wolfram, Walt, and Natalie Schilling-Estes. 1995. "Moribund Dialects and the Endangerment Canon: The Case of the Ocracoke Brogue." *Language* 71: 696–721.

———. 1996. "Dialect Change and Maintenance in a Post-Insular Island Community." In Schneider, 103–48.

Wolfram, Walt, Natalie Schilling-Estes, Kirk Hazen, and Chris Craig. 1997. "The Sociolinguistic Complexity of Quasi-Isolated Southern Coastal Communities." In Bernstein, Nunnally, and Sabino, 173–87.

Wolfram, Walt, and Erik R. Thomas. Forthcoming. *The Development of African American English: Evidence from an Isolated Community.* Oxford: Blackwell.

Wolfram, Walt, Erik R. Thomas, and Elaine W. Green. 2000. "The Regional Context of Earlier African-American Speech: Evidence for Reconstructing the Development of AAVE." *Language in Society* 29: 315–55.

Woods, Howard B. 1979. "A Socio-Dialectal Survey of English Spoken in Ottawa: A Study of Sociological and Stylistic Variation in Canadian English." Ph.D. diss., Univ. of British Columbia.

———. 1991. "Social Differentiation in Ottawa English." In Cheshire, 134–49.

———. 1993. "A Synchronic Study of English Spoken in Ottawa: Is Canadian English Becoming More American?" In Clarke, 151–78.

Wyatt, P. J. 1976. "Wichita Dialect: A Study in a Kansas Urban Community." Ph.D. diss., Indiana Univ.

Zeller, Christine. 1993. "The Investigation of a Sound Change in Progress: /æ/ to /e/ in Midwestern American English." Paper presented at the 22d meeting on New Ways of Analyzing Variation in English (NWAVE 22), Ottawa, Ontario, 14–17 Oct.

INDEX OF SPEAKER NUMBERS

PUBLICATION OF THE AMERICAN DIALECT SOCIETY

Editor: RONALD R. BUTTERS, *Duke University*
Managing Editor: CHARLES E. CARSON, *Duke University*

THE AMERICAN DIALECT SOCIETY

Membership is conferred upon any person interested in the aims and activities of the Society. Dues are $35 annually for regular members, $20 for students, and $5 extra for members outside the United States. Life membership is available to individuals for $700. Members receive all publications: *American Speech*, its monograph supplement Publication of the American Dialect Society (PADS), and the *Newsletter*. Institutional subscriptions are also available. Address payments to Duke University Press, Journals Fulfillment, Box 90660, Durham NC 27708-0660; phone (888) 387-5687 or (919) 687-3617. Questions concerning membership or the Society should be addressed to the Executive Secretary, Allan Metcalf, Department of English, MacMurray College, Jacksonville IL 62650 (e-mail: AAllan@aol.com).

Officers for 2001

President: DENNIS R. PRESTON, *Michigan State University*
Vice President: MICHAEL B. MONTGOMERY, *University of South Carolina*
Past President: RONALD R. BUTTERS, *Duke University*
Executive Secretary: ALLAN METCALF, *MacMurray College*
Delegate to the ACLS: JOAN H. HALL, *Dictionary of American Regional English*
Executive Council Members: LISA ANN LANE, *Texas A&M University* (2001); WILLIAM A. KRETZSCHMAR, JR., *University of Georgia* (2002); KIRK HAZEN, *West Virginia University* (2003); BEVERLY FLANIGAN, *Ohio University* (2004)
Nominating Committee: WALT WOLFRAM, *North Carolina State University* (chair); RONALD R. BUTTERS, *Duke University*; JOAN H. HALL, *Dictionary of American Regional English*
General Editor, ADS Publications, and Editor, PADS: RONALD R. BUTTERS, *Duke University*

STATEMENT FOR AUTHORS

The object of the American Dialect Society, as stated in its constitution, "is the study of the English language in North America, together with other languages influencing it or influenced by it." The monograph series Publication of the American Dialect Society (PADS) publishes works by ADS members in (1) regional dialects, (2) social dialects, (3) occupational vocabulary, (4) place-names, (5) usage, (6) non-English dialects, (7) new words, (8) proverbial sayings, and (9) the literary use of dialect. Models for these kinds of studies may be found in issues of PADS. PADS does not publish articles on general grammar without dialect emphasis or articles on literary figures not known as dialect writers.

The general policy of PADS is to devote each issue to two or three long articles or, more commonly, to a single study of monograph length. Shorter articles and book reviews should be submitted to *American Speech,* the journal of the American Dialect Society.

Manuscripts submitted to PADS and *American Speech* should be styled following *The Chicago Manual of Style* (14th ed., 1993). Documentation must be given in the text itself using the author-date system (chap. 16), with the list of references at the end prepared in the humanities sytle (chap. 15).

Manuscripts for *American Speech* and PADS may be submitted to Charles E. Carson, Managing Editor, American Dialect Society Publications, Duke University Press, Box 90018, Durham NC 27708-0018. Telephone: (919) 687-3670. E-mail: carson@duke.edu.

Index to

AN ACOUSTIC ANALYSIS OF
VOWEL VARIATION
IN NEW WORLD ENGLISH

ERIK R. THOMAS

North Carolina State University

Publication of the

American Dialect Society

·

Number 85

·

Published by Duke University Press
for the American Dialect Society

INDEX

Abel, Ken, 74–76
"abnatural" changes, 55
acoustic methods, 11–14
African Americans, viii,
    1, 3–5, 16–18, 19,
    24–27, 29–32, 34,
    38, 40, 41, 46, 48,
    49, 58, 161–84
Alabama, 137
    Anniston, 2, 29, 116
    Birmingham, 74,
        116–17
    central, 17
    Dallas County, 166
    Montgomery, 38,
        113–16
    north-central, 113
    northern, 37, 117
    Piedmont, 113–14
    Plains region, 114
    southern, 23, 105,
        114
    Talladega, 114
    Tuscaloosa, 116
    Tuscaloosa County,
        116
Alberta, southern, 60,
    61
Allen, Harold B., 17, 30,
    72
Anderson, Bridget L.,
    viii, 11, 38, 55, 176,
    198
Anshen, Frank, 122
antiformants, 52, 200
Appalachians, 17, 19,
    37, 45, 46, 48, 117–
    22, 166, 176; see also
    mountains
archival recordings, viii
Arizona, vii, 185, 186
Arkansas, 23, 30, 45,
    133, 140
    White County, 134

Armour, Malcolm, 16
Ash, Sharon, 2, 20, 26,
    29, 33, 41, 47, 50–
    53, 70, 72, 74, 77,
    78, 81, 103, 106,
    113, 116, 119, 161
Asian Americans, vii, 29;
    see also Japanese
    Americans
Atal, B. S., 12
Avis, Walter S., 26, 32,
    59, 61, 64
Ayres, Harry Morgan,
    69, 71, 110, 144
Bahamas, 19, 26, 29, 32,
    42, 48, 49, 106–7,
    163
    Abaco Island, 106–7
    Cherokee Sound,
        107
Bailey, Charles-James N.,
    55, 59, 105
Bailey, Guy, viii, 3, 18,
    26, 29, 47, 48, 51,
    135, 137, 138, 140,
    161, 170, 174
Barbados, 163
Beason, Larry, ix
Benson, Robert, ix
Bermuda, 106
Bernstein, Cynthia, 26,
    51, 138, 140, 172,
    174, 176, 178, 186
Bhasin, Neeta, 76
Bills, Garland D., 185
Blacks, 106; see also
    African Americans
Bloomfield, Morton W.,
    59
Boberg, Charles, 2, 20,
    21, 23, 26, 29, 41,
    47, 51–53, 61, 69,
    70, 72, 74, 77, 81,
    83, 90, 94, 103, 113,

119
boll weevil, 165
Bowie, David, 51
Brahmin speech, 67
Brazil, 133, 137–38
    Americana, 138
breaking, 19, 21, 22,
    105; see also triph-
    thongs
British Columbia
    Vancouver, 2, 60, 61
    Victoria, 60
British English, 21, 22,
    24
    dialects of, 25, 70
Brown, Cynthia, 74
Brown, Vivian R., 52
Buckingham, Andrew,
    16
"bunched-tongue" /r/,
    44, 75–76
Butters, Ronald R., viii–
    ix
Cajun English, 133,
    102–3
California, vii, 17, 21,
    30, 33, 51, 185, 188
    East Palo Alto, 3
    Los Angeles, 3, 102,
        190
    Sacramento, 103
    San Francisco, 102–3
    San Francisco Bay
        area, 16, 18, 29,
        41, 54, 103
    southern, 103
Callary, Robert E., 78
Canada, 16, 21, 29, 33,
    39–40, 59–61, 64,
    81; see also Alberta,
    British Columbia,
    Newfoundland,
    Ontario, Quebec
    western, vii

1

ABOUT THE AUTHOR

ERIK R. THOMAS is associate professor in the Department of English at North Carolina State University, where he works with the North Carolina Language and Life Project, an investigation of dialectal variation in several communities in North Carolina. He received his Ph.D. at the University of Texas at Austin in 1995 under the direction of Robert D. King. He has published a number of articles on phonetic variation in North American English, including (among others) several on African American or Mexican American English. Most recently, he has coauthored, with Walt Wolfram, *The Development of African American English: Evidence from an Isolated Community* (Malden, Mass.: Blackwell, forthcoming).